The Vatican Papers

By Nino Lo Bello

NEW ENGLISH LIBRARY

First published in Great Britain by New English Library,
Mill Road, Dunton Green, Sevenoaks, Kent, a division of
Hodder and Stoughton Ltd, in 1982

ISBN 0 450 04882 9

Design and production in association with
Book Production Consultants, Cambridge.

Printed in Great Britain by The Thetford Press Ltd, Thetford, Norfolk

Bound by Weatherby Woolnough, Northants.

To Susan and Doug, who taught me
much about life

OTHER BOOKS BY THE SAME AUTHOR

The Vatican Empire
Vatican, USA
European Detours

Contents

'In the Vatican everything is forbidden, and everything is possible.'

— *Vatican saying*

'What would Christ do if He could see? What would He, who rode on an old donkey, think about the luxurious car, with the ornate throne as a seat? What would He say, if He saw the portfolio of the Vatican shares? What would He do if He saw all the treasures of the Vatican, treasures which could be used to alleviate ignorance by improving education? What would be His reaction to the comfortable lives of the members of the Curia? If Christ suddenly appeared in the middle of Saint Peter's Square and said: "Leave your riches and follow me," I wonder how many would. I'd like to know what would happen to Him if He knocked on the Vatican door saying: "You speak in my name. You invoke me. I have come to tell you that you are misinterpreting my teachings." But I know exactly what would happen. The authorities would instantly call the Roman police, in accordance with the Lateran Agreements of 1929, and accuse Him of being anti-establishment, and of disturbing the peace. He would not be judged as before, however, but sent to a mental ward and classified as a maniac impersonator of Jesus Christ.'

— *Monsignor Semprione*

'Cosa farebbe Cristo se potesse vedere? Cosa penserebbe, Lui che cavalcava un vecchio asino, della macchina lussuosa con l'enfatico trono come sedile? Cosa direbbe se vedesse la cartella azionaria vaticana? Cosa farebbe se vedesse tutti i tesori del Vaticano, tesori che potrebbero essere usati per migliorare l'istruzione, alleviando l'ignoranza? Come sarebbe la Sua reazione devanti alla vita confortevole dei membri della Curia? Se Cristo apparisse improvvisamente in Piazza San Pietro e dicesse: "Lasciate i vostri beni e seguitemi," io mi chiedo quanti sarebbero a seguirLo. Mi interesserebbe sapere cosa Gli accadrebbe se bussasse alla porta del Vaticano dicendo: "Voi parlate in mio nome. Voi mi invocate. Sono venuto per dirvi che state sbagliando l'interpretazione del mio ammaestramento." Ma so perfettamente cosa accadrebbe. Le autorità chiamerebbero subito la polizia romana, in conformità con gli accordi Lateranensi del 1929 e L'accuserebbero di essere un rivoluzionario e di turbare la pace. Lui non sarebbe comunque giustiziato, come la volta precedente, ma messo in manicomio dove verrebbe considerato come una personificazione maniaca di Gesu Cristo."

— *Monsignor Semprione*

CHAPTER I

Introduction

IN NOVEMBER 1974 when Vittorio De Sica died, none of the obituaries or laudatory pieces about him made mention of the 73-year-old Italian director's film that was never shown to the public at all, his all-time favorite. It was a motion picture he made for the Vatican in 1945, financed entirely by papal money, but when Church officials evaluated his finished product, the black-and-white movie was never released for distribution.

Bearing the Italian film archive register number of #562, De Sica's flick, which took nearly two years to make and cost the Vatican less than $40,000 to produce, was titled *The Gates of Heaven* [*La Porta del Cielo*], with a script by Cesare Zavattini using a strong religious theme along lines suggested by Pope Pius XII. The Vatican never gave any reason, either publicly or privately, to De Sica himself, as to why the first movie it had ever produced was 'killed.'

This virtually broke De Sica's heart because he not only considered it a cinematic neo-realism masterpiece, on a par with his *Bicycle Thief, Shoe Shine*, and *Two Women* (the last named won Sophia Loren an Oscar in 1961), but he also was convinced it was the finest film he had ever made. He remained convinced of this until his death.

This is also borne out by his son, Christian, who owns the only extant copy of *The Gates of Heaven* outside of the Vatican itself. It is a 16mm print, the first 13 minutes of which are faulty in that the film jumps when projected. In his downtown Rome apartment, Christian De Sica gave me a private showing of *The Gates of Heaven* on his home projector. For obvious legal reasons, the copy Christian has cannot be shown in any theatre, nor is he prepared, for the time being, to reveal how he came by his copy.

'My father often spoke of this film at home,' Christian explains. 'He saw the finished, edited version only once in his life, but my mother [actress Maria Mercader] has viewed it several times and agrees that it was his best movie ever. She is of the opinion that if *The Gates of Heaven* were ever to be released, despite its now being nearly 40 years old, it most certainly would receive a nomination for an Oscar as one of the best foreign films of the year.'

Ironically, the man the Vatican placed in charge of the production — and who was, in effect, De Sica's boss on the set — was a lesser Church official, a young cleric by the name of Father Giovanni Montini, who 18 years later was to become Pope Paul VI in 1963. De Sica used to tell an anecdote about Padre Montini: when the young priest visited the set for the first time, he asked if he could look through De Sica's camera. Italian filmmakers have a custom that whenever anyone looks through a camera for the first time, he has to buy drinks or coffee for everyone in the crew. A good sport, and at great expense to himself, though he was then desperately poor, Father Montini took the company to the Rome train station bar, fished into his purse and found enough coins to pick up the tab, including a beer for the amused American soldier assigned to guard the set.

Years later, after Montini had become Pope, De Sica had reservations about inquiring of him privately as to the fate of *The Gates of Heaven*, because he was a non-practicing Catholic by then and had married Maria Mercader while still legally wed to another woman. Defying the Vatican's and Italy's no-divorce laws of the time, he became, legally, a French citizen while still living in Rome and married in France where he had obtained a divorce. So meeting the Pope was then a no-no. And Miss Mercader, De Sica's third wife, was a co-star in *The Gates of Heaven*, together with Massimo Girotti and Marina Berti.

Lasting an hour and 25 minutes, the film deals with several people on a train from Rome to Loreto who seek a miracle at the famed sanctuary of 'The House of Mary,' brought to Italy from Nazareth in the year 1294. The movie shows one old woman traveling to Loreto to pray that the family she has served as a governess for many years will find peace among its ever-quarreling members. On the same train is a young laborer, recently blinded in a factory mishap (which we are shown in flashbacks), and with him is a colleague tormented by the fact that he was directly responsible for the accident. The film sequences also include a young pianist who does not believe in God; he too is on his way to Loreto to seek some kind of miracle to bring back the use of his hand which has become paralyzed. In the same car is an orphan boy, accompanied by a young girl, herself an orphan and not yet ten years old, who is watching over the boy; the two meet a semi-paralyzed business man who takes a liking to the two children and decides to bring them into his home and support them. How each of the train's passengers finds his own miracle, even before the train reaches Loreto, is the main thrust of the film.

'Papa', adds Christian, 'used to make a kind of wisecrack about *Gates*. Several times I heard him say: "To get that film into the theatres, it probably will take God *and* a miracle!" '

Vittorio De Sica's affair with the Vatican was not unique, in the sense that he was the victim of Vatican secrecy. Vatican officials have centuries and centuries behind them, and secrecy is a way of life in the tiny Catholic city-state. Indeed, secrecy behind the bronze doors is a cardinal rule. So secret are the activities of the labyrinth of Vatican offices, which act independently from each other, that when something of importance breaks within one office, it is usually a secret to the other Vatican departments. This obsession for secrecy is shored up by an aspect of Italian culture that influences the Vatican since the majority of people who rule and who work there are themselves Italians: simply put, Italy and the Italian government have a long tradition of keeping the people uninformed. Unlike the atmosphere in the United States where citizens feel they have a right to know, and politicians and government leaders ostensibly cater to this feeling, in Italy and in the Vatican there is no formal policy to give out information to the public. If anything, it is the other way around — the assumption on the part of the Church is that most matters pertaining to the Church are the Church's business and these matters ought not to be made public.

Newspapermen covering Rome and the doings of the Vatican have always complained about the lack of official information that is given out by Church officers who influence the lives of nearly 700 million Roman Catholics in over 2000 dioceses and archdioceses around the globe. Although American and British editors — who respect the public's right to know — are eager for hard news on Vatican events of all kinds, the world's largest charity organization does not care if anything is ever reported to the press. Newsmen who regularly cover the Vatican are forced to engage in unorthodox methods to get information because of the Vatican's incredibly poor press relations. Up until just recently the Vatican did not have a press officer or an authorized spokesman whom correspondents could question. When finally a press office was set up in the late 1950s, the spokesman — a clergyman from Yugoslavia who had no feeling for the problems of newspapermen and very little empathy for pressmen in general — usually knew nothing. And when he did, he was afraid to make a comment. Invariably, he would tell reporters that he could reveal nothing because of the Vatican's secrecy rules. The press officer gave no press conferences, never tipped correspondents off when a major statement from the Pope was expected, and at important public functions in Saint Peter's could not even get newsmen seats or make press accommodations. He also had a policy of keeping the press office closed in the afternoon or evenings, the very times when correspondents would most likely show up to ask a question or seek background information.

No small wonder, therefore, that the working press in Rome was forced to create a network of Vatican tipsters, cajole amenable Vatican officers with outright bribery or, by using ingenious sales talks, work out a deal to purchase information.

Covering Rome in the 1950s and 1960s was unlike any other situation, and veteran reporters admitted that even the Soviet Union and Nazi Germany did not engage in so much secrecy about so many things. About the only real plus Vatican reporters had going for them during this period were the calculated official leaks by the Vatican, a hot disclosure from one of the factions or a good tip via disgruntled clerics within the sacred enclave — but that meant usually only one reporter would get the story, while the others helplessly had to report what a competitor publication had already divulged.

The Vatican secrecy that plagued reporters after the war in Rome still plagues them today, but perhaps not so intensely. Things have loosened up a bit, and now copies of the Pope's speeches are made available, for instance. Nevertheless, covering the Vatican is generally considered journalism's toughest, most demanding and most frustrating assignment.

Although it tarnishes its image in today's world, the Vatican will not eliminate its mania for secrecy in the foreseeable future. Instead of realizing that, sooner or later, most of the Vatican secrets get out anyway and that before they do, there are often distorted and damaging accounts from deadline-pressured newsmen, the Church remains oblivious. It alienates the faithful, generates mutual suspicion and destroys the confidence of the people. The ill-effects of secrecy in the nerve center of Catholicism are the same whether the reasons for secrecy are justified or not.

Its preference for secrecy now an accepted fact, the Vatican — let it be said here, however bluntly — does not always believe in the truth. It believes in its own truths, half-truths and non-truths — those 'truths' which foster its points of view and shore up its status in the eyes of the faithful. This has always been and is so today. This may be the *raison d'être* for the secrecy.

One of the things most Roman Catholics are not aware of is the fundamental dishonesty of the Vatican. Like many governments, it lies and distorts facts when it suits its particular point of view. For instance, Catholics today are told by their leaders that the Church has always condemned birth control (not true), that Catholicism has never recognized divorce (equally not true), that women have never been ordained as priests (also not true), and that priests have always been celibate (not true, either). Truths and historical truths are often unpalatable to Vatican and Catholic Church officials, and most often Catholic leaders attempt to cover these up in the name of God or Christ.

Let's look for a moment at four lies Catholics are told these days: (1) birth control — all through the nineteenth century the Church played down its teachings on birth control. In discreet replies to the bishops of France, for instance, the Holy Office advised them to proceed very cautiously lest they disturb the conscience of married couples. In his encyclical on Christian marriage, Pope Leo XIII did not even mention the subject at a time when birth control was almost universal among Catholics in France; (2) divorce — for the first 1000 years of Christian history marriage was not regulated by the Church but by civil authority, and divorce by mutual consent was permitted; (3) women as priests — the historical facts show that women have not only been priests but have served as bishops, too. Both Saint Bridget of Kildaire and Theodora of Smyrna were priests, and both of them performed the roles of bishop, though in Bridget's case she was never actually appointed a bishop; (4) celibacy — there are innumerable examples of priests being allowed to marry in Catholic history, not to mention some prominent cardinals of the past who had wives and children — and mistresses.

Although many decisions made today by priests are correct in terms of present-day Vatican rules, it is patently absurd to attempt to shore up certain of these rules by saying they have always been that way in Catholic history.

In the belief that there is 'a time to keep silence and a time to speak' Pope Paul VI in March 1974 ordered the issue of a three-page memo whose purpose it was to tighten, even more so, the Vatican's secrecy methods, so that leaks to diplomats, spies, journalists and 'other outsiders' could be curtailed or prevented long enough for the Pope himself to reveal first what he intended to reveal. The confidential circular was aimed at eliminating embarrassment for the Pope, his staff and the princes of the Church, and it came after the Vatican found out that its telephones had been tapped. Three of the some 2000 extensions within the Vatican had indeed been bugged (permanently), and there was no way for Vatican security officers to know just how long the illegal monitoring had been going on. Nor was there any way to determine who was involved in bringing about this undercover surveillance, despite the fact that the Vatican is well aware that a Vatican tipster system exists. The identity of these tipsters who sell their usually reliable inside information to major newspapers with news bureaus in Rome, to news magazines with correspondents stationed in The Eternal City, to the wire services like Associated Press, United Press International, Reuters and ANSA (the Italian news agency) and to certain people in the diplomatic corps, is a long-standing mystery that the Vatican has never been able to resolve successfully.

It might be mentioned here, as an aside, that when I was associated with the Rome bureau of the late-lamented *New York Herald Tribune*, the bureau chief had a thoroughly trustworthy Vatican tipster who received a monthly payment for his services, even when he had not come up with any news. To the chagrin of the *Trib's* last bureau chief, Sanche de Gramont, an author who now calls himself Ted Morgan (and to its previous long-time bureau chief before that, Barrett McGurn), when the Herald Tribune closed down for good in 1966, we learned that the *Trib's* Vatican tipster had also been, quietly, the Vatican tipster for another major, competitive publication! My guess is that he is still serving in that capacity right now — and wouldn't the Vatican like to know who he is.

Although the papal security service — ever vigilant but not so efficient as a Pope would pray for — has indeed tracked down various sources of leaks in the past, including the three bugged telephones, the Vatican at times can be like a sieve. One can understand why Pope Paul wanted to put a stop to it, as best he could. His 1974 instructions instigated punishments for violators, ranging from reprimand and suspension from work to salary docking and excommunication. The people bound by pontifical secrecy (the Vatican's own expression for top security) would include cardinals, bishops, high prelates and major and minor officials of the Church's central administrative body, the Curia. Lower level personnel were included in the memo, but these people are not made to take a long Latin oath (the way all priests have to) to keep Church business under wraps.

The following matters were listed by the Pope's memo as coming under pontifical secrecy: the preparation and editing of papal documents placed under the seal of pontifical secrecy; Church business transacted by the Secretariat of State; revealing documents and publications brought to the attention of the Doctrinal Congregation; revealing information on accusations made against Church authorities concerning offenses against the faith and morals; reports from apostolic delegates, nuncios and other papal envoys on classified matters; information concerning the proposed naming of new cardinals; information concerning appointments to be made to the Curia or the selection of major officials for special assignments, and coded correspondence that would include inter-office memos of a critical nature.

Idiosyncratically, one of the strengths of the Vatican — some would say, weakness — is that it just does not care what the effects of its standard rule of thumb on secrecy produces. It does what it does because it does it, and because that is the way it has always been.

The purpose of this book is to penetrate the purple curtain and get behind Vatican secrecy — and to inform people about the Vatican, non-Christians and Christians alike — on a variety of subjects the Vatican has preferred to keep more or less to itself. My feeling is that everybody knows of the Vatican, but far too many people know little about the Vatican. Part of the fault lies with the Vatican itself, and part lies with the press which prefers to report on major Vatican events in detail and takes little time to investigate some of the minor issues. This book concerns many small issues, as well as the major. Today, with this book in the last 20 years of the twentieth century, I hope to inject a flow of fresh air into the Vatican; it is a long time in coming and it is most needed.

As one whose assignment in Rome was to keep a continous radar eye and a well-focused microscope on the Vatican for nearly a decade, Vatican secrecy was the bane of my existence. The ploys, diversions and tactics of Vatican bureaucrats invariably threw sand into my gears, and my only consolation was that I was not alone in Rome's frustrated press corps which is mostly housed at the *Associazione della Stampa Estera* (Foreign Press Club) on Via della Mercede where two floors of facilities are in operation. But God provides for those who provide for themselves, and like my two highly respected bureau chiefs in the Rome office of the *New York Herald Tribune* — both McGurn and de Gramont — I activated, in addition to my own sources inside the Vatican, people in the bureaucracy who were willing to talk to me if I did not name them. These contacts were based on mutual trust and friendship, some of which was enhanced by a hobbyist gourmet-cook-wife who, like Benito Mussolini before her, knew the value of gastro-politics and the 100 per cent gastro-rapport that often comes with the dessert on a slow-going Sunday afternoon or an equally slow-going Saturday night. Thus it was no accident that I became good friends with such angelic men as Cardinal Tizio, Bishop Caio and Monsignor Semprione, without whom this book could never have been written. The last-named gave me the benefit of his careful reading of the finished manuscript.

Not everyone who should be thanked can be named here — but there are others, of course, whom I can mention whose aid was invaluable. Particularly do I want to mention dear friends and colleagues like Desmond O'Grady, Paul Hofmann, Wilton Wynn, Milo Farneti, Sam Waagenaar, Mike Wilson, George Weller, Peter Nichols, Emilio Verani, Ettore Petta, Fausto Bonato, Rabbi Elio Toaff, Bruno Tedeschi, Roberto Mayr, Bruno Brovedani, Malcolm Farr, Henry Tanner, Peter Hebblethwaite, Joan Lewis, Charles Mitchelmore, Sanche de Gramont, Barrett McGurn, Gene Di Raimondo, George Armstrong, Corrado Pallenberg, Anna Brady, John Earle, Walter Galling, Eva Layi, Christopher Matthews, Jack Payton, Curtis Bill Pepper, Claire Sterling, Peter Tumiati, David Willey, Leo Wollemborg, Daniel Madden, Marc Anthony Messina, Joseph Wechsberg, Alan Levy, Monica Emmer, Carl Clemens, Maureen Burns Walther, Roswitha Haller, Inge Pohl, Günther Anger, Norman Shetler Sr, Charles De Mangin, Joseph Mack, Patricia Wise, Bertha Smyth, Emilie Rooney, Susan Lo Bello, Douglas Heckathorn, Lucille Cipriano Szabo, Anny Paulick, Laurana Mitchelmore, Paul Gitlin, Gene Winick, Bennet Bolton, Charles W. Bell, Simon Wiesenthal, Hans Küng, Dunwoodie Hall and Stephen Klaidman.

My debt to these individuals is great, but I alone must bear the responsibility for the contents. Finally, due credit is given with heartfelt thanks to my devoted colleague and editor, Irene Rooney Lo Bello, who, during her sympathetic editing of the various drafts, advised, admonished and at times harangued me. Her critical eye applied to the pages and their webwork revisions, undertaken with enthusiasms and applied skills, has, I trust, enriched the book.

I have drawn from the views of social scientists without necessarily accepting their theoretical frameworks; thus in the background are elements of Weberian analysis and Parsonian theory.

So let the chips fall where they may. There will be attackers who will find ammunition to come at me strong, and there will be defenders who will have a lot to defend. Nevertheless, I hope that this book will reach readers beyond them and provide cause for contemplation. Amen.

— Nino Lo Bello
Vienna: March 1982

CHAPTER II

A Woman, A Mouse and the Bones of Saint Peter

UNDERNEATH THE mighty Saint Peter's Basilica lies a city. It is the city of the dead, and as such constitutes one of the best sources for Vatican inside stories. Down below in the crooked subterranean street between two rows of dust-pocked mausoleums, one can peer through a small, barred opening. This is the site of the grave of the first of the apostles, Saint Peter. His bones are still there — and the story behind those bones is one that has yet to be told, for the mystery of these bones, and their eventual authentication, was one that plagued Vatican officers for centuries. Only when a woman and a mouse came into the picture was the mystery finally solved.

The story began with the crucifixion of Peter in Nero's Circus and his burial on the Vatican hill. Centuries and centuries went by and not until May 1942 did any kind of official announcement come from the Vatican as to where Saint Peter's bones were buried. On May 13 of that year Pope Pius XII announced on the radio that the bones of the first Roman pontiff, the first Bishop of Rome, had been found. Then towards the end of 1950 Pius once again spoke on the subject in his Christmas message: 'The excavations under the Altar of the Confession, at least as regards the tomb of the apostle, a search on which we set our heart from the very first days of our pontificate, and their scientific study have been happily concluded. The essential question, then, is whether Saint Peter's tomb has now really been found. To this question, the final conclusion of our studies provides an answer — a very clear Yes. A second question subordinate to the first one regards the relics of Saint Peter. Have they been found? On the edge of the sepulchre have been found remains of human bones which, however, cannot be proved with certainty to belong to the body of the apostle.'

Fully 18 years later, Pius' successor, Pope Paul VI formally let it be known that the bones of Saint Peter had indeed been found. In a public declaration on June 26, 1968, Paul VI declared: 'new and very patient and very accurate inquiries have been carried out: the relics of Saint Peter have been identified in a manner which we consider convincing.'

Quite frankly, Pope Paul on this day was not being thoroughly honest, for he led the world to infer that the Saint Peter's bones he had talked about were the same bones that Pope Pius had talked about in 1950, when in fact two different sets of bones were involved. The ones that Pius had talked about turned out to be, after thorough inspection, not those belonging to Peter. No complete or clear announcement, however, was ever made about this. The two papal announcements, however welcome they were to the Christian world, did not indicate at all the series of absolutely incredible blunders the Vatican committed, the truly fantastic detective work and superb piece of scientific detection by a stubborn woman who would not take No for an answer, and the tiny mouse which came to the rescue when all seemed lost.

Three months after becoming Pope in June 1939, Pius XII — eager to resolve once and for all the mystery behind Saint Peter's bones — asked Monsignor Carlo Respighi, who held the office of Secretary of the Pontifical Committee for Sacred Archeology, to institute a formal attempt to uncover Saint Peter's tomb underneath the main altar in the Basilica. Although the Curia was very much against any kind of excavation underneath the altar because of the stupendous weight of Bernini's bronze and marble canopy that embraced the general area, Pius pushed his weight around on this one and took the full responsibility for any such consequences. He even promised that if the sum of money set aside for the excavations ran out, he would have the work continue with money from a personal bank account he still had under his family name of Pacelli. Still the Curia fought him and sought to block the diggings, but in the end Pius won and the shovels began.

In 1940 four archeologists, three Italians and a German Jesuit, were given the job that was to run for about nine years, and they were assisted by a team of the Vatican's best carpenters, ironworkers, plumbers, masons and electricians — known inside the Vatican as *sampietrini*; these workers were under the direct supervision of Monsignor Ludwig Kaas, a thoroughly efficient German or so he thought himself to be, whose efficiency almost proved disastrous during the course of the work. Two blunders that Monsignor Kaas committed were his failure to keep a proper day-by-day logbook of the work and his failure to take photographs of the work under way. Monsignor Kaas was also responsible for the lack of coordination between his crew of workers and the four archeologists. But his biggest blunder was yet to come.

The archeologists — Antonio Ferrua, Enrico Josi, Bruno Apolloni-Ghetti and Engelbert Kirschbaum — discovered that substantial portions of a monument known by historians to have been built by Emperor Constantine to honor Saint Peter had been used as the basis upon which to build Saint Peter's Basilica, with the main altar being placed on the site of the monument itself. Incorporated into this monument was a much smaller, somewhat primitive monument built earlier, a small niche dug into a brick wall, flanked by two small marble columns supporting a slab of travertine and resting on another slab which covered a hole in the ground that had been cut away to look like a trench. Although the archeologists spent almost nine years getting down into Peter's original tomb, when they finally reached it, it was empty.

But close to the tomb was a small collection of human bones that had been placed in a small arch, and these were taken away by Monsignor Kaas, placed into a zinc box and eventually put behind lock and key in his office. As luck would have it, Monsignor Kaas allowed one of the archeologists, Father Engelbert Kirschbaum, to take a photo of a fragment of a humerus and a femur. The bones remained in Monsignor Kaas's cupboard and would have probably remained there forever, if Pope Pius had not one day just happened to have seen the two photographs taken by Father Kirschbaum. Pius asked his personal physician, Dr Riccardo Galeazzi Lisi, for an opinion on the bones.

Even though more than 80 per cent of the bones were missing for any kind of meaningful reconstruction of a skeleton, Dr Galeazzi Lisi arrived at the conclusion that the bones belonged (1) to one man; (2) to an elderly man; and (3) to a man of sturdy build. This fit Peter's description quite well. There was only one fly in the ointment — a subsequent examination of the bones revealed that they actually were the bones of two men and a woman. But in the meantime Pope Pius had already announced in 1942 that the bones were of Saint Peter. So, in his 1950 announcement, he simply said the bones 'could not be proved with certainty' as belonging to Peter, letting the world infer what it wanted.

It is at this point that an incredible series of events follow in which a woman — Dr Margherita Guarducci, then a professor of Greek epigraphy (the study of inscriptions) at the University of Rome — intruded into the history of Peter's bones and became a legend in her own right within the Vatican (one of the few women ever to do so).

Guarducci had read in 1952 in a Rome newspaper an article on Antonio Ferrua, the Italian Jesuit who comprised one of the quartet of the Vatican archeology team. What caught her attention was a casual reference to Father Ferrua that an inscription had been found on the wall, inside the recess, which had Greek letters that read: PETR on one line and ENI on the other line. Since she was an expert on Greek inscriptions, she asked the Vatican if she could study this. As was to be expected, Professor Guarducci was repeatedly turned down by Vatican bureaucrats. Rebuffed but undaunted, and then 67 years old, she managed to see Monsignor Giovanni Montini, then Substitute Secretary of State, later to become Pope Paul VI. With Monsignor Montini's help, Professor Guarducci obtained a private audience with Pope Pius and convinced him that she should take a close look at the inscription. In May 1952, the double-locked section of the secluded excavations were opened to her, but alas and alack, the PETR and ENI inscription were nowhere to be found. When she sought out Father Ferrua, he assured her he had personally seen the letters himself and bemoaned the fact that they had not been photographed. What had happened to the inscription?

It took Professor Guarducci nearly two years of persistent hunting, but eventually she discovered that Monsignor Kaas had stored away — once again in his cupboard — a tiny chunk of plaster from the wall that came unstuck. Guessing that this piece could very well have the Greek letters on them, she sought to get Monsignor Kaas to let her look at it. He refused. There was nobody who could get the headstrong monsignor to change his mind. So back to Monsignor Montini went Professor Guarducci who once again went to see the Pope, who then ordered Monsignor Kaas to comply. Sure enough, there were the elusive letters. Study of the Greek letters led Guarducci to interpret the inscription: 'Peter is in here.' It took her another six years of intensive study of the faded graffiti that the early Christians had scratched on that wall to solve the riddle. She did this mostly by using enlarged photographs of the graffiti and studying them almost daily in her home and in her office.

Professor Guarducci then made a most revealing discovery. After considerable study on the spot (for now she had been given access to the excavations any time she wanted), she deciphered an incription written in the form of P E. With the help of her sister Maria, she pored over the strange criss-cross of signs and letters in the grottoes beneath the altar and compared them with those in the catacombs in and near Rome. They found significant repetitions and meanings, and now a special line was beginning to take shape.

During the second century, the Christians who had gone underground as a result of systematic persecutions, developed a mystical code. They had symbols such as the Greek chi rho — a combination of the first two Greek letters of the word Christ to form a ☧. Similarly, early Christian worshippers and pilgrims used the Latin letters P and E for Peter, M for Mary and T for the Cross. These were often inserted in the names of the worshippers and those they wished to commemorate. Thus, if a Christian's name was Paolo, beneath the

P in that name, an E was drawn in to signify Peter's crucifixion. If the Christian's name was Claudia, than this name was written with a Greek X fused with the P, making the chi rho and indicating Claudia's devotion to Christ.

The PE symbol in various combinations occurred again and again in the crypt beneath the confession altar. Peter's name was not spelled out, and this was why none of the archeologists was able to find it. But it was there in monogram form at the foot of the P to make it look like a key — PE. Underneath were some letters that could have been an abbreviation of the Greek word, *Enesti*, which when taken together with the monogramic letters would mean, 'Peter is buried here.'

In demolishing a segment of Constantine's wall, the Vatican workers uncovered another odd find, besides the graffiti — a horizontal slit in the wall. When they made it bigger, they discovered a small recess behind it in the form of a rectangular box, lined with marble slabs that had been bricked in. The archeologists put down in their notes that the recess was empty, 'except for the remains of organic matter and bones, mixed with earth, a strip of lead, two small skeins of silver thread and some coins dating from the 10th Century.'

As luck would have it, one day in September 1953, Professor Guarducci was on her knees studying the graffiti on this wall with a magnifying glass, and a foreman of the *sampietrini*, Giovanni Segoni, was standing watching her. She asked Segoni if the excavators had found anything else in the recess, besides the objects already known about. Much to her surprise, Segoni said there was indeed some other stuff (yet another box that Monsignor Kaas had squirreled away), a wooden box in a damp cellar in front of the chapel of Saint Colombanus. Segoni led Guarducci to the box, and inside was the most incredible assortment of objects, consisting of many human bones, some bones of cats and dogs, ancient coins, tiny shreds of woolen cloth with golden threads and the almost complete skeleton of a mouse.

It was not fully clear why Monsignor Kaas had not reported these objects to any of the four archeologists when the diggers had uncovered them; he apparently had stuffed them into a box, forgot to label them, made no record of them in a ledger and took no photographs. These objects at first did not indicate in any way that they might be the bones of Saint Peter, partly because the animal bones would hardly be mixed up with the remains of the saint and partly because of the coins and other objects that were not of the era of Saint Peter. Guarducci, nevertheless, routinely submitted the bones to an anatomy expert in Sicily, Professor Venerando Correnti of Palermo University. After several years of study, Professor Correnti reported that the bones comprised a nearly complete set that belonged to one person and those bones were of an old man. His report also showed that the age of the man was between 60 and 70 years and the height between 163.6 and 167.9 centimeters (between 5ft 4½ in and 5ft 6in).

With this information, Professor Guarducci began to think that the bones could be Peter's. She surmised that when Constantine's workers opened Peter's original tomb, they found his skeleton covered in earth, and in order not to damage the relics, they picked up the whole lot and placed both the earth and bones intact inside Constantine's monument. What baffled Guarducci, however, were the animal bones, 29 in all. Further examination by Professor Correnti, helped now by Professor Luigi Cardini of Rome University, identified the bones as those of a hog, a rooster, an ox and sheep. The remaining 19 bones belonged to one animal, the mouse.

But there was something very special about the rodent's bones. Unlike the others which were yellowed and encrusted with earth, the mouse's bones were very white and clean. The riddle Guarducci faced was: what was the meaning of all these animal bones that were mixed with those of Peter and that had been so carefully hidden and protected inside Constantine's monument? For most of a summer Guarducci wrestled with this question and could find no solution. She decided to put the question to some of her professional friends in Academia, especially archeologists who had had a lot of experience digging in the Rome area. She asked them if they ever had occasion to find animal bones mixed in with human bones, and one of her friends said that in cases like that, it usually meant that a body had first been buried on farm land, among the carcasses of dead farm animals, and then later disinterred and reinterred together with the farm soil and the animal bones.

Slowly the pieces to the jigsaw puzzle seemed to be falling into place. Guarducci learned that the body of the martyr had first been buried in a simple trench on a farm until Constantine decided to move it to a safer and more sumptuous place. And there the whole collection remained for 1600 years. Professor Guarducci undertook further scientific tests. Experts were consulted on the other materials found inside the recess. Soil analysts reported that the earth found in the recess very likely came from the soil in which the first century tomb was dug. Chemical analysis showed that the cloth in which the bones were wrapped had a fine plate of gold, other threads were made of pure gold and some of the linen showed traces of having been gold-plated. But perhaps the most important fact to emerge from the chemists' research was that the wool had been dyed with a deep purple which in Peter's time was the most expensive dye and was reserved for royalty and high Church dignitaries.

There remained one stumper: the presence of coins from the tenth century and how they came to be inside a recess that had supposedly never been opened since the days of Constantine the Great (288–337 A.D.). The bones of the little mouse finally solved the question and gave Guarducci her final clue as to the authenticity of the bones of Saint Peter. Since the bones of the mouse were whiter than the other animal bones and since there was a lack of earth encrustation on the skeleton, the mouse had obviously infiltrated the recess after it was built and then perished there. With his wriggling to get into the recess from above, the mouse (Guarducci surmised) helped some of the coins, which were very thin and small in diameter, to slip into the tiny space. Coins were apparently thrown on to the church floor by pilgrims, and the janitors of the basilica swept these into receptacles — but some slipped unnoticed into the cracks in the floor and gradually dropped downwards over a century or so.

Professor Guarducci finally solved a mystery that had plagued the Vatican for centuries. But, in so doing, she upset an ecclesiastical applecart that meant a big embarrassment for Vatican officials. For centuries the Saint John Lateran Church in Rome had kept the 'skull of Saint Peter' in a silver container, to which millions of believers had gone to pay homage. Guarducci's final report made it plain that this was a false relic. When Pope Paul VI announced that Saint Peter's bones had been discovered, no mention was made of the skull. Nor was any mention made of Professor Margherita Guarducci.

CHAPTER III

The Bitter Pill of Pope Paul

POPE PAUL VI had an idiosyncracy that was kept from the public: he often wore a hairshirt studded with metal points that scratched his skin. Paul, who had the build of a professional wrestler and the well-muscled arms of an athlete (which the public of course never realized), began wearing his hairshirt as a young priest. After his election as Pope in 1963, he even wore it underneath his rich robes on every important occasion. When he opened the Holy Year in 1975, his tired and wan appearance brought mass feelings of compassion for him, but nobody could have imagined that his torso was wrapped in a hairshirt with metal points that were pressing and penetrating his flesh. Vatican staffers could never quite accept this self-torture.

No amount of self-torture, however, could ever come close to the torture that Paul underwent with his so-called birth control encyclical cum inner-Vatican politics that crushed him like grapes in a wine press. To Catholics throughout the world, not acquainted with the phenomenon of political action within the Vatican itself — just as deadly as politics anywhere else — it would come as a shock to learn that behind the papal throne this disturbing dirty game is frequently played. Political maneuvering is practiced by the Curia strongmen whose Catholicism, often cast in a medieval mold, is not above the fine Italian art of conspiracy. No matter how scandalous these intrigues would be if known to the outside, the orthodox cardinals who represent the old guard and who run the gamut from conservative to reactionary keep a sharp eye on the Holy Father when it comes to sensitive matters.

At their very best and at their very worst, popes are political beings (perhaps the word 'politician' sounds too harsh — but that is what a pope is and has to be, whatever euphemisms are used). As Pope, the individual who rules over nearly 700 million Roman Catholics and over his immediate domain inside the Vatican walls — where he is the chief executive, the legislature and the judiciary — is necessarily mixed up in the give-and-take of the game of politics. Sometimes he gives, and sometimes he gives in. Set aside any feeling of shock you may have and recognize that the orthodox cardinals and bishops who form a cocoon around Catholicism's chief shepherd do not hesitate to badger him. Such was the case of Paul on the question of contraception.

After the Second Vatican Council, Pope John XXIII appointed a commission of bishops and laymen to consider the question of birth control, a debate that had raged for years among Catholics everywhere. The Papal Commission on Birth Control, which was limited to an advisory capacity, set about making a thorough study of the issue in 1964 meeting in secret for many sessions. When it submitted its report to the pontiff in the middle of 1966, it consisted of a majority statement and a minority statement. The Vatican never made the report public, and Pope Paul remained silent while he gave the report intensive study with an eye to issuing a crucial encyclical on the controversial matter of birth control among Catholics.

An unidentified member of the papal commission made a copy of the report in Latin available to Desmond O'Grady, the Rome correspondent of the *National Catholic Reporter*, a liberal, independent weekly newspaper based in Kansas City, Missouri. Using its own English translation from the Latin, the newspaper printed the full report in its issue of April 19, 1967; its editor, Robert G Hoyt, justified the publication of a Vatican secret document on the grounds that the text would be a service to its readers and that birth control as an issue was nobody's monopoly, 'not even those ramifications of it which touch on the meaning of the Church's teaching authority.'

The report showed that a majority of the bishops favored birth control. The majority based its argument for using means of contraception, other than the rhythm method, almost entirely on the need for fulfilment in marriage, which it said included sexual fulfilment and the right to plan the number of children the family can care for and prepare 'for a truly human life'.

Although acceptance of contraceptive pills had been considered a possible avenue for the Catholic Church to take, in abandoning its opposition to mechanical means of contraception, the majority did not mention the pill or differentiate between it and other means of contraception. The majority stated: 'The regulation of conception appears necessary for many couples who wish to achieve a responsible, open and reasonable parenthood in today's circumstances. If they are to observe and cultivate all the essential values of marriage, married people need decent and human means for the regulation of conception.' Defending the importance of sexual love in marriage, the majority added: 'Through developing their communion and intimacy in all its aspects, a married couple is able to provide that environment of love, mutual understanding and humble acceptance which is the necessary condition of authentic human education and maturation.'

In their minority report, the conservative bishops stood firmly on the past teachings of the Church. Arguing that contraception was evil in itself, they said: 'Something which can never be justified by any motive or any circumstances is always evil because it is intrinsically evil. It is wrong not because of a precept of positive law, but a reason of natural law. It is not evil because it is prohibited, it is prohibited because it is evil.' The minority then added: 'If we could bring forward arguments which are clear and cogent based on reason alone, it would not be necessary for our commission to exist, nor would the present state of affairs exist in the Church as it is.'

The conservative bishops saw serious theological implications in a change of position in the Church. 'For the Church to have erred so gravely in its grave responsibility of leading souls', the minor paper stated, 'would be tantamount to seriously suggesting that the assistance of the Holy Spirit was lacking to her.' The minority report also contended that the condoning of artificial contraception in marriage would open the door to approval of extramarital sexual relationships, sterilization and unnatural sex acts.

The Vatican's reaction to the unauthorized publication of the commission's report, before the pontiff had had a chance to study it in full, was that it was leaked to put pressure on Paul to make a decision. *L'Osservatore Romano*, commenting on the leak, said that the Holy Father had reserved for himself the right to provide a solution to the serious question without his enemies seeking to force the issue.

Not until late July 1968, more than 14 months after the *Reporter* had spilled the beans, did Pope Paul finally make a decision and promulgate his encyclical, *Humanae Vitae* [Of Human Life], which banned the use of effective birth control procedures for the spacing of children and the control of population. It was greeted with anguished protests from the Catholic community all over the globe, and though priests in support of the Pope were given ample press coverage, there were nevertheless equally strong protests from the Catholic clergy, especially in the United States. The hostile lay reaction was immediate and it burgeoned — one newspaper poll reported that 94 out of every 100 practicing Catholics disagreed with the pontiff. Even to this day the angry protests and challenges still continue over Paul's fateful blunder. Many Catholic laymen and a large number of priests were driven out of the Church because they felt that birth control was not a matter of Christian faith.

What had happened inside the Vatican? Why had Pope Paul,

whose hobby was the reading of sociology books (as he once personally told me in Milan shortly before his election to the papacy), gone against the majority of bishops and knowledgeable laymen who had recommended that the Church change its position on birth control? Had he come under the influence of conservatives within the Vatican system while he was pecking out his seventh encyclical on a battered Olivetti portable?

Pope Paul, himself duly impressed with the logic of the majority report and the sound sociology it displayed, wanted the question of contraceptive uses left up to the conscience of the individual, with strong warnings to the effect that the use of such devices were permissible in some circumstances and only when necessary to preserve and foster the values and sacredness of marriage. But he was overruled. Hemmed in by the Curial structure, which at that time constituted a majority of elderly Italian cardinals who were very conservative, Paul gave in to the concentrated pressure and finally agreed to accept the view of the minority bishops on the papal commission — even though he knew fully well that the encyclical would have a disastrous effect within the ranks of Roman Catholics, cause untold agony for nameless millions and have a shattering effect on the ecumenical movement.

The fuss and feathers even involved the US Secretary of Agriculture in President Gerald Ford's cabinet in 1974 when he (Earl Butz) made a remark about birth control in connection with a speech Pope Paul had made at the World Food Conference in Rome that Mr Butz had been attending. Borrowing a remark he had overheard from an Italian woman at the conference and embellishing it with a mock Italian dialect of his own, Secretary Butz said at a breakfast table meeting with some newsmen that as far as Pope Paul's controversial birth control encyclical was concerned, 'He no playa da game, he no maka da rules!' Later he apologized for the ethnic slur, but the basic message, without the accent, was there.

CHAPTER IV

The Encyclical That Was Never Published

AN ENCYCLICAL from Pope Pius XI entitled, *Humani Generis Unitas*, which dealt in part with the issue of anti-Semitism, was snuffed out by the Vatican shortly before the Pope's expected death. It should have been entitled, *The Encyclical That Was Never Published — And Should Have Been*, for had it appeared in 1938, as planned, it might have saved the lives of millions of people. The unpublished papal document, apart from the historic and social impact it would have had in the uneasy, war-worried world of 1938, gives an unflattering glimpse of the inner workings of the Vatican as a place of intrigues.

In June 1935, the ailing Pius XI commissioned an American Jesuit priest, Father John LaFarge (who died in 1963 at the age of 83), to write the text of an encyclical attacking racism and anti-Semitism. This order came nearly a year and a half before the outbreak of the Second World War. Author of several books on race and founder of the Catholic Inter-racial Council of New York City, Father LaFarge was an editor of the Jesuit magazine, *America*, and a restless crusader in the fight against racism in the United States. His draft contained an explicit condemnation of anti-Semitism and would have made binding on all Roman Catholics obedience to its various major points. Though couched in the usual ecclesiastical verbiage, its language made quite clear that Hitler's anti-Jewish policies were intolerable to the Vatican and to all Roman Catholics. Since more than half of Hitler's soldiers were Catholic and nearly all of Germany's southern regions (especially Bavaria, which also embraces a goodly chunk of Austria) were strongholds for Catholicism, the encyclical *Humani Generis Unitas* [The Unity of the Human Race] would have had considerable influence in Germany — and perhaps even on Hitler who was himself a Catholic. Had it been published in late 1938 or early 1939, it might have saved many of the six million Jews slaughtered during the course of the war. In 1938 Hitler had only just begun to move into full-scale persecution of the Jews and had not yet started his program of extermination. Given the moral weight of the papacy at that point in history, the publication of the encyclical might have helped save hundreds of thousands of lives, and perhaps even millions.

LaFarge's draft, once it got into the Vatican, became the victim of two related and separate Vatican intrigues. The first was that the finished manuscript had to be submitted 'through channels' to LaFarge's Jesuit superior general, Rev Wlodimir Ledochowski, despite the fact that the Pope had ordered it directly from LaFarge. Father Ledochowski, a Polish count before he went into the clergy, came from a country that has the reputation (if Simon Wiesenthal's appraisal as the world's foremost Nazi hunter has any value) of being statistically the most anti-Semitic Western country of all. Therefore it is not beyond the realm of possibility that he shared some of his people's negative feelings toward the Jews, though there is no proof of his ever having uttered any kind of anti-Semitic remark while in the embrace of his Church. Whatever Father Ledochowski's attitudes towards the Jews, the fact remains that he held on to the LaFarge essay for three whole months. The Pope at the time was sick, and it is not known if he saw the LaFarge text or whether he knew that LaFarge had completed it.

The second intrigue concerns French Cardinal Eugene Tisserant's suspicion that Benito Mussolini had Pius XI assassinated to prevent him from openly denouncing Fascism (see Chapter X). Quite possibly Mussolini moved faster than he might have simply because he knew of the proposed encyclical. There is also good reason to suspect that Il Duce had a full copy of the LaFarge text delivered to him by one of his Vatican spies. Mussolini himself was not an anti-Semite and he had strong reservations about Hitler's persecution of the Jews; but, to keep Hitler contented, he began to carry out Germany's racial laws in Italy, admittedly at a snail's pace, but with enough eyewash to keep Hitler happy.

Father LaFarge's text distinguished between false and justified human groupings, and he made clear that racism and anti-Semitism involved false concepts. He called on people of good will to eradicate from public life all distinctions based on race, for 'such distinctions can only be felt as defamatory and discriminatory'. Explaining that racism easily gave way to anti-Semitism, he said that it was clear that the struggle for racial purity 'ends by being uniquely the struggle against the Jews'. He then quoted a 1928 Vatican attack on anti-Semitism. The text continued that no political solution concerning the Jews was the 'true solution' if it contradicts the demanding laws of justice and charity.

The draft's section on Anti-Semitism was entitled 'The Jews and Anti-Semites', and pointed out that contemporary anti-Semitism had historical roots: 'Save for the systematic cruelty, this struggle, in true motives and methods, is no different from persecutions everywhere carried out against the Jews from antiquity. These persecutions have been censured by the Holy See on more than one occasion, but especially when they have worn the mantle of Christianity. . . .

'As a result of such a persecution, millions of persons are deprived of the most elementary rights and privileges of citizens in the very land of their birth. Denied legal protection against violence and robbery, exposed to every form of insult and public degradation, innocent people are treated as criminals though they have circumspectly obeyed the law of their native land.

'Even those who in time of war fought bravely for their country are treated as traitors, and the children of those who laid down their lives on their country's behalf are branded as outlaws by the very fact of their parentage. The values of the Jews, this flagrant denial of human rights, sends many thousands of helpless persons out over the face of the earth without any resources. Wandering from frontier to frontier, they are a burden to humanity and to themselves.'

The LaFarge text also called anti-Semitism 'misguided and harmful' in the light of Church teaching about the Jews, which demonstrated the need for energetic measures to preserve both the faith and morals of its members and society itself against the corrupting influences of error. Anti-Semitism, said the document, was not only pitifully inadequate but also defeated its own purpose, producing in the end only greater obstacles to cope with. 'The Catholic Church habitually prays for the Jewish people who were the bearers of divine revelation up to the time of Christ. . . . Actuated by their love, the Apostolic See has protected this people against unjust oppression and just as every other kind of envy and jealousy among the nations must be disapproved of, so in an especial manner must be that hatred which is generally termed anti-Semitism. . . .

'Anti-Semitism is an assault, under the pretense of protecting society, an evocation of limitless hatred, a license for every form of violence, rapacity and disorder, and an engine against religion itself. Thus we find that anti-Semitism becomes an excuse for attacking the sacred person of the Saviour himself, who assumed human flesh as the son of a Jewish maiden; it becomes a war against Christianity, its teachings, practice and institutions.'

The main slant of the proposed encyclical dealt with the extreme disorder found at that time in the social life of man and mentioned three attempts to create a new unity. These were references to Germany, Italy and the Soviet Union. The draft called excessive nationalism 'a real perversion of the spirit' and classified totalitarianism as being a type of government that was contradictory to natural law. It said that totalitarian governments fostered nationalism, racism and anti-Semitism in an effort to create a sense of unity among their peoples; this type of unity was fallacious and contradicted the real unity of the human race, all of which was 'an outrageous denial of the spirit of God'.

Unlike popes before him (and those who followed him), Pius XI was a man noted for his strong language among his colleagues while at work, and this type of talking was often reflected in his encyclicals which were most often not couched in vagueness of thought or indirectness of language. LaFarge, knowing this, permitted himself to put down in the manuscript the kind of direct, hard-hitting language that would maintain papal dignity, of course, but would pull no punches. Whether Pius would have accepted the entire LaFarge text is an academic point, since the encyclical was never issued. Rev LaFarge, by the way, did not write the proposed encyclical alone; he was assisted by a German Jesuit priest, Father Gustave Gundlach, a professor of the Gregorian University in Rome. The two men met in Paris during the summer of 1938 for the writing; Gundlach prepared the first part of the manuscript on totalitarianism and racism, while LaFarge dealt almost exclusively with the portion concerned with anti-Semitism.

LaFarge, Gundlach and a French priest worked on the encyclical for eight weeks, and, when it was ready, LaFarge personally delivered it to his Father General on or about October 1 and continued on his way to New York. On October 16, Father Gundlach wrote Father LaFarge saying that he distrusted Father Ledochowski because he seemed 'bent on sabotaging the encyclical', a point he repeated in a subsequent letter dated January 28, 1939. Gundlach had heard inside the Vatican that Ledochowski was of the opinion that the world situation was then too critical to allow the Pope to publish such a sharp document.

In the meantime, on November 25, 1938, Pius had suffered two heart attacks, and although he made an apparently good recovery, his asthma worsened because of his bad heart, and his health from that day on was not very good. He died the following year in the early hours of February 11, before he was to make a key speech to the Italian bishops. As late as the first week of January, Pius had not yet received the manuscript.

On March 2, 1939, Cardinal Eugenio Pacelli of Milan, who had once been the papal nuncio in Germany for 12 years where he had cultivated a growing admiration for the German people, was enthroned on the Seat of Saint Peter as Pope Pius XII. He had been

Pope for less than six months when World War II broke out, after Hitler's invasion of Poland and Czechoslovakia. On October 20 Pius XII issued his first encyclical, *Summi Pontificatus* (most of which was written by Father Gundlach), and it drew heavily on the LaFarge-Gundlach manuscript, which Pius had managed to read shortly after his predecessor's death. *Summi Pontificatus* stressed the 'unity of the human race', condemned totalitarianism and the outbreak of war and offered to use the office of the papacy as an agent of mediation.

It left out the heart of LaFarge's text — the part on anti-Semitism.

CHAPTER V

The Vatican and the Jews

THE 22-YEAR-OLD medical student wore a gray, baggy-trousered uniform of a street cleaner. In his pocket were two battered books of poetry. He was an unlikely killer, but the time was World War II when men like him in Rome were made into assassins. He pushed his cart up the cobblestone slope of Via Rasella on that warm, spring afternoon of March 23, 1944, and once in front of Number 156, he stopped, browsed through one of his poetry books and waited for the German SS company, three abreast, to come by singing in time to the rhythmic thud of their boots.

The young student touched a match to the tobacco crumbs and paper in his pipe, put the pipe to a fuse leading to the cart and walked briskly away. Inside the cart were 40 pounds (18 kg) of TNT, and there was an explosion as the German soldiers marched by. Thirty-two SS troops died on Via Rasella. In reprisal the German command in Rome ordered 10 Italian males killed for every dead soldier. The next day the Gestapo and the Italian Fascist police scoured Rome, rounding up as many Jews as they could find — 70 in all. When no more could be located, men was taken at random. Altogether, 335 men were brought in, 15 more than was required by the Commandant. The ages of these men ranged from 15 to 74. Herded into sealed meat trucks, the hostages were trundled off to the Ardeatine Caves outside Rome where there is a network of grottoes among the catacombs which was used by the Christians to bury their martyrs 1900 years earlier. One by one the 335 male hostages were shot. After the war the victims of the Ardeatine Caves massacre became Italian heroes, and the caves have been made into a national monument, visited by hundreds of thousands of Italians every year.

Brooklyn-born author Robert Katz wrote a book about the massacre, called *Death in Rome*, which was later made into a film in 1973, *Massacre in Rome*, for which Katz also wrote the script. Carlo Ponti produced the movie in which both Marcello Mastroianni and Richard Burton starred. In both the book and the film, Katz alleged that Pope Pius XII had reliable information of the Commandant's plans for reprisals on the Via Rasella ambush but did nothing to stop them when he was fully aware that action on his part might prevent the reprisals. In the book, Katz also suggested that Pius remained silent when Roman Jews were rounded up and taken to their death in concentration camps.

Although the book had been out for a few years already, nobody in the Vatican made mention of it, but on the first day of the showing of the film, Countess Eleonora Rossignani, a niece of the late Pope, was outraged. Almost immediately, she filed criminal libel charges against Katz, Ponti and the film's director, George Pan Cosmatos, stating that both the film and the book, from which the screenplay had been taken, were 'an ignoble denigration of our beloved and heroic Pope Pius XII'. During the trial the prosecution contended that the book and movie represented 'the forces of evil' and that Katz's book 'should be burned at the stake'. The trial lasted 21 months, and the three men were convicted. In 1975, the American author was fined 400,000 lire and sentenced to 14 months in prison, and Ponti and Pan Cosmatos to seven months each. Although the sentences were suspended, Katz appealed the verdict, and in July 1978, an appeals court reversed the lower court's ruling and acquitted him and the other two men.

The Ardeatine Massacre was one of the incredible tragedies of wartime Italy, but I wonder if there exists a more unbelievable story from World War II than the events following Germany's invasion of Yugoslavia in the spring of 1941. After Yugoslavia's capitulation, the new State of Croatia was formed, and this gave rise to a band of Catholic fanatics, the Ustashi, who decided to eliminate all non-Catholics in Croatia. Thus all men, women and children who were Jews, gypsies or Orthodox Serbs were slaughtered by the thousand. In one morning alone, inside an Orthodox church in the village of Glina, the Ustashi brutally murdered more than 700 Serbs. The killings not only had the backing of the local Roman Catholic priests, but were carried out by a large number of priests and friars leading the killer gangs. Even more terrible were the Catholic priests who became concentration camp directors and carried out the torture and murder of thousands of people. To mention a few by name, there was a Jesuit priest by the name of Rev Dragutin Kamber, Father Braanimir Zupanic, Father Zvonko Brekalo, Father Zvonko Lipovac, Father Srecko Peric and the monk, Miroslav Filipovic, a Franciscan who was made Commandant of the Jasenovac concentration camp which equalled Dachau in horror and who was responsible for the deaths of 40,000 people.

With a file containing thoroughly documented evidence of the

Catholic Church's responsibility for the Ustashi's crimes, the Yugoslav Chapter of the International Red Cross sent one of its polyglot staff workers, Branko Bokun, to Rome with the object of persuading the Vatican to end the atrocities in Croatia. This could have been done if the Vatican had spoken out against them, for it was the belief of the Red Cross that the Ustashi would have obeyed a pontifical command. Bokun spent nearly four years in Rome during which time he managed to see several of the Vatican's officials. With a letter of introduction to Monsignor Giovanni Montini (the Vatican Secretary of State in 1941, later to become Pope Paul VI), he got into the Apostolic Palace, but the only official he could see was a young priest who treated him coldly and would not let him in to see Montini. The young cleric agreed to take Bokun's file on the Croatian disaster and place it on Monsignor Montini's desk, suggesting that he come back in a week. Which he did. Once again, Bokun was unable to see Montini, but the priest said that the Secretary of State had given the matter his careful consideration and had had a word with the Croatian ambassador, who had explained that the atrocities detailed in the file were the work of the Communists, maliciously attributed to the Catholics. Bokun was also informed that the Vatican had no diplomatic relations with Croatia and that therefore nothing further could be done. When Bokun tried to explain that the Vatican had daily contact with the papal legate in Zagreb and could order him to order the Catholics to stop the butchery, he was told by the priest, in an irritated manner, that the matter was considered closed.

Finding himself frustrated by the Vatican bureaucracy, Bokun then decided to see Pope Pius XII personally and show him the file. He would go to the Wednesday semi-public audience, known as the *bacciamano*, to which only some 30 people were allowed at a time; when he kissed the Pope's ring, he would then hand over the file. On October 8, 1941, having made arrangements through friends of friends he entered the majestic Sala Regia, and after the Pope entered with raised arms, he proceeded to pass down the reception line. When it was Bokun's turn, he kneeled, kissed the ring and received the blessing. Then Bokun presented the file to the Pope (speaking to him in Italian), but after listening and nodding, the Pope made the sign of the cross over it and rhythmically moved on to the next person. He paid no attention whatever to Bokun's nervous voice which asked the Holy Father to look at the file and consider its important contents. One of the documents in it was a letter to Pius from the former minister of the Kingdom of Yugoslavia. It read:

'Your Grace: I write this to you as man to man, as a Christian to a Christian. Since the first day of the Independent Croatian State, the

Serbs have been massacred and this massacring has continued to this day. . . . Why do I write this to you? Here is why: in all these unprecedented crimes, worse than pagan, our Catholic Church has also participated in two ways. First a large number of priests, clerics, friars and organized Catholic young actively participated in all these crimes, but more terrible even Catholic priests became camp and group commanders and as such ordered or tolerated the horrible tortures, murders and massacres of a baptized people. None of this could have been done without the permission of their bishops, and if it was done, they should have been brought to the Ecclesiastical Court and unfrocked. Since this did not happen, then ostensibly the bishops gave their consent by acquiescence at least. . . . It is the duty of the Church to raise its voice: first because it is a Church of Christ; second because it is powerful. I write to you this, about such terrible crimes, to save my soul, and I leave it to you to find a way to save yours. [signed] Prvislav Grizogono, Former Minister of the Kingdom of Yugoslavia. At Zemum, February 8, 1942.'

Repeated attempts after that to get through the labyrinthine red tape of the Vatican were fruitless. As time went on, Bokun received information from Yugoslavia that more than 700,000 Orthodox Serbs had been murdered as well as nearly 90,000 Jews and gypsies. Improbable as it may seem, Bokun found minor Vatican officers with whom he talked totally apathetic; he came away from his conferences with the impression that the priests who worked inside had forgotten humanity and were pursuing worthless goals with their wartime politicking. The mass killings and atrocities in Croatia did not stop, and most of these went on without the knowledge of the rest of the world. Not a single member of the Ustashi Catholic clergy was ever called to task, nor was anyone unfrocked by the Vatican. Or excommunicated.

After the war had ended, nobody was much interested in the grotesque events. Nor did the Vatican ever make mention of the chaos in Croatia, even after Hitler's legions had been destroyed. Bokun had painfully kept a diary of his stay in Rome, and when he tried to sell his book to more than 30 publishers, nobody showed much interest. It had to wait as late as 1973 before Praeger Publishers Inc of New York put the diary out, but it got few reviews and caused less than a ripple.

Contrast this experience with another book written by the long-time Israeli Consul in Italy, Pichas E Lapide, *The Last Three Popes and the Jews*, in which he contended that the Roman Catholic Church 'saved more Jewish lives during the war than all the other churches, religious institutions and rescue organizations put together. Its record stands in startling contrast to the achievements of the International

Red Cross and the Western Democracies. . . . The Holy See, the nuncios and the entire Catholic Church saved some 400,000 Jews from certain death.'

Another prominent writer, Member of Parliament Maurice Edelman, president of the Anglo-Jewish Association told the London Council of the Association that the intervention of Pius XII during the war saved tens of thousands of Jewish lives. Mrs Golda Meir, when she was Prime Minister of Israel, cordially thanked Pius for having raised his voice so often in favor of the Jews. And in gratitude for the way the Vatican sheltered some 5000 Jews during the German occupation of Rome, the American Jewish Welfare Board wrote to Pope Pius in July 1944 a letter in which the following sentence appeared: 'We are deeply moved by this remarkable display of Christian love, the protection afforded to Italian Jews by the Catholic Church and the Vatican during the German occupation of Italy — particularly as the risks incurred by those who gave shelter were immense.' Other commendations from Jewish sources, inspired by the Pope's humane work on the behalf of European Jewry and the financial donations made by him, have sought to give credit to Pius and the Vatican for its fine conduct in the charitable traditions of the Catholic Church.

Behind these favorable public pronouncements of gratitude on the part of Jews, there is, however, another story. And it is one that contradicts the popular image of the Vatican's part in helping Jews. Whereas Jews in many parts of the world have been lavish in their praise towards the wartime Pope, the Jews of Rome view things rather differently. When you strip away the façade the Vatican has successfully put up, you find that the Vatican does not deserve the credit that many Jews, unaware of the total facts, have acknowledged. The Vatican has the full story, but it has not seen fit to release it, nor is there any indication that it will do so.

It needs to be said first that the Vatican has not had any compunction about lying, has not had any compunction about withholding information that would change its image and has not had any compunction about letting Jews and other people all over the world infer that every individual act of wartime charity ever bestowed on the Jews by Catholic priests or nuns was instituted by the Pope. Vatican propagandists have been quite successful in whitewashing Pius XII's wartime role regarding the Jews.

Eighteen days after the Germans had overrun Rome in September 1943, the new commander of the SS in Rome, Major Herbert Kappler told both Ugo Foà, president of Rome's Jewish community, and Dante Almansi, president of the Italian Hebrew Union, that he wanted within 36 hours a total of 50 kilograms of gold (about 110 lbs) from the Jewish community in exchange for 200 Jews who were to be deported to Germany. Major Kappler set a deadline of 11 am for Tuesday, September 28. With time pressing them, Foà and Almansi knew that there was nobody in the Jewish community who had 50 kilograms of gold stashed away at home. Their only hope was to get individual Jews — and perhaps some Catholic friends — to contribute wedding rings, earrings, bracelets, cigarette cases, watches, gold coins and some gold-plated spoons. But would there be enough of these items to make up a total of 50 kilos? Perhaps the Vatican would help out in this case, in the form of a loan that would be paid back in better times? The Vatican was approached through Father Borsarelli who got an appointment with Pope Pius that very morning. Father Borsarelli came back with a rather substantial offer: if any gold was lacking by the time of the deadline, the Vatican would lend up to a maximum of 15 kilos (33 lbs).

Almost immediately word of the German demand had spread around Rome, and not only did Jews go to the synagogue on the Tiber to deposit their gold donations but many Catholics as well. Things moved rapidly, but on the last morning, nevertheless, Foà went to Major Kappler and obtained an extension until 4 pm. At 4 o'clock the two Jewish leaders presented themselves with more than enough gold to meet the commandant's requirements. Having collected sufficient gold to cover more than the stipulated weight, the two leaders decided to play it safe, and when they presented the precious cargo to Kappler, the final weight came to 50 kilos and 31 grams. It had not been necessary to put into use any of the 15 kilos the Vatican had offered.

Years later, stories began to appear in the press that the Vatican had given over 15 kilos of gold to Rome's Jewish community. In an important history by British scholar Anthony Rhodes, *The Vatican in the Age of the Dictators*, an erroneous statement about this gold was published as documented fact — that the Vatican immediately contributed 15 kilograms of gold towards the final sum. This was indeed not the case, for not a single gram of Vatican gold was ever included.

The story of the Jews and the Vatican, however, does not end here. On April 17, 1955, on the occasion of the tenth anniversary of Italy's liberation from the Nazi yoke, thousands of Italy's Jews gathered to pay homage to those who had genuinely assisted — to 'the Priest of the Jews', Father Maria Benedetto, and to 21 other Catholics who had risked their lives to save Jews during the War. Gold medals were awarded that day. Each medal had on it a symbol of the Ten

Commandments and the seven-armed candelabra with the words, 'From the Jews of Italy — In Gratitude'. Father Benedetto was given a citation which read: 'Incomparable in his rescue work, he succeeded in bringing his great arduous task to a successful end — contemptuous of danger, with strong will-power, and a noble joy in the helping of others — deserving of everlasting gratitude. . . .' The daily newspaper of the Christian Democratic Party, *Il Popolo*, headlined the event with 'The Thanks of the Jews Who Were Saved By The Christian Courage of the People'.

In neither the newspaper account nor in any of the speeches or presentations was any mention ever made of the Vatican. Whether this was done deliberately or not might be hard to say, but one thing is certain: the Italian Hebrew Union, which awarded the special gold medals, saw no reason to offer either Pope Pius or any Vatican officer an award of any kind. The Catholic persons getting the medals — which included, besides Father Benedetto, three other priests, the Rome chief of police, and a number of private citizens — were the ones recognized by the Jews of Italy and especially the Jews of Rome. These were the people of non-Jewish faith who put themselves out for thousands of Jews to save them from the German concentration camps.

As for Father Benedetto — the so-called Priest of the Jews — his work on behalf of the Jews is too complex to be described here, but suffice to say all of it was done right under the noses of the Nazis and at great risk to his life. That the Vatican, after the war, sought to take all the credit away from him is not one of that organization's most noble moments. That the Vatican attempted to attribute much of Father Benedetto's accomplishments to the quiet hand of Pius XII is also a low point in Vatican history. The Jews of Italy, almost to the last man and woman who survived the holocaust, were — and still are — virtually unanimous in their opinion that the Vatican behaved unethically when the war was over and the plaudits were being handed out. The Vatican gave Father Benedetto no recognition, and he died unknown to the rest of the world — but a hero to the Jews. Sad to relate, even the alert, estimable *New York Times* failed to publish an obituary.

Father Maria Benedetto was a Frenchman born in 1895 with the name of Pierre Peteul. During World War I, he was wounded in action, fighting as a warrant officer and at the war's end was awarded the Croix de Guerre with five citations for bravery under fire, in addition to the esteemed Medaille Militaire. When he became a Capuchin priest, he began his church duties under the name of Father Marie-Benoit, later to be changed to Maria Benedetto while serving in Italy. Shortly after Father Benoit/Benedetto had been transferred to Rome by the Father General of his order, an old acquaintance of his, an Italian Jew who had been for many years the director of the Credit Franco–Italian bank in Nice, visited him on an important mission. Since the war was not going well for the Germans, the leaders of the large number of Jewish refugees in southern France were afraid that the Nazis would undertake an invasion of the Italian-occupied French provinces. This would have been a total disaster for the mass of Jews there. Some very vital information had to be imparted and four crucial suggestions had to be made to the Pope; Father Benedetto undertook the responsibility of presenting them to His Holiness in a special audience, despite the fact that Father Benedetto and the various French Jewish organizations hiding out in Lyon knew that the Pope had never had done much to help the Jews anywhere.

Father Benedetto was frankly disappointed in the Pope's reaction, but he nevertheless left with him a document from the Rabbis of Lyon which contained clandestinely obtained information on the concentration camps in Upper Silesia (Auschwitz and Treblinka) and details on how deportations of Jews were organized in France. The report was handed to Pius on July 16, 1943. In later years the Vatican was to announce that the reason it had taken no action, nor made any public condemnation of Auschwitz or Treblinka — a considerable time before the rest of the world was to hear of these two notorious death-camps and their extermination activities — was that ecclesiastical authorities could not 'verify the veracity of the report'.

The four suggestions for the Pope's study and consideration were: (1) the possibility of the Vatican getting news on the fate of approximately 50,000 French and foreign Jews who had been deported from France; (2) the possibility of getting help from the Vatican in obtaining better treatment for those Jews who were in concentration camps in France; (3) the possibility of the Vatican, through its diplomatic contacts of getting neutral Spain to extend protection to those Jews in southern France who were of Sephardic extraction (those European Jews that had originally settled in Spain and Portugal); and (4) the possibility of the Vatican helping those Jews stranded in the Italian-occupied French territory to get back into Italy where they were sure to be safer.

On the first, second and fourth suggestions there was no Vatican response at all, much to the bitter disappointment of Father Benedetto. As for the possibility of getting Spain to protect Sephardic

I acknowledge my indebtedness re information in the preceding pages to my good friend and Rome colleague Sam Waagenaar, who was a personal friend of Father Maria Benedetto.

Jews, the Franco government issued orders providing for protective papers to be given to any Jew who could prove his Spanish affiliation. But by the time that order came out, the Germans had removed the occupation duties from the Italians. The stateless Jews in France who claimed Spanish nationality were not given any recognition and were treated as stateless Jews by the Nazis, which meant subsequent deportation for most of them. Altogether, nearly 50,000 Jews were trapped in southern France, most of whom fell victim to Hitler's Final Solution.

Convinced that getting Vatican or papal help for the Jews was a blind alley, Father Benedetto decided he would do what he could do on his own — without papal assistance. Accordingly, he installed himself solidly in the Capuchin Convent on Rome's Via Sicilia, a stone's throw from Via Veneto and practically under the shadow of the Nazi high command in Rome. It was at this address that the friar became deeply involved in the housing of huge numbers of refugees: since there were far too many to be lodged in the convent itself, many of them were put into small pensions and hotels. Often large bribes and extra payments had to be made to let Jews stay on without registering with the Italian *Questura* (Rome police department) as required by law. An even greater problem was in the feeding of these people because food in Rome was severely rationed. None of the refugees had ration cards, which could be obtained only if one had already registered with the *Questura*. But Father Benedetto found ways in a city where residents had for centuries made their own successful approaches to bureaucratic mazes and entanglements, a not unfamiliar phenomenon throughout all of Italy, wartime or no wartime. Italians had centuries of experience in this kind of thing and kept the Germans constantly confused by keeping one step or a half dozen steps ahead. Father Benedetto, though no Roman, had become one — a master of bureaucratic legerdemain.

By luck, one day, Father Benedetto found a dilapidated old printing press among some old furniture in one of the convent's closets. With the help of a refugee typographer Father Benedetto printed up false French identity cards for many Jews. By using a 'rubber stamp' which had been fashioned by inking the dial of a pocket watch, filling in the letters with a toy printing set, and affixing French fiscal postage stamps (which had been bought from a philatelic store in Rome), the Capuchin priest produced identity cards on which he himself blithely signed in the name of appropriate French authorities. These 'official documents' fooled Swiss, Rumanian and Hungarian legation officers to get some 200 Jews out of Italy and into the safety of those countries.

As for the Vatican that gave Benedetto no help, the Swiss playwright, Rolf Hochhuth, was one of the first to suggest that the Church had fumbled the ball. In a controversial drama, he gave fictional treatment to Pope Pius's silence on the Jews. Called *The Deputy* in the United States when produced on Broadway in 1963 and *The Representative* in England when staged in the West End the same year, the play — whose explosive blank verse was translated into some 20 languages — depicted the wartime Pope as cynical, money-minded and callous as regards the Nazi persecution of the Jews. Though his play was called historically inaccurate, Hochhuth at the time defended himself not on the grounds that he was using poetic license but that certain confidences had been made to him by a disgruntled member of the Curia who had not wished his name to be revealed. Hochhuth had his own tipster inside the Vatican.

Not until Act IV does *The Deputy* make its explosive point. In that scene the Pope comes on stage conversing about the stocks and bonds in which the Vatican has invested and whose value is in effect being influenced by the Allied bombings of Italy. The Pope says he is disturbed by the destruction of 'our factories', adding that the Germans have been 'more friendly than the destroyers of San Lorenzo' [the Allies]. The Pope then talks of selling some of the Vatican shares to 'influential men around Roosevelt', since this would no doubt bring on a decrease of the air raids on Rome. Just then an aide comes into the room to inform the Pope of the extermination camps in Poland, but the Pope shows no interest in this news. Meanwhile, through the Pope's window one can see the SS rounding up Jews for shipment to Auschwitz. Hochhuth's comment on this callousness: 'Perhaps never before in history have so many people paid with their lives for the passivity of one single politician.'

The outcry and furor over Hochhuth's play broke all decibel counts in the theatre, but it was Pope Paul VI who had the last word. He wrote a letter in June 1963 while he was still Cardinal Montini of Milan and it was received by *The Tablet* in London on the same day he had become Pope Paul VI. Had Pius XII done what Hochhuth castigated him for not doing, wrote Paul, 'his action would have led to such reprisals and devastations that Hochhuth himself — the war being over, and he now possessed of a better historical, political and moral judgment — would have been able to write another play, far more realistic and interesting than the one he has in fact so cleverly, and also so ineptly, put together. What is the gain to art and culture when the theatre lends itself to injustice of this sort?'

Yet there are deeper waters for Pius XII to swim through. That he had not known the Nazis had already begun exterminating Jews in certain concentration camps is a false inference that followers of the Catholic religion have been led to make. As early as January 1943, Pius had in his hands a letter from Wladislas Rackiewicz, president of the Polish government-in-exile in London, in which he said: 'The extermination of Jews, and with them of many Christians of the Semitic race, has only been a test for the systematic application of scientifically organized mass murder. . . . Hundreds of thousands of people are killed without due process. . . .'

There are masses of papers in the Vatican that show that the Pope knew of the exterminations and that he had been advised not to speak out. For instance, President Roosevelt's envoy, Myron Taylor, went from Washington to Rome three times in 1942 (the last time he stayed in Vatican City for 11 days) to supply Pius with oral and written information about the Jews and the Nazis. This was also true of the British minister to the Holy See, Sir D'Arcy Osborne, who returned to Rome on June 29, 1943, after a three-month stay in London where his superiors briefed him, among other things, on Hitler's program for the Jews. Sir D'Arcy even asked a Vatican officer, 'Why does not the Holy See intervene against the terrible slaughter of the Jews?' Even Cardinal Tisserant, in a letter to the Archbishop of Paris, admitted he had requested the Pope to publish an encyclical on this question, adding that there was a danger to the Church in that 'history tomorrow should not be allowed to reproach the Holy See with having followed a line of political convenience which was serving its own advantage exclusively. . . .'

Firmly holding to his belief that to break his silence on the Jewish exterminations would have been both useless and dangerous to the Jews, Pius had another reason for not speaking up. This reason never came to public attention at the time. Having received confidential reports from Germany that Hitler had a plan to kidnap him when the time was ripe and the occasion was equally ripe, Pius was truly worried that Hitler would abrogate an article of the 1929 Concordat in which the German government collected a compulsory Church tax from its citizens each year. Fifty per cent of this sum was turned over to the Catholic Church in Germany and the rest went to Rome. The tax total collected in 1943, for instance, amounted to some 450 million marks, which at that time was worth over $100 million. Because of the huge sum of money involved, and because of the dire results the loss of this money might have had on the German Catholic Church, Vatican officials believed it deserved major consideration, for Hitler indeed was the kind of leader, once unduly upset, who would put a stop to the Church's share.

When the war ended in Europe, many were the apologists who

sought to give defense to Pope Pius's stand on the Jews and the Nazis. Nearly all of these defenses, some more vociferous than others, supported the Pope's refusal to speak up on behalf on the Jews. Pius himself finally got into the act. On Easter Sunday 1945, he addressed close to a half million people who had gathered in Saint Peter's Square, and on the subject of Germany's treatment of the Jews, he expostulated:

'Those who let themselves be seduced by the instigators of violence and who followed the band so unwisely, now finally begin to wake up from their illusion, astonished to see how far their servile docility has led them. For them there is no other way of salvation, but to repudiate once and for all the idolatry of absolute nationalism, of pride in the superiority of race and blood.'

For many Jews who heard those words that day or read them in the papers, the statement must have had a phony ring to it, for they were words that were said too late and words that were uttered once the danger had vanished. The holocaust had taken place, and now the Pope was speaking out, for the first time, against Hitler's treatment of the Jews.

It took Rev Robert Leiber, a Jesuit professor of ecclesiastic history at the Pontifical Gregorian University — and an extremely close confidant of Pius XII throughout most of his reign — to become the foremost spokesman and apologist for the Vatican. He was also dishonest in what he published. His first article appeared in March 1961 in the Jesuit monthly, *Civiltà Cattolica*. Entitled, 'Pius XII and the Jews of Rome 1943–1944', the article successfully twisted history around and created a myth that was a staggering evasion of hard fact. His words have been quoted over and over again as the official Vatican stand. Five years later, Father Leiber repeated some of his statements in an interview in *Look* magazine. Essentially, he stated that there had been during the German occupation two special pontifical organizations in Rome to help the Jews — the Delasem and the Opera di San Raffaele. However, neither of these two organizations was a Vatican organization and neither received financial assistance from the Pope.

Delasem, Father Leiber maintained, had begun in Genoa as 'a Jewish organization' that became a Vatican institution when the Germans occupied that city. Except for money contributed by some Jews and other Church institutions in Rome, 'the rest was totally donated by Pius XII'. In the *Look* interview Father Leiber added that 'the Pope spent his whole private fortune' to help the Jews. Since none of this was true, executive members of the Jewish community in both Rome and Genoa, astounded by the statement, drafted a letter of protest to be published in *Civiltà Cattolica*. In the letter the Jewish leaders of both cities who affixed their signatures stated bluntly that Delasem — which had been run by Father Benedetto — had never been a pontifical organization and had always been, and remained till the end, a Jewish organization. The letter also stated that Delasem never received any money from Pope Pius but got money instead from Italian citizens, both Jewish and Catholic. *Civiltà Cattolica* never published this letter. The only answer the Jewish leaders got was from Father Leiber who, ignoring all the corrections and counter-statements, said in a very short note that the events had taken place so many years before that by now it was not worthwhile discussing the matter any further. Even the intervention of Father Benedetto had no effect: he told a Vatican officer that during the nine months of the German occupation while he was acting as president of Delasem, 'no money whatsoever had been received from the Vatican'.

As for the other organization that helped Jews in Rome, Opera di San Raffaele, Father Leiber stated that some 2000 persons, the great majority of whom were Jews, were able to travel to Brazil with help from that organization with money that came from the Vatican. This was a misleading statement: the head of that organization, German Pallottine Father Anton Weber, pointed out that the Opera di San Raffaele 'only took care of Catholic-baptized Jews of non-Italian nationality, never of *real* Jews'. As for the money that was supposed to have come from the Vatican to carry out this noble work, Father Weber said that Leiber's declaration gave the wrong impression because the money only came through the Vatican serving as a transfer office or clearing house, a step which the war had made necessary. The actual funds, amounting to $125,000, came from the Chicago section of the United Jewish Appeal and had been delivered to the Vatican by Monsignor Bernard Sheil of Chicago. Father Weber's clarification was also not published in *Civiltà Cattolica*.

Additional misrepresentations by Father Leiber raised Cain with Italy's Jews, but the Vatican never repudiated any of his statements. For instance, Father Leiber, praising 'the lonely admirable priests, strong in a laudable religious devotion', said that their work had been done on orders from the Vatican. 'Pius XII had made it known,' Leiber wrote, 'that the religious homes could and should give Jews refuge.' Yet all of the priests who were active in helping Jews find secret hiding places said they never got any such papal instructions and that they acted individually and spontaneously on their own, though they were sure that they had the Holy Father's silent consent.

One of the persons who escaped was Catholic atomic physicist Enrico Fermi, accompanying his Jewish wife.

Still another statement by Father Leiber reported that of the 4500 Jews hidden in various clerical hideouts in Rome, many of these were hidden within Vatican walls. This Leiber declaration also is an exaggeration, for neither the Chief Rabbi of Rome nor any of the important members of the Jewish community of Rome could report of ever having heard of a single Jew who had been hidden inside the Vatican itself. One reporter in Rome, seeking to verify this, spent a lot of time tracking down what he thought was the only known family, 11 Jews in all, which had been given a four-months' haven inside the Vatican — but that appeared to be a special case because one of the daughters in the family had been engaged to marry a Catholic who had been befriended by a priest living inside the Vatican. The other exception was a converted Jew who made a large sum of money as a manufacturer of ready-made clothing, and when he died in 1949, he left all his possessions to Pius XII, as per promise.

Another propaganda gimmick used by Father Leiber was to give prominent mention to the conversion of Chief Rabbi Italo Zolli to Catholicism, as some kind of ultimate proof of what the Church did for the Jews. As well as Father Leiber's declarations, the Vatican got into the act too and tried at the time to make the most of this conversion. In so doing, the Vatican created and perpetuated a number of calculated fabrications designed to convince the world that it was pro-Jewish.

Rabbi Zolli had disappeared from view on September 8, 1943, when Nazi troops took over Rome completely. Not until June 1944, when the Allied armies took Rome over, did Rabbi Zolli re-surface. It was said at the time, and the Vatican inferred it was true, that Rabbi Zolli had been housed clandestinely inside the Vatican. Rabbi Zolli had in fact not been hiding inside the Vatican but had hid himself in various different places in Rome during the some ten months he was not to be found anywhere, despite efforts on the part of the Nazi commandant to ferret him out. When the Germans retreated from Rome, Rabbi Zolli, then 68 years old, sought to take up his duties once again as the Chief Rabbi of Rome, but Rome's Jewish community resisted because the people felt that their chief rabbi had left them in the lurch when they really needed him.

Rabbi Zolli, together with his wife and daughter Miriam, had himself baptized in the Catholic rites early in 1945. The Vatican let it be known that Rabbi Zolli, in becoming a Roman Catholic, had made a vow to convert to Christianity if God would guide him safely through the holocaust. The Vatican did not make any mention of the fact that Zolli had been attracted to Christianity as a youth. Shortly after his conversion, Zolli was appointed Professor of Hebrew and

Testamental Literature at the Pontifical Biblical College of Rome.

Zolli, one of six children of the family Zoller, had been destined by his deeply religious parents to become a rabbi. Though he was a superb scholar and a humanist, Zolli was not considered a good rabbi by his peers, nor even by his daughter. True, he showed great skills while teaching Old and New Testament theology at the University of Padua, during which time he was taken by the idea of establishing a bridge between the Jewish faith and Christianity, a point of view he brought forth in his book, published in 1938, *The Nazarene*, and in his dissertation entitled, 'The Holy Alliance Between the Ancient and New-Testamentary Literature'.

As Chief Rabbi of Rome, however, Zolli never quite found his place in that city's community, the oldest Jewish community in the world. 'There was no contact', his daughter Miriam told Rome journalist, Sam Waagenaar, in an interview. It was not unexpected, therefore, that Rome's community went against him when he reappeared after the Nazis' departure. Embittered and torn with his own inner struggle concerning the 'religious bridge' he wanted to erect between the religion of his parents and the religion of the popes, Zolli became an outcast among his own people. After he was informed by a prominent Roman Jew in 1944 that he had better search around for another arrangement, Zolli over-reacted and told the representative that if Rome's Jews wanted to put him out to pasture after he had spent 40 years working for Judaism, 'they will pay dearly for it'. Several years later, in an interview with an Israeli newspaper, Zolli told a correspondent: 'Heaven is my witness that what I did was not done out of self-interest. I simply became a convert to Catholicism as the result of a profound religious conviction that developed in me over a period of years. . . . The knowledge of Catholicism and my love for Christ and for the Gospels could merge in my soul without any contrast. . . . I feel as if I were born a Catholic.'

Having milked the Zolli affair dry, Father Leiber never let up on the propaganda, stating that the Jews were grateful to the Pope 'for the help they received from him during the war'. He reported how in 1945 a group of Jews who had come out of the death camps thanked the Pope in a private audience for his help, how the Israeli Philharmonic Orchestra gave a concert at the Vatican in May 1955, how the Chief Rabbi of Rome, Elio Toaff, wrote in an article commissioned by *L'Osservatore Romano*, the Vatican's semi-official daily newspaper, that 'more than anyone, we have had the occasion to appreciate the great compassionate goodness and magnanimity of the Pope during those unhappy years of persecution and terror, when it seemed there was no escape for us. . . .'

Father Leiber forgot to mention that *L'Osservatore* did not publish the second half of Dr Toaff's article in which he diplomatically expressed the view supported unanimously by Rome's Jewish community, that so much more could have been done by the Vatican. His carefully chosen words were: 'We prefer to remember what the Pope *has* done for the Jews, instead of thinking about what he has *not* done. . . .'

The Pius apologists continued to take up the cudgels on his behalf as late as the fall of 1981 when a new book by J Derek Holmes, a Roman Catholic priest, suggested that the wartime pontiff jeopardized his reputation in order to save the lives of thousands of Jews then being concealed by the Vatican. By wisely not condemning Nazi atrocities, the Pope laid himself open to subsequent allegations that he lacked courage, but this was done with an ulterior motive. In his book, *The Papacy in the Modern World*, Father Holmes, a British historian, said that Pius's 'own work on behalf of the Jews might have been endangered by a public denunciation of the Nazis, even though such a denunciation might have justified his moral reputation in the eyes of mankind.' Rev Holmes maintained that Pius was faced with a simple choice: 'Was his own moral reputation more important than the life of a single Jew?' The Pope, according to Father Holmes, sheltered some 400,000 Jews from German deportation. Moreover, when the Nazis demanded 50 kilograms of gold in exchange for the lives of 200 Roman Jews, Father Holmes stated, the Vatican was quick to supply the ransom. Another error in the Holmes book is the assertion that more than half the Jews in Rome were being sheltered in ecclesiastical buildings that had been opened to them on the instructions of the Pope himself.

Was Pius's silence on the persecution of the Jews a scandalous blot on an otherwise impressive pontificate? Careful diplomat that he was, the Pope was convinced that a public accusation against the German chancellor would be fatal to Vatican neutrality, in addition to which a pontifical conscience statement against the Third Reich would not really change matters. Whatever his personal feelings about Hitler, to the very end the Pope considered Soviet Russia to be the real danger to Europe. For this reason he avoided causing a breach with Germany which he believed was destined to lose the war eventually. With the final collapse of the Nazi armies, the Pope feared that the Soviet occupation of Central Europe was an event that would be irrevocable.

Even though Pope Pius failed when he was confronted with a choice that was beyond a single individual's capacity, what weighed heavily on him were the inept attempts on the part of the Vatican after 1945 to conceal the truth. At that time an open explanation of the reasons that lay behind his conduct and his understandable human failure would have been widely welcomed by Jews and Christians alike. But the Pontiff never gave any explanation or admitted any regrets, behaving as if there had never been any kind of silent collaboration between the Vatican and the Nazi regime. How far the Church should open itself to the people, especially to the people who support it — namely, is it a government first and a religious institution caring for its flock second, or vice versa — is a dilemma the Vatican has yet to deal with in terms of the staggering, unforeseeable upheavals that have taken over today's world.

CHAPTER VI

The Monastery Route For Ex-Nazis

ONE OF the black marks the Vatican may never erase from its record is the help it gave to Nazis on the run, war criminals who wanted to reach a safe haven in South America after the end of the Second World War. These 'runaways' were helped through a connection between the Vatican and ODESSA, which had set up a so-called monastery route between Austria and Italy and several Fascist countries in South America. Hitler's deputy, Martin Bormann, escaped through this route and is presumably still alive somewhere in Argentina and/or Paraguay and/or Uruguay and/or Brazil — or a rotating combination of them.

The Vatican priests who helped runaway Germans flee the Continent were prompted by a sense of Christian compassion, but in the case of Bormann a sizable sum of money was turned over to a Franciscan friar of German background who — possibly unknown to the Pope at the time — involved himself in such matters. Without his help and his Vatican connections, ODESSA might not have successfully swifted so many Nazis away from Europe at a time when the authorities of West Germany, Italy, Austria, France, the United States and the Soviet Union were seeking to round up the Nazi regime big shots suspected of major holocaust crimes against the Jews. To all intents and purposes, once their job was done, ODESSA quietly dissolved itself after it had shuttled several hundred Nazi war criminals to safety, during the 1960s and part of the 1970s, in such places as South America, Spain, the Middle East and Africa.

ODESSA, whose initials resembled the word for a well-known resort on Russia's Black Sea, was no doubt a unique travel agency. The six capital letters, initials for protection society formed by affluent ex-Nazis after the war, stood for *Organization Der Ehemaligen SS Angehörigen* (Organization of Former Members of the SS). Operating with Masonic secrecy and the ruthless efficiency that made Himmler's SS the most dreaded force in Germany, this underground organization provided false papers, ready cash, hideouts and transportation. All members of the team are still wanted by European police.

ODESSA had contacts with professional smugglers in all frontier areas, and good connections with certain South American embassies in Europe and with the Vatican. Their operation needed money, but this was no problem, for when it became apparent that Hitler was going to lose the war, smart Nazi money got busy. Large funds and deposits were transferred early in 1944 to neutral or non-belligerent countries. It is not known when exactly ODESSA came into operation, but with astronomical sums of German money that had been squirreled away before Hitler's final defeat, the underground organization had no trouble starting off on the right financial foot.

So efficiently and so clandestinely did ODESSA do its job of hiding Nazis and getting them away from Europe that the Allied intelligence services knew nothing about it. Neither did Interpol, nor the FBI nor the KGB. Well-camouflaged, as befitted Germany's sense for efficiency, ODESSA was master-minded by a Dr Johann von Leers, who was known in his heyday as the Jewish Expert of Joseph Goebbels' propaganda factory and was a wanted war criminal himself. The holder of six degrees from different universities, von Leers operated virtually as a one-man team, though he had some trusted helpers in Buenos Aires, Cairo and Rome. He was never caught, and the last report had him living quietly somewhere in a friendly Middle East capital where his racist views on the Jewish people find a hospitable climate.

Not until the late 1960s and the early 1970s did any clues about him and his underground organization emerge. One of the first reports came during the Düsseldorf War Crimes trial from Fritz Paul Stangl, who was charged with the responsibility of murdering at least 400,000 persons in the Sobibor and Treblinka concentration camps. Stangl testified in court that he escaped from a prison camp in Austria after the war and reached Damascus with a Red Cross pass obtained for him by an unidentified Austrian bishop. Later, his wife Therese let it be known in her testimony that her husband had received 'some help' from the Vatican which had assisted 'a great many Germans' to flee to Brazil after the war. In a later testimony, Stangl admitted he had got a 'Vatican passport' which enabled him to reach Brazil from Damascus. Then, as now, Vatican passports are extremely difficult to come by, since they are issued only for strictly limited reasons. It is hard to say whether Stangl was telling the truth, though under oath, and how he may have got the Vatican passport, for no further information is available.

During the period that ODESSA was in operation and at the time that Stangl made his getaway with the organization's help, the Vatican was in the process of aiding thousands of persons of many nationalities, including those made stateless by changing frontiers. The Vatican Migration Bureau, which later changed its name to the International Catholic Migration Commission, was enmeshed in helping refugees in every possible way, advising people on job opportunities, giving out food and clothing and helping refugees obtain travel papers. In a few cases the Vatican gave out travel documents of limited duration to enable certain refugees to leave for another country, but most of these were isolated mercy gestures. Since Vatican priests observed a policy of never checking out a refugee's political beliefs, many refugees were people who favored the Axis as well as the Allies. Ironically, while the Vatican may have been aiding ex-Nazis, a large number of Jews were also being helped. Ex-Nazis and Jewish travelers spent the night in a small inn near Merano in Italy's mountainous north region, unaware of each other's presence. The Nazis were housed on the ground floor and were warned to stay inside; the Jews were hidden on the upper floor and were similarly briefed to remain indoors. Stangl spent a night at this inn before he went to South America.

No doubt the most prominent ex-Nazi who made his getaway with the help of ODESSA and through the Vatican was Martin Bormann, easily the biggest Third Reich fish still at large today. Bormann had become a fairly good friend of Pope Pius XII when Pius was the papal nuncio in Germany for 12 years, and this may have played a role in the way the Vatican treated his case after the war. In May 1948 Bormann — dressed in the garb of a Jesuit priest, sported Vatican papers to show he was a stateless person (they carried the official number 073.909 with Pope Pius's signature). Strangely enough, for one dressed as a Jesuit, Bormann's papers showed him to have been born in Poland with the name of Eliezer Goldstein, a name usually thought of as Jewish. It got him to Brazil, nonetheless. It also got five of his children away from Europe later on, in 1950, after they were housed for several days in the Pallottine Order's monastery in Rome. Carrying American passports in false names that were arranged by the Catholic Church, the Bormann children left for South America.

During his services as Hitler's secretary, Bormann became one of the most powerful men in Berlin. Exercising considerable influence over Hitler, he was a guiding force in the persecution of Jews and the exploitation of slave labor. On May 2, 1945, he left the bunker where Hitler had committed suicide and tried to escape. Fellow fugitives later reported that he had died when a German tank blew up near him after being hit by a Soviet shell. But the Nuremberg war crimes tribunal found the evidence of his death 'not conclusive' and convicted him in absentia of war crimes and crimes against humanity in 1946. That Bormann was able to get into Argentina by some devious routing can be attributed to the Vatican's rapport with that country's former president, Juan Perón.

Far too many are the Nazis who were helped by the Vatican after the war. But one case in particular should be mentioned, because it demonstrates that when money comes into the picture, the Vatican responds. This is the case of Paul Touvier of France, the Nazi collaborator who received a presidential pardon after pressure from the Vatican. Touvier was second-in-command of the pro-Nazi militia in Lyon during the occupation. Twice tried in absentia after the war and twice sentenced to death for war crimes, Touvier somehow evaded arrest and then vanished — for 25 years. His escape came as a result of a deal he made with the Vatican. By agreeing after the war to give the Vatican all the militia money left over from the war, he was assured on the word of God that he would be protected. The militia money in question came from the looting of Jewish properties and homes during the occupation. Touvier himself took over the Lyon apartment of a Jewish textile millionaire and installed his mistress in the home of another Jewish businessman.

With Vatican help Touvier managed to elude the authorities. Calling himself Paul Berthet, he had identity papers which gave his address as that of the Archbishop of Lyon. Quite often he wore the cassock of a priest, and there were at least a dozen clerics who looked after him while Resistance groups kept searching for him. Though he was completely forgotten and could have continued to live a quiet, retired life under Vatican protection, he emerged in 1962 with a plea that French President Georges Pompidou grant him a complete pardon — which got the open support of the French cardinal in his area who sought supportive information for Touvier's rehabilitation process. Shortly after the cardinal was moved to an important post inside the Vatican, Touvier got his presidential pardon. Touvier, however, could not stay in Chambery to enjoy his pardon long because many enraged Resistance men and women sought revenge. Touvier went into hiding again in 1972 at the age of 57. Nothing has been heard of him ever since.

For the Vatican and Pius XII the Second World War was Topic A every day in one form or another. Particularly noteworthy were the Vatican's secret attempts to put an end to the war. It is not generally known that the Vatican made several concerted efforts to persuade Benito Mussolini and Italy to drop out of World War II in 1943. Pope Pius talked with Mussolini secretly several times during a period that ran from March 1939 to December 1940 on the problems involving the anti-Semitism practised by the Nazis and the Fascists, the treatment of war prisoners on both sides, the suffering of innocent populations (the Jews and the gypsies) and the fate of the Poles. In later talks that covered the period of November 1942 through December 1943, Pius devoted his efforts to extricating Italy from its alliance with the Germans and to save Rome from being bombed, whether by the Allies or by Axis planes.

In the Vatican files there is a private letter written in July 1943 by Monsignor Angelo Roncalli (later Pope John XXIII), who was then the apostolic delegate to Turkey, to Monsignor Giovanni Montini (later Pope Paul VI), who was then the Vatican Under-Secretary of State. Monsignor Roncalli's letter reports a meeting with German diplomat Franz von Papen who talked about the Russian slaughter of thousands of Polish officers buried in a mass grave at the Russian village of Katyn, near Smolensk. Von Papen said he believed the Poles, once fully aware of the slaughter, would side with the Germans for their own protection.

'I replied with a sad smile', Roncalli's letter reads, 'that it would first of all be necessary to make them forget the millions of Jews sent to Poland and killed and that in any case this was a good occasion for the Third Reich to change its methods of treating the Poles.'

There was, however, another attempt on the part of the Vatican to get Italy to remove itself from the war. Vatican archives show that this was initiated by President Franklin D Roosevelt. Late in 1939, after Hitler's troops had suddenly moved into Poland — thereby opening the Second World War — Roosevelt sought to bring about a diplomatic arrangement with the Vatican, inasmuch as he considered it a vital listening-post that would benefit the United States. Although he could not officially recognize the State of Vatican City, he nevertheless appointed Myron C Taylor as his 'Personal Representative' (the quotation marks were his) and gave him all the privileges of an ambassador. Instead of taking up residence in the Vatican, Taylor kept a low profile, stayed in the United States and made periodic visits to the Pope when required.

When the Mussolini regime issued a declaration of war against the United States, the American Embassy in Rome was closed down, and since Taylor now could no longer make his periodic visitations to the Pope, the White House felt it would lose its liaison with the Vatican for as long as the war went on. However, the Vatican, too, did not want to lose contact with Washington, and so it suggested that Roosevelt consider the advisability of appointing a charge d'affaires to the Holy See. That way, the US representative could take up residence inside the Vatican under the same protection given to the charge d'affaires from the United Kingdom, Poland and France.

Neither the Mussolini nor the Hitler regimes would offer any objection, a Vatican officer explained to Roosevelt, nor would the Nazis ever violate the neutral status of Vatican City. Accordingly, Roosevelt appointed Harold H Tittmann, Jr, a Protestant, who had been for a dozen years an officer in the American Embassy in Rome and had been named Taylor's aide in February 1940. The White House gave Tittmann's appointment a top-security hush-hush so that the US Senate would not have to carry out its constitutional right of confirming the appointment. Tittmann took up residence inside the State of Vatican City in mid-December of 1941. During his stay there, which lasted until the summer of 1944, Tittmann had many conferences with the Pope and with high-ranking Holy See officials, one of whom was Monsignor Montini.

Apart from a number of routine matters that had to be dealt with, as befalls any 'ambassador', Tittmann had a very special job to perform, one that was Roosevelt's pet. His was the job of getting Pope Pius to encourage some changes in Italy's politics and to convince the Italians that if they abandoned the war, the US government would make it worth their while at war's end. What carried prime urgency was that Italy should get out of the war immediately in any way that it could, even if this meant the displeasure of Hitler and/or the removal of Mussolini as chief of state. No small task this — but the Pope was amenable and cooperative. His efforts, however, were met with blocks, and Roosevelt was of the opinion that His Holiness was not trying hard enough. So in one of the boldest diplomatic moves ever made by an American president in time of war, FDR took a risk and sent Ambassador Taylor, secretly, back to Rome in September 1942 — after ten months of fighting between American troops and Italian soldiers in North Africa.

The Holy Father — a Roman-born Italian and a super-patriot of Italy — was worried that Mussolini's blind adherence to Hitler would bring nothing but total disaster on the Italian people. Pius was also of the view that although Hitler was respecting the boundaries of the State of Vatican City, partially because at least half his army was Roman Catholic and partially because it was sound politics on his part, Third Reich ideology was basically anti-Christian in nature. Taylor's assignment was to convince the Pope that he should now put pressure on Italy to break diplomatic relations with Nazi Germany and therefore abrogate its alliance with the Third Reich.

Although Pope Pius never succeeded in convincing Italy or Mussolini to withdraw from the Axis, the events that transpired nevertheless precipitated a mid-stream switch in tactics on Italy's part. Allied troops entered Rome in June 1944 as the Nazis retreated to the Gothic Line further north. (Ambassador Taylor returned to Rome and continued serving in the same capacity under President Harry S Truman until he retired in 1951.) Italy surrendered to the Allies, on September 8, 1943, became an 'enemy' of the Third Reich, and dispatched many of its soldiers to serve with American and British troops in the European campaign.

CHAPTER VII

Eva Perón's Body and the Vatican

NO STRANGER story in Argentina's turbulent history exists than that of the macabre odyssey of Eva Perón's embalmed body which for some two decades had been traveling secretly in various parts of South America and Europe. Even stranger is the direct role the Vatican played in this drama, a role that never got any publicity. The Eva Perón saga is a perfect example of the efficiency of the Vatican's secrecy tactics and skills.

In more than two decades from the day of her death on July 16, 1952, at the age of 33, Evita's body was surrounded constantly by mystery and intrigues. Her corpse, which was secretly shipped from one country to another — five in all — had been perfectly preserved by a special embalming process (the same technique used to keep Lenin's body intact). Known as the patroness of the Argentine people and a crusader for the underdog, the beloved wife of Juan Perón has found a final resting-place in a tomb of the Recoleta Cemetery in Buenos Aires.

Eva was the illegitimate offspring of a farmhand and a coachman's daughter. Her mother ran a boarding house in a small pampas village 150 miles west of Buenos Aires. When Eva was 15 years old, she ran off to Buenos Aires to try her luck in show business. Struggling hard for a number of years, she managed to land several small parts in B films. Not until she went into radio, however, as a broadcaster did she make any kind of impact. Eva Duarte had a warm, alluring voice that at times could be almost hypnotic, and before long she had a solid following, becoming known as Señorita Radio. In 1944, when she was 25 years old, Colonel Juan Perón, who had just effected a successful coup d'état, asked her to make a radio appeal on behalf of the thousands of homeless persons caught in an earthquake.

Colonel Perón married Miss Duarte a short time later, and though she was extremely cautious about trying to stay in the background, she became a power in her own right. Her public appeal lay with the poor of Argentina, whom she often called 'my dear shirtless ones'. They in turn created the cult of Eva Perón. Her political and social philosophy was known to everyone, thanks to her book, *La Razón de Mi Vida* (The Reason for My Life).

Through the Eva Perón Foundation, which she ran on a personal basis, often sitting up until 3 or 4 am to dispense money and gifts to persons who came to see her with convincing stories of sorrow, Eva won the adoring support of the working class. Several times, however, she came very close to depleting the national treasury in her quest for money, despite the fact that she virtually bled the big corporations with repeated demands for contributions. Affectionately known as Evita, Argentina's one-woman welfare organization built hospitals, set up children's playgrounds, provided clothes for the needy, dispensed toys for destitute children and at Christmas sent out thousands of gift packages to families down on their luck. Small wonder that Evita was looked upon as Lady Bountiful by the *descamisados* (the shirtless ones). In June 1974 Mrs Perón, during a successful European tour, had a state audience with Pope Pius XII, and as a result, her image, on her return, was ever greater.

During the early 1950s, Eva Perón was struck by cancer at the age of 29. Despite unsuccessful surgery for cancer of the uterus, she managed to continue with her public life, even accompanying her husband in an open car on the occasion of the inauguration for his second presidential term. Wrapped in furs, she tried to camouflage the fact that her once-plump body had become frail and that she, now a dying woman, was down to 80 pounds (less than six stone). A month after attending Perón's swearing-in, Eva died. She lay in state in the national congress hall in a flowing white tunic with her natural blonde hair spread out across a small pillow. For two weeks there were mile-long lines of people (often during heavy rain) waiting to pay their last respects.

Argentina came to a full stop — factories, offices, stores, schools and theatres all closed. The country was flooded with a cascade of commemorative pennants, medals, pictures, keyrings, plaster busts, records and postage stamps. Extra copies of her book were sold by the thousands every day. Streets, squares, schools, rivers and mountains were named after her. Even the City of La Plata was given a new name, Ciudad Eva Perón — and Pope Pius was petitioned to consider her for sainthood.

Many of these events were dramatized in a much-publicized musical hit called *Evita*, which opened in London in mid-1978, bowed on Broadway with equally great box office receipts and swept throughout the world. Told with minimum sentiment and maximum music, the 46-member musical — written by Tim Rice and Andrew Lloyd Webber and directed by Hal Prince — gave no hint as to what happened to Evita after her death. This aspect of the Evita story is perhaps even more fascinating, however macabre the details.

It began with the decision by Perón, as another step in the deification process, to have her body scientifically preserved for all time. He called Pedro Ara, one of Europe's greatest pathologists, to do the embalming. Dr Ara, a Spaniard, had closely studied the preservation process used on Lenin in Moscow and was certain he could do the same for Eva. Paid a fee of $100,000, he took a year to work on the corpse. First, he replaced the blood with alcohol, and then he pumped in glycerine at a temperature of 140 degrees Fahrenheit (60 degrees Celsius) through her heel and ear. At normal room temperature the glycerine solidified, leaving the body partially embalmed. The skin and the internal organs remained intact. Then the body was subjected to a series of carefully controlled immersions in special liquids, so that, although the corpse diminished a little bit in size, the skin took on a near-transparency and a surprising elasticity. Her lips remained very red, and her hair as rich and as blonde as when she was alive and in good health.

In September 1955 when Juan Perón was overthrown, he fled to Paraguay, leaving behind his wife's body. Perón's successors, aware that Eva could become a political hot potato, were not quite sure how to deal with her earthly remains. They needed time to work out something, and in the meantime they ordered a medical commission to determine 'the authenticity of the corpse'. When in November of that year a military junta replaced the provisional government and General Pedro Eugenio Aramburu took over Argentina's reins, Eva Perón's body was suddenly 'kidnapped'. The kidnapper was Colonel Moore Koenig, an arch foe of Perón who had personally directed mortar fire on many of Eva's monuments. As part of his revenge on Perón, Koenig said he was going to give Eva a 'Christian burial', the same as for any ordinary human being. The dead woman was placed in a cheap coffin and turned over to Major Antonio Arandia, who put her into the back of any army truck, which he parked overnight at a busy street corner and then drove to a warehouse. After being taken to five more hiding-places, the body was transferred to a large packing case and kept in Arandia's apartment in Buenos Aires.

By this time news of the so-called kidnapping had leaked and thousands of Eva's faithful followers, many of them armed, relentlessly searched the city for the coffin. Arandia took to sleeping every night with a pistol under his pillow. Awakened one morning before dawn by some strange noises, he whipped out his pistol and shot twice at the outline of a human form that appeared in the doorway of his bedroom. Unfortunately the figure he shot down was that of his pregnant wife who had gone to the toilet. She was killed outright. Forced to get the coffin out of his house, Arandia sneaked it off to a military building, where he stacked it on the fourth floor among boxes that were labeled 'radio sets'. But the body was discovered by President Aramburu's secret service chief, while on an inspection tour of the fourth floor.

Wanting Mrs Perón's preserved remains out of the country once and for all, President Aramburu asked the Vatican for help. Pope Pius took a personal interest in the case: with the Pope's envoy to Argentina, the Most Rev Mario Zanin, acting as the middleman, Eva (now in a packing case) was on her way to Europe by September 1956, where in a classic cloak-and-dagger maneuver, she made a stop in Brussels and another stop in Bonn. In West Germany, the body was stored for two months among old furniture and old office files belonging to the Argentine Embassy.

The next stop for Eva was Rome, where she was temporarily placed in that city's only Protestant cemetery, a few yards from where the English poet John Keats is buried. Her grave, bearing a fictitious name, was the Vatican's way of throwing any would-be searchers off the trail, since the Holy See had agreed to be the guardian of Eva Perón until further notice. When a left-wing Roman newspaper got wind that Eva Perón was buried somewhere in Rome, the Vatican exhumed the body and sent it to Milan accompanied by a nun from the Society of Saint Paul, Sister Giuseppina Airoldi. She had been told the body in the coffin was that of an Italian widow called Maria Maggi who had died in Argentina and who had requested in her will that she be buried in her home city of Milan. Sister Giuseppina took care of the burial in Milan's Musocco Cemetery where Eva remained for 14 years in Plot 86, Garden 41.

In April 1971 a new Argentine regime decided to restore Eva Perón to her original status of 'Señora Numero Uno' — but no one in Buenos Aires knew where Eva was. Not even Juan Perón, who was in exile in Madrid, knew. Paid spies, Perón's closest cohorts and private detectives now took up the search, scouring Rome, Buenos Aires and Madrid. All in vain — Eva Perón was nowhere to be found.

It is not quite certain who in the Vatican was responsible, but one of Perón's paid agents learned from 'a senior papal aide' where exactly Eva Perón was buried. So in July 1971 a man describing himself as Carlos Maggi, brother of the fictitious Maria, appeared at the cemetery in Milan and, with written notarized permission, was able to exhume his 'sister's' remains. The rotting, black wooden coffin was put into the hearse of a Milan undertaker and driven to the French border. With the apparent cooperation of the Italian, French and

Spanish frontier police, thanks to some Vatican magic, Eva Perón's body crossed the border without a single delay or search. As Eva passed into Spain, waiting were two truckloads of gendarmes who forthwith escorted her for the final 450-mile (725-kilometre) lap to Madrid. At 9 pm the strange convoy rolled through the gates of Number 6 Calle de Navalmanzano, where Juan Perón was waiting on the steps for his dead wife.

The body was removed to a basement, and Dr Ara began a close examination. He noted that his work had held up exceedingly well, despite the fact that both knees had been broken, the chest was marked by five perforations and the nose had been smashed. In addition, the blonde locks had been cut off to the neckline, but the color and texture of Eva Perón's skin were so natural it looked as though she was merely asleep.

When I asked a Vatican spokesman not long ago if he had any comment to make on the saga of the body of Mrs Perón, he said he had no knowledge of the body, nor did he know where it had been all those years. When I suggested that Pius XII had played a key role in the body's secret burials in Rome and Milan, his answer was that popes never concern themselves with matters of that nature.

CHAPTER VIII

The Big Lie About Columbus

SINCE THE Vatican has no compunction about controlling the dispensing of facts to the world or perpetuating a falsehood when its interests are to be served, it is no wonder that one of the most freakish fibs in all history deserves the honor of being perhaps the Vatican's best-kept secret, based on a historical quirk that it, the Vatican, did not set in motion. Simply put, Christopher Columbus did not discover America on October 12, 1492, as every schoolchild knows and as everybody takes for granted today — but one whole day later, on October 13.

Columbus set sail from the harbor of the sleeply little town of Palos de la Frontera, Spain, on the morning of August 3, 1492, to cross the Atlantic Ocean. With the Pinta, the Niña and the Santa Maria, Columbus reached the Island of San Salvador (in the Bahamas) on the morning of October 13, 1492 — but a historian by the name of Fra Bartolomé de las Casas, who later became Bishop of Chiapas, gave out the word that Columbus had landed on October 12. He had a motive for doing this, and when the Pope was informed that the date had been moved up by one full day for a number of good reasons of special interest to the Church, the Vatican gave its approval and the gigantic falsehood was kept perpetuated.

To understand how this historical white lie came about, one must take into account the era and the atmosphere in which Columbus undertook his fateful expedition. It was an age when the masses had been plagued by epidemics and costly wars. This explains why credence was given to the most absurd ideas and endorsed with blind conviction. For example, the number 13 was considered an evil omen. Known as the numeral of Judas, it was looked upon as an anti-Christ sign. In those days, when people counted, they invariably said, '. . . ten, eleven, twelve, *that other*, fourteen. . . .' Even the largest school in Spain, the University of Salamanca, did not teach the subject of mathematics, for it was considered 'the devil's science.' These were some of the factors that Fra Bartolomé weighed before he took it upon himself to doctor the date, and there were others that influenced the

Spanish historian's bold decision.

Columbus (whose given name Christopher meant 'Bearer of Christ') had made his trip in the name of the Trinity — the Father, the Son and the Holy Ghost — so as to give his project the protective charm of a good-luck symbol. He had left Palos on a Friday and had returned to Spain on March 15, 1493, which was also a Friday. Since October 13 had fallen on a Saturday, the cleric reasoned how much more symbolic it would be if the world were told that the 'holy trip across the ocean' had also terminated on a Friday, a day viewed in that period as the holiest one of the week because Jesus Christ had died for humanity on a Friday. Moreover, through a stroke of coincidence, Friday, October 12, happened to be the day of the patron saint of Spain's Ferdinand and Isabella, the Catholic rulers who allegedly financed the trans-oceanic venture.

Bartolomé de las Casas figured that a trinity of Fridays with reference to Columbus's controversial voyage would be regarded as a mystical note by a populace that had had from the beginning some misgivings about the Genoese seafarer's gamble. Columbus must have thought the change was a wise one, especially since the Vatican had gone along with the deception, for he never once refuted the monk's announcement about Friday the 12th, and nobody paid much attention to the fact that the Pinta, the Niña and the Santa Maria journals and logbooks had not been made accessible to the general public.

The full truth about Columbus is not yet fully known by the world, for the Vatican wants to keep as quiet as possible certain details about the revered seaman. Contrary to what is taught in school, Columbus's benefactor, Queen Isabella of Spain, did not pawn her jewels to finance his trip. She offered to but never did. Columbus got the money for his first voyage from the endowment fund of the Santa Hermandad police force. The sum of 250,000 maravedis ($2,100) was lent to him by the police, and it was subsequently repaid by Isabella.

Another side to Columbus's 'Catholic trip' across the ocean that was kept very low-key by Vatican clerics was that he and the men who traveled with him brought syphilis to Europe. Columbus's men contracted it from the women of San Salvador, and, when they returned, they infected some prostitutes with it. From them, the disease spread.

CHAPTER IX

'E Pur Si Muove! . . .'

ON MARCH 12, 1737, when the body of Galileo was moved from a tiny chamber in the belltower next to the Chapel of Saints Cosimo and Damiano for final burial in Pisa's Church of Santa Croce, a fanatic admirer of Galileo — a nobleman by the name of Anton Francesco Gori — cut off three fingers from the astronomer's right hand to keep as relics. Two of the fingers are today in the private possession of a doctor and his family, while the right middle finger is in the Museum of the History of Science in Florence. One flight up in Room 6, the withered phalanx is in a showcase enclosed in an egg-shaped, gold-decorated glass container atop a cylindrical piece of marble, on which a Latin sentence by an astronomer of the University of Pisa has been inscribed. The finger, indeed a curiosity, is pointing skyward toward the heavens and toward heaven in silent, fourth-dimension irony.

In November 1979 in Room 6, which is also crammed with many of Galileo's personal possessions (a lens, a compass, two telescopes, thermometers, a chair and four wooden bedlegs), a most significant ceremony was held on the occasion of a most significant event: after three and a half centuries, Galileo Galilei had been rehabilitated by the Vatican and Pope John Paul II had made the public proclamation. Galileo had been condemned in 1632 for proving that the earth revolved around the sun, a thesis that went against official Church doctrine, and for which Galileo had spent the last nine years of his life under house arrest.

Contrary to popular myth, Galileo never actually dropped unequal weights from Pisa's leaning tower to prove or discover certain basic laws of gravity. Vatican condemnation came to him for supporting the heliocentric theories of Nicolaus Copernicus. Although he made a public recanting, at his trial he declared: *'E pur si muove!'* (Nevertheless, it does move!)

Galileo's case rested in limbo within the Vatican until Napoleon took the original trial transcript to Paris, as part of his Italian booty. After the French monarchy was restored, the dossier was returned to the Vatican in 1846 on the condition that it be made available to

French scholars at any time they wanted to study it. The Vatican agreed. No French scholars bothered with the documents until the early 1960s when Father Dominique Dubarle got permission to look at them. An atomic scientist who was deeply concerned with reconciling the Catholic Church with science, Father Dubarle put together a legal brief defending Galileo on canonical law and petitioned the Vatican to reopen the proceedings. No pope (neither Pope John XXIII nor Pope Paul VI) showed much sympathy for the Dubarle–Galileo cause until the arrival of the present Polish Pope, who has always had a special interest in the scientific work of Copernicus, a fellow Pole who studied at the University of Cracow.

What upset the Grand Inquisitors of the Roman Catholic Church's Holy Office some 350 years ago was the ailing Italian astronomer's theory that the earth and planets of the solar system revolved around the sun and that the sun — not the earth — was the center of the known universe. Galileo developed this theory after making multiple observations through his telescope based on calculations carried out nearly a hundred years before by Copernicus. In 1616 the Inquisition declared Copernicus' theory in error and the Pope warned Galileo that he should not defend or teach it any longer. Galileo agreed not to mention it, but after some 16 years of continued observations through a telescope that magnified 32 times, he published a report in 1632 saying he was convinced that the earth revolved around the sun. Brought to trial in front of seven of the Vatican's most important cardinals, Galileo — then suffering from various illnesses in his advanced years — sustained two days of interrogation, much of it under the threat of torture and the fear that as a heretic he could be burned at the stake. Finally, when he could no longer go on, Galileo fell to his knees, recanted his theory and begged the mercy of his inquisitors. Because of his abject public renunciation, he was not ordered to be burned at the stake but sentenced to unlimited imprisonment which was commuted to house arrest in Florence and Siena.

Even while under house arrest, Galileo wrote a most poignant letter to the Holy Office in which he pleaded his innocence. 'I am not of this opinion,' he stated, 'and have not been of the opinion of Copernicus, since I was ordered to abandon it. Besides I am in your hands. You may do as you please. . . .'

One of the ironies of Galileo's case, perhaps typical of the way the Vatican sometimes does things, is that the Vatican's denunciation of Copernican theory was withdrawn in 1835, while Galileo's conviction remained. Well, the dust finally settled, and on November 10, 1979, Pope John Paul II addressed 70 members of the Pontifical Academy of

Sciences and announced Galileo's rehabilitation. In his speech the Pope said:

'Just as religion needs religious liberty, so science legitimately claims freedom of research.' The Pope also said he hoped an interdisciplinary study by historians, scientists and theologians would banish the mistrust of science which existed in some minds.

One is almost tempted to respond to Galileo's noted retort:

'E anche si muove il Vaticano!' (Even the Vatican moves!)

CHAPTER X

Murder in the Vatican

ON THE last day of his life, Albino Luciani of Venice — who 34 days before had been elected Pontiff on the fourth ballot and had taken the name of John Paul I — arose at 5 am, a routine he had established almost from his first day in office. The early morning hours was the time he enjoyed most, partly because of the quiet and partly because of the freedom from distractions. After celebrating Mass in his private chapel a few yards from his bedroom, he took a light breakfast and went back to the bedroom to do some work. At 8 am he went into his office to begin work. It was Thursday, September 28, 1978.

On the last day of his life, John Paul I had an audience with ten Philippine prelates and told them in his charming textbook English that while Jesus spoke of justice and social liberation, He did not remain silent about the fullness of life in the Kingdom of Heaven. That morning was average, heavy with a schedule of 13 official audiences. In between John Paul I managed to scan four Roman newspapers, and he paid special attention to the Italian correspondents' reports on the Middle East, a subject that interested him personally.

On the last day of his life, the new Pontiff met with Patriarch Hakim who represented the Melchite Catholics now scattered across Syria and Lebanon; Hakim presented John Paul I with an icon of Christ and another of the Virgin Mary. The day before John Paul had enchanted more than 10,000 pilgrims in the modern, auditorium-like Nervi audience hall. It was to be his last general audience. As was his custom, he interrupted his prepared remarks and summoned a fifth-grade student, Daniele Bravo of Rome, to the podium. Lowering the mike to the boy's height, the Pope proceeded to interview him about school during which the lad said he always wanted to be in the fifth grade because he would then not have to change teachers. Chuckling, the Pope said, 'Well you are different from the Pope. When I was in fourth grade, I worried about making it to the fifth, and when in the fifth, about passing to the sixth. . . .'

On the last evening of his life, the Pope had a light supper at 8 pm of sliced veal, vegetables, salad and a glass of white wine. After eating, he chatted with his Secretary of State (Cardinal Jean Villot), and at 10 pm he retired, taking with him to his simple, four-poster bed a copy of a fifteenth-century book by Thomas Kempis, *Imitation of Christ*. A little while later, just before 10.30 pm, his secretary, Father John Magee, phoned him to report that a left-wing student had been murdered that evening in downtown Rome. 'Are these young people shooting each other again? Really, it is terrible,' the Pope said. Those were the last words anyone was to hear him speak.

The next morning, when Mother Vincenza — who had cared for the former Venetian cardinal for over ten years — did not see him emerge from his room by 5.30 to go to his private chapel to say Mass, she went to the bedroom door with his usual cup of coffee. After she knocked and got no reply, she summoned the Pope's private secretary, Rev Magee. He knocked at the bedroom door and waited a good 30 seconds before knocking again, this time somewhat harder. He waited some more and knocked anew. Still no answer. Father Magee cautiously slid the door open, apologizing as he stuck his head in. He saw that John Paul was slumped over his open book — the light was still on. When the Pope did not wake up, Father Magee knew that something had befallen him. Cardinal Villot was immediately summoned. It was later determined that Pope had been dead for some hours. To a stunned and shocked world, the death announcement was made at 7.42 am by the Vatican's press officer, Rev Romeo Pancirolli. The cause of death was announced as having been either a stroke or a heart attack.

In the next few days when confusion reigned as to what had caused the Pope's death, a traditionalist Catholic organization, *Civiltà Cristiana*, formally petitioned the Vatican authorities to undertake an inquest into the Pope's death. Suggesting that an autopsy be done, the organization said the world wanted to know 'the true reasons for John Paul's death'. Italian newspapers picked up the cudgels, and a growing controversy began when Vatican officials declared there would be no autopsy. The Vatican would not say why. Italy's leading newspaper, Milan's *Corriere della Sera*, ran a front-page article with the headline, 'Why Say No To An Autopsy?' and pointed out there were no Vatican rules against autopsies; neither was there any kind of precedent against them. The paper cited that an autopsy had been conducted in 1830 on the body of Pope Pius VIII who died at the age of 69 only 18 months after he had been elected. *Corriere* asserted that the world would indeed welcome any medical information which would in no way interfere with religious or spiritual matters. The paper felt the Church had nothing to lose and in fact everything to gain, especially since none of the 15 doctors who belonged to the Vatican's health services would comment on the Pontiff's death. In diplomatic language, *Corriere* added that the 'era of crimes at the Vatican' was a thing of the past but curiosity on the unexpected death of John Paul was quite understandable.

In Turin, Italy's second-most important daily, *La Stampa*, made an even bolder statement, opining that the Vatican's untenable decision 'makes the situation appear suspicious'. None of Italy's newspapers, however, went so far as to suggest that the Pope had been murdered. Ignoring all such demands, the Vatican said that any further explanation about the Pope's death would be an embarrassing capitulation to popular pressure. The Vatican explained that the use of the Latin phrase, *mysterium mortis*, by a cardinal to describe John Paul's death was not a reference to the circumstances of his death so much as it was a way to describe the 'mystery of death' in general — how no one knows the hour, how death comes in and how inscrutable are 'the workings of God'. The Vatican also pointed out that Article 17 of the apostolic constitution implicitly ruled out papal autopsies. In heavy rains and with at least 100,000 people present, while hundreds of millions watched on satellite television, the funeral of the 65-year-old Pontiff was solemnized.

After the Pope was buried and his successor named — the first Polish pope in history and the first non-Italian pope in 455 years — the questions of the autopsy and the cause of death and the suspicions of foul play died down. But several disturbing facts about the late Pope then emerged. For one thing, when he had been chosen by the Conclave of Cardinals, almost as an unknown quantity, he was believed to be a confirmed conservative — an ecclesiastic version of Barry Goldwater. It looked at first as if John Paul's firm hand would guide Peter's boat away from the dangerous rocks of the modern world. *L'Osservatore Romano* painted a picture of John Paul as an ultra-conservative; what he actually did was take the world by storm with his engaging smile and friendly, unpretentious manner that made it appear that even such a beloved Pope as John XXIII would soon be cast into the shadows. This new, 263rd Pontiff of the Roman Catholic Church possessed a quiet charisma, and like John XXIII came across as a pastoral leader and not an intellectual.

The first surprise came to Vatican insiders a few days after he was enthroned when in an address to the College of Cardinals, he discarded a prepared speech because it was 'too Curial' in style and spoke extemporaneously and from the heart. Still later, there were some more surprises about the former patriarch of Venice whom so few of the cardinals really knew because he was not a Curial cardinal but a cardinal with a proven pastoral track-record, for which he had been a compromise selection at the Conclave having got the support of two powerful cardinals — Franz Koenig of Vienna and Giovanni Benelli of Florence.

When Cardinal Luciani's dossier had been looked into some more after his election to the papacy — a different picture of him began to emerge. The Curia cardinals, who control the Vatican and very often the Pope himself, began to find out about the man who now wore the tiara. Albino Luciani in Venice was a man who was quick to entertain the most progressive ideas. For one thing, in a newspaper interview some years earlier, Luciani endorsed the ideas of a nineteenth-century work called 'The Five Wounds of the Church', which advocated the direct election of bishops by clergy and people. Luciani approved in principle of the participation of the people and the local clergy to select a bishop from four or five proposed candidates. This whole idea has always been repugnant to controlling members of the Curia. As a non-Curial cardinal Luciani — despite his pastoral wisdom and gentleness — would have enemies inside the Vatican, as all popes eventually have. In the Vatican there are, to be sure, enemies and more enemies.

As one who deliberately stayed out of the intrigues of his fellow Italian clerics, especially those involving the Curia inside the Vatican, Luciani was a kind of ecclesiastical loner who followed his own path without making waves either in Venice's multiple canals or in Rome's channels where the waters are even more dangerous behind the Leonine Walls. Luciani's contacts were mostly with German and Belgian bishops and European theologians, not excluding local Italian clerics of all stripes. A believer that the Roman Catholic Church should always be genuinely poor, the way Christ was poor all his life, Luciani never publicly endorsed any of the Vatican's business and finance endeavors, even if the earnings from such were used for charitable purposes. Moreover, he often sought to convince priests in formal chats that they should abandon their old manuals and read instead a relatively progressive Italian magazine called, *Nuova Teologia*, selected copies of which are banned from the Vatican Library.

In Albino Luciani's case, his posture as a conservative — which had been totally misrepresented by *L'Osservatore Romano*, even grotesquely exaggerated — was not helped by the startling revelation inside the Vatican that the new Pope John Paul I was planning to re-examine the controversial, 1968 birth control encyclical of Paul VI. Cardinal Luciani had not been a member of the Pontifical Commission on Birth Control and therefore had never signed any document connected with it. Aware of the pastoral difficulties Pope Paul's encyclical had brought not only to his priests in Venice but also to priests in all churches and parishes over the world, John Paul I would apparently not have condemned the encyclical *per se* but would have studied its mitigating clauses carefully to find a possible way out. Once, in a remarkably mild reference to *Humanae Vitae* in a Venice church, the Cardinal said he was sure that no one would ever be hounded out of the Church for dissenting. This statement may or may not have come to the Vatican's attention at the time, but Vatican politics being what they are, it reached the Curial controllers soon after the man had been enthroned.

So we come now to the crunch about Albino Luciani's death and the Vatican's refusal to undertake an autopsy. For what reason or reasons — never made clear or intimated — did the Vatican refuse the inquest? The answer is not known. Nor is it known if Pope John Paul I was poisoned in his papal palace in AD 983, and an autopsy by five during his 34 days as Pontiff. Although I had thought I had come fairly close to pinning down a hard answer, I could not substantiate it. So we have no proof of foul play.

Foul play inside the Vatican is not unknown. Pope Benedict VII was poisoned in his papal palace in A.D. 983, and an autopsy by five German scientists on Pope Clement II, who died in 1047, showed that a poison had caused his death. Clement was Pope for one year before he became the assassination victim of a rivalry that existed between Germany and Rome. The circumstances of the poisoning could not be established, but the many reforms that Clement introduced created for him a number of enemies within the Vatican. In the sixteenth century, the Vatican was the scene of a murder attempt on Pope Leo X, and this affair ended in the execution of the conspirators, among whom were two cardinals. Another Pope, Lucius II in 1145, died a violent death when the brother of an anti-Pope declared himself ruler and Lucius led an assault of papal troops on Rome. The exact circumstances of Lucius's death are not clear, but the Vatican once made an official admission that he died as a result of a wound from a stone.

No such violence surrounded the unexpected death of John Paul I. Having suffered a heart attack, the Pontiff then apparently worked himself to death. Just three days before he died, his personal physician warned him to slow down. But John Paul did not listen. He kept up his grueling work schedules, working till past midnight (sometimes while sitting in his bed).

John Paul's death was no mystery to his brother Edoardo. He told me that there had been three other cases of sudden deaths in his family in which there was no warning and each had been about the same age as his brother. On the Pope's maternal grandmother's side, two sisters died similarly. The father of his maternal grandmother also died in the same manner. The Pope's sister, Antonia Luciani, told me that her brother had been hospitalized eight times in his life and that he did not enjoy full, complete health, though he was not in any way sick when elected Pope.

Perhaps one of the reasons why there was great secrecy surrounding John Paul's death is that when Pope Pius XII died, there was something of a scandal stemming from the sale of photographs of the dying Pontiff. The only time in Vatican history when it called in a private detective was in this case, to avoid a massive scandal over the photos. Worried about the ramifications, the ecclesiastical authorities during Pope Pius XII's administration hired a 'divorce detective' by the name of Tom Ponzi. He was to find the culprit who took the pictures and keep the secret so tight that it would never explode all over the world.

The brewing scandal had its original roots in Pius's first serious illness in October 1953 when the Pope's personal physician, Dr Riccardo Galeazzi Lisi, called in Dr Paul Niehans. He was noted for his cellular therapy rejuvenation clinic that he maintained on Lake Geneva and for having numbered among his patients such notables as Winston Churchill, Somerset Maugham, Germany's Chancellor Konrad Adenauer, the Aga Khan, Gloria Swanson and Christian Dior. Looked upon by many as a miracle worker, other members of the medical profession, however, considered Niehans a quack and a charlatan, mostly because the so-called rejuvenation cells he injected into his patients were extracted from the fetuses of sheep.

Dr Niehans raced to the Vatican and gave His Holiness a number of injections, which apparently improved the Pope's condition. But a year later, the Pontiff fell sick again, this time more so than the last, and again Niehans was summoned to treat Pius with his controversial injections. Again, the Pope showed considerable improvement, and he was able to return to his desk where he worked in good health until November 1954, at which time he once again became extremely ill. Once more was Dr Niehans called in by Dr Galeazzi Lisi. However, someone else in the Curia summoned Dr Raffaele Paolucci, then Italy's most foremost surgeon. So both Dr Niehans and Dr Paolucci gave the Pope a thorough examination, and both men found him suffering from a serious hernia. The doctors differed as to the treatment, however: Paolucci recommended immediate surgery, and Niehans felt that what the Pope needed were more of his youth-cell injections. Galeazzi Lisi sided with Niehans, and when two other famed specialists were called in, neither of them would commit himself. Disgusted, Dr Paolucci left the Vatican in a huff, Dr Niehans made the injections, and the Pope recovered.

Let it be noted that the former Eugenio Pacelli, the brilliant Roman nobleman who became Pius XII had a number of idiosyncrasies, of which his preoccupation with his health was only one. Pius, for instance, had a complex about house flies which he bad-mouthed as carriers of disease. Whenever he spotted a fly in his office or bedroom, he chased after it with a flyswatter he carried at all times on a belt underneath his robe. Although this was a harmless idiosyncrasy, the Pope's hypochondria, on the other hand, was a serious matter, for among his imaginary illnesses were a chronic toothache of mysterious origin, irregular pulse to a suspected heart condition, bilious attacks or some other hepatic disorder, enlargement of the prostate gland and anemia.

Though all of the above were only imaginary ailments, Pius did suffer from an inflamed colon and chronic gastritis, but these Galeazzi Lisi believed were the direct result of the Holy Father's hypochondria and from the administration of a vicious system prescribed by one of the Pontiff's dentists. Preoccupied with his teeth from early youth, Pius cleaned them several times each day in a long and complicated ritual. First, he brushed his teeth with a toothpaste that had been concocted especially for him by a chemist he trusted; then he washed out his mouth with a strong astringent preparation, and followed this up by massaging his gums with sterilized cotton swabs which he dipped in a disinfectant solution.

Despite these elaborate dental rituals, the Pope was nevertheless convinced that something was seriously wrong with his gums. Although he was assured by his dentist that there were no organic causes for his worries, the Pope never accepted his dentist's clearance.

Much against the advice of competent Vatican doctors, the Pope therefore sought the aid of an obscure Roman dentist who came up with a 'remedy' for his presumably bad gums. This dentist, however, really was a quack and he gave Pius a strong preparation that was a solution used mainly to tan hides, chromic acid. Not only is chromic acid harmful to sensitive gums but it is also, when taken internally, a slow-working poison. Over the years Pius swallowed substantial quantities of this remedy, and it was responsible for the stomach disorders which sapped his strength and eventually killed him. Pius's gastritic condition stemming from the intake of chromic acid became much worse and more complicated by painful spasms of the diaphragm that induced attacks of hiccups.

Pope Pius managed to keep going fairly well, however, until late September 1958, and then while vacationing at the papal summer place in Castelgandolfo, he was once more seriously stricken.

Although Dr Niehans was called in again, this time with several other specialists, Pope Pius grew steadily worse, and on October 9, 1958, he died at the age of 83 in great pain, the victim of the alchemists and quacks whose help he had sought. Dr Galeazzi Lisi was of the view, which he made public, that Pius XII's death was caused by the quacks.

Some sensational accounts about Pius's strange death began to appear in Italian newspapers, which were topped with increasingly scurrilous and exaggerated items about the Pope's condition at the time of his death. As efficient and as effective as the Vatican's intelligence service was, it was unable to discover who was responsible for what went on. Whoever the tipster was, he was making a lot of money from editors in various parts of Europe for the sensational reports. But what upset the Vatican inner circle more than anything was the biggest shocker of all — someone had made a candid home movie of the dying Pope that showed him in agonizing stages, right up to the final moments of his death. The movie was being auctioned off to the highest bidder by a person or persons unknown. Through a front man, the Vatican outbid everybody and eventually bought this film outright.

The special assignment of private eye Tom Ponzi was to identify the newspapers' phantom tipster. Top secret was the order of the day, for if it ever got out that the Vatican had hired a private detective to discover who was divulging secrets, the Church would become a laughingstock in the eyes of the world. For this reason, Ponzi had to undertake the investigation with the maximum discretion and in absolute confidence. He was faced with the fact that some of the clinical reports on the Pope had been accurate, though several had been distorted or embellished with innuendos. Ponzi surmised that the tipster was one who had had access to the Pontiff's sick room and who knew something about medicine. Since so many doctors had been called in for consultations and because there had been a number of nursing nuns and even cardinals and priests from the papal staff involved, not to mention some members of the Pontiff's immediate family, Ponzi's job was not going to be an easy one. The main suspicion, however, fell on Dr Niehans who had a dubious reputation because he constantly sought publicity. Mixed into the investigation was that nearly all the sensational stories about the Pope made favorable mention of Niehans' cellular-therapy — even stating that he had saved the Pope's life twice. But, as things turned out, the first to be suspect was the first to be cleared, for Ponzi's dogged research showed conclusively that Dr Niehans had definitely not been the culprit.

One by one, others were eliminated from Ponzi's suspect list, and eventually he zeroed in on the person responsible. His voluminous report to the Vatican and the succeeding Pope (John XXIII) made eyes pop. The Vatican mystery had been solved. The phantom tipster was one of the least suspect on Ponzi's initial list, but the hard facts made it certain that Pius's personal physician, Dr Riccardo Galeazzi Lisi, was the villain. Almost instantly he was barred from the Vatican for life, and swiftly did a hastily convened meeting of the Rome Medical Association remove him from their rolls, after a full hearing in closed session — an action that was tantamount to revocation of his license to practice medicine in Italy. Dr Galeazzi Lisi left Italy immediately thereafter and set up his own rejuvenation clinic in a small town just over the Italian–French border. To stop any similar occurrence, Pope Paul VI instituted a number of strict regulations into the apostolic constitution.

The subject of papal medical doctors and murder is by no means unknown; the death of Pius XII's predecessor, the former Achille Ratti (Pope Pius XI), had political implications since the name of the game was murder, Vatican style.

The murder of Pius XI became a Vatican problem after Cardinal Eugenio Tisserant died in a clinic in Albano Laziale. Virtually within minutes after Tisserant's death was known, Vatican officials rushed to the cardinal's quarters inside the Vatican to get his diaries, in which he had written daily notes and comments about Vatican affairs for over 60 years. But they were too late. For someone had already stolen off with the Tisserant papers, moments before Vatican agents got to the room. The Pope had ordered that Tisserant's notes be confiscated and put into cold storage because he was recognized as being utterly frank and straightforward and because, among other things, he had known far too many details about the murder and murderer of Pope Paul XI in 1938, which the Vatican wanted to continue to keep quiet.

It did not take the Vatican long to figure out, through its spy network, just who was responsible for whisking away Tisserant's papers. He was a French monsignor by the name of Georges Roche, who had been for years a close friend of Tisserant and who had been called in by Tisserant to administer Extreme Unction to him (the last rites). Monsignor Roche had been instructed by Tisserant to collect his diaries before the Vatican got their hands on them and to hide them where nobody could find them. The Tisserant documents made it quite clear that Pius XI was put to death by a Vatican medical doctor, Professor Francesco Petacci. Dr Petacci, who was the father of Mussolini's mistress, movie actress Claretta Petacci (shot to death with Il Duce in April 1945 and hung upside down alongside her notorious lover in a public square in Milan), died in July 1970, 19 months before Tisserant's death.

Pius XI was 64 years old in 1922 when he became a surprise choice to be the successor to Pope Benedict XV. A compromise candidate pushed by Pope Benedict's Secretary of State, Cardinal Pietro Gasparri (whom later Pius XI was to dismiss summarily), Pius XI was an unknown quantity at the time of his election, since he had spent most of his adult life as a librarian. For 25 years he had worked in the Ambrosian Library in Milan and later was the chief of the Vatican Library for five years (during which time he encouraged a young French scholar, Father Eugenio Tisserant to become a librarian). Library work occupied most of his time, and his only outside interest was mountain-climbing.

When elected to the papacy, Papa Ratti (as the Italians affectionately knew him) promised to continue Benedict's policies, but it was clear soon after his assumption to the throne that his was a rather complex character. He was a man with an unusually strong personality and some clear-cut ideas as to what he wanted to do: he had every intention of solving the so-called Roman Question, which had set the Holy See at odds with the Italian State. He also intended to strengthen strengthen the international role of the Holy See. The goals were, of course, related, but it meant that an agreement would have to be reached with Benito Mussolini who had seized power in Italy.

Mussolini expanded the role of his Fascist regime but was shrewd enough not to antagonize the Vatican because the masses behind him were at the same time avid Catholics. He himself detested all religions, and though he never embraced Catholicism *per se*, Mussolini recognized it as a political force that could serve his purposes if it collaborated with him, or vice versa. Since the Pope was of the same view and recognized Mussolini as the Vatican's 'man of destiny' who could heal the unnatural breach between the Church and the State, how much better for the Vatican to work out a truce, however uneasy, between the Church and Italy.

Such was the background against which the Lateran pacts of 1929 were signed, concluding the Roman Question and founding the formation of the State of Vatican City which now could deal, diplomatically and politically, with every other country on an equal basis. Pius is supposed to have said at the time that he would sign a pact with the devil 'if it were for the good of the Church'. And maybe he did.

Whereas the concordat policy was designed to reach agreements on disputed questions between Church and State, the dictatorial regime was often offending basic human rights and violating agreements.

Disputes over youth groups and Catholic Action came up, as the Nazis in Germany were becoming aggressively racist in their policies. In March 1937 Pius XI published two strong encyclicals, one written in German and entitled, *Mit Brennender Sorge*. Both of them condemned divinization of a race and constituted the first papal confrontation with Nazism. At the same time the Holy Office, in June 1937, came out with strongly critical remarks against a book by an Italian author who was preaching Hitler's racial theories which, when applied to Italy, were supposed to benefit that country.

Although the condemnation did not deter the Fascists from acting out Nazi racial theories in Italy, it provoked considerable friction between the Mussolini regime and the Vatican. Fascist biggies insisted that the Vatican stay out of politics, as agreed upon in the Lateran pacts, whereas Vatican spokesmen repeatedly maintained the matter was not political but spiritual. The Pope made a series of speeches in the summer of 1938 in which he blasted Italy's 'exaggerated nationalism' and the ever-growing racist policies of a regime that was beholden to Hitler. Pius also summoned the American Jesuit scholar, John LaFarge, and told him he wanted an encyclical written against racism, anti-Semitism and totalitarianism. (See Chapter VI The Encyclical That Was Never Published.) When Cardinal Innitzer, archbishop of Vienna, described the German occupation of Austria as 'providential', the Vatican made it clear publicly that it had no responsibility for the statement, summoned Cardinal Innitzer to Rome and prevailed upon him to repudiate the statement.

Enmeshed in the brouhaha, Pius XI visited the Canadian College in Rome on February 3, 1939, for its 50th anniversary, and in a speech he made it clear that he would give the College another audience. Two days later, however, Pius had a serious collapse, and apparently aware that he was dying, he confided to Vatican officials that he had one great desire that he knew God would grant him; he wanted to last until Saturday, February 11, the anniversary of his coronation and the 10th anniversary of the reconciliation with Italy. On Thursday of that week, he had two heart attacks and on the night of the 10th, his condition deteriorated rapidly. At 5.31 in the morning, on February 11, Pius XI died at the age of 82.

The Tisserant papers indicate Benito Mussolini had a motive for wanting to do away with Pius XI. Though he was in failing health, the octogenarian Pontiff had called together a special conclave of Italian bishops for Saturday, February 11, at which time he had planned to make a formal attack on Fascism and denounce the Concordat on the basis that Il Duce (at Hitler's behest) had pushed through a set of racial, anti-Semetic laws. Having struggled so hard back in the late 1920s to get the Vatican lined up with his regime, through the signing of the Concordat in order to gain better support from the Italian people, Mussolini now did not want the Pope to renege on the Concordat ten years later, especially since his country had formed an alliance with Nazi Germany and was now at war with England and France. For his image among his own people, he needed the Vatican on his side in appearance if not in fact.

When he suspected that Pius's open letter to the meeting of bishops would denounce both Fascism and the Concordat, Mussolini gave the order to his informers inside the Vatican to find out for certain what the Pope was writing in his letter. Despite the fact that top secrecy prevailed on the Pope's new statement, there were some intimates who knew — among them Cardinal Tisserant. Efforts were made to persuade the Pontiff not to go through with his conclave on Saturday, but though his heart was in very bad shape, he worked on his speech every night, while Vatican medical doctors attended the dying man. Tisserant was then chief librarian of the Vatican Library, but as a friend of Pius, he had more access to the Holy Father than any previous Vatican librarian had had.

About 24 hours before Pius was to make his defamatory speech, Dr Petacci — who had previously never been inside the Pontiff's bedchamber — went to him and gave him an injection that would kill him. Pius died the next day, exactly on the morning he was to have read his speech. The written speech itself was never found — so there exists no hard proof that Pope Pius XI had written the denunciation. Neither is there actual proof that Mussolini had the man erased.

CHAPTER XI

The Vatican and the Kennedys

WHEN COUNTRIES do not have formal diplomatic relations with the Vatican but maintain a friendly liaison and a mutual respect for each other, the pope does not appoint an ambassador (nuncio) to represent him but an apostolic delegate, whose duty it is to watch over the condition of the Church in the territory assigned to him. Like an ambassador, the apostolic delegate keeps the pontiff informed from his area about the area. Although the apostolic delegate is not a diplomatic envoy in the technical sense of the word and does not enjoy diplomatic privileges and immunities, the United States (as do another 15 countries) extend diplomatic courtesies to the apostolic delegate.

The office of the apostolic delegate to the USA was established by Pope Leo XII in 1893. At the very outset this apostolic delegate, in matters involving diocesan problems, was granted the power of final decision-making without having to communicate with Rome. To understand this delegation of power by the Pope to another man, one must understand that for a long time the Catholic clergy in the United States lived through a state of confusion, largely because there was an absence of a central administrative authority present on American soil. This confusion was heightened at the outset by the innumerable immigrant divisions of the Church which spoke different languages and often pushed nationalistic interests that competed with one another. Even today there still remains a degree of antipathy among Irish–American Catholics (who dominate the American clergy, especially at the top), and three other large ethnic groups — Polish–American Catholics, Italian–American Catholics and German–American Catholics. The rivalry, such as it is, is quite an understandable phenomenon, since the internal political power of the American Catholic Church to all intents and purposes is vested in the hands of Americans of Irish background. Witness the fact that the great majority of the clergy, including the cardinals and archbishops, is of Irish descent. This Irish domination of the American Church has for nearly a century stuck in the craw of the sovereigns who reigned in the Vatican.

It is no wonder, therefore, that the apostolic delegate who occupies the spacious building at 1312 Massachusetts Avenue NW, the general headquarters of the Roman Catholic Church in America, has nearly always been Italian. In this way have popes made sure that the 'Irish heresy' of American Catholicism remained under the control of a man whose first allegiance was to Rome. The apostolic delegates to the United States have been Archbishops Francesco Satolli, Sebastiano Martinelli, Diomede Falconio, Giovanni Bonzano, Pietro Fumasoni-Biondi, Amleto Cicognani, Egidio Vagnozzi, Luigi Raimondi and Jean Jadot. The apostolic delegate to the United States today is Monsignor Pio Laghi.

Matters of a social nature are the concern of an apostolic delegate, but in recent years — with the Vatican's rise as a multi-national power — affairs involving the subject of money and finances are a major concern of the papal representative and he has to be expert in economic matters. Egidio Vagnozzi was such a man. Having served as the apostolic delegate to the United States for nine years (and before that an additional ten years in Washington in the office of the apostolic delegation), Cardinal Vagnozzi was the Vatican's 'finance minister' in Rome for many years until he died in December 1980. It was John XXIII who appointed Vagnozzi as the apostolic delegate to the United States to replace Amleto Cicognani, when the latter went back to Rome to take up his duties as Vatican Secretary of State. Although Cardinal Vagnozzi was formally trained in philosophy and theology, he became a sharp observer of the American economy and a keen admirer of the 'American way of doing business'. With the help of Cardinal Spellman of New York (himself an expert on financial matters) and a volunteer team of advisers from the business milieu, Cardinal Vagnozzi kept abreast of events in the business and financial world. Not without reason, therefore, was it believed that no single person inside the Vatican had the extensive knowledge of business practices as had the Pope's 'finance minister'. It was Cardinal Vagnozzi who gave 'a negative report' to the Vatican on John F Kennedy when he was running for president. It was Vagnozzi's considered professional judgment that although Kennedy was a practicing Roman Catholic and came from a family that had been overly generous to the Church in donations, he would never become 'the Vatican's man in the White House', nor would he be of much use to the Vatican itself when and if a crunch came. Vagnozzi was right in this analysis.

An incident that took place in November 1961, which the Vatican succeeded in keeping out of the public prints, bears this out. In that year the former apostolic delegate to the United States, Cardinal

Cicognani (who had become the Vatican Secretary of State) made an attempt to see President Kennedy on the occasion of a return visit to the United States. He tried to get an appointment for a courtesy call to the Chief Executive but was informed that Mr Kennedy, occupied with pressing matters, could not see him. A second attempt by His Eminence also met with frustration when a White House officer bluntly reminded him that the US government did not officially recognize the government of the State of Vatican City and that a visit by its Cardinal Secretary of State would embarrass the president.

Deciding to pull some strings, the then-Bishop Vagnozzi persuaded Cardinal Cicognani to stay in Washington an extra day. The former got a prominent figure in the Kennedy Administration, a convert to the Catholic religion, to bring about a meeting. The White House finally yielded and set an appointment for the Holy See's Secretary of State, provided the visit be classified as a personal one. Accompanied by Apostolic Delegate Vagnozzi, Cardinal Cicognani arrived at the back door of the White House (as per instructions) and was escorted to the front door where the president greeted him formally. For the approximately 20 minutes that Mr Kennedy stayed with the Vatican's representative, news photographers were denied anyopportunity to take pictures. Nor were any reporters allowed to be present.

During his long residence in Washington as apostolic delegate, Cardinal Cicognani had been received by several US presidents of Protestant affiliation. The Catholic officer, therefore, had not expected the White House to give him a cold shoulder. But things got worse. Eight days later when Protestant Evangelist Billy Graham paid a courtesy call to President Kennedy, the carpet was literally laid out for him at the front door, in spite of the fact that Graham had gone to bat for Vice-President Richard M Nixon during the 1960 presidential campaign. Dumbfounded to note that the White House had permitted lensmen to shoot many pictures, Bishop Vagnozzi became even more disenchanted with JFK when he refused to grant federal aid to parochial schools. Because Protestant presidents like Hoover, Roosevelt, Truman and Eisenhower had been more charitable towards the Church than Kennedy had, the name of John F Kennedy became mud inside the Vatican.

Perhaps oblivious to the low esteem her husband was held in, Mrs Jacqueline Kennedy nevertheless wanted something from the Vatican a year later, and she quietly approached Pope John XXIII, through devious political channels to get him to do her a personal favor — one that required the Pope to break or bypass some Church rules. At the time that she initiated her campaign she had not met Pope John so she took her case to influential friends with access to the

Pope. What she wanted was to get a Vatican annulment of the first marriage of her sister Lee to Michael Canfield, an American. Lee wanted to regularize her status because she had married Prince Stanislaus Radziwill in a civil ceremony. Her wedding to Canfield took place in Virginia in 1953 and was dissolved under civil law in 1958.

Under the advice of a noted Roman lawyer, Professoı Fernando della Rocca — who was associated with the Vatican's Sacra Rota — Mrs Kennedy undertook the following plan. She wrote a letter on White House stationery to the then President of Switzerland, Phillip Etter who had agreed to present the request to Pope John in person. The plea on behalf of Princess Radziwill concerned itself with the woman's faith and her hope that she would be admitted anew into the Church. In November 1961, having assured Mrs Kennedy that he would do his best to 'achieve what you and your sister have so much at heart', Etter took the message to Pope John. But the plan did not work, for the Pope was indignant. He told Etter that he could not personally occupy himself with the question, that it was a matter of the competent authority, the Sacra Rota.

Mrs Kennedy did not give up. On March 10, 1962, she was received by Pope John in a special audience. He was at his most charming and even told the First Lady something about her husband that she did not know: when John F Kennedy was 22 years old, in 1939, he posed for a sculptress working on a wooden panel which was to become part of an altar that is today in the Vatican. Kennedy posed for a Polish-born artist, Irene Baruch, who was married to a career diplomat, John Cooper Wiley, then serving as US Minister to Latvia and Estonia. Needing a model for the angel in one of the 12 panels surrounding a life-sized statue of Saint Therese, Mrs Wiley found Jack Kennedy's curly hair and youthful serenity of expression just what she wanted to depict in the angel. The particular panel shows the winged angel (Kennedy) hovering over Saint Therese while she is writing a book; he has one hand on her shoulder and the other hand cupping the edge of the book. Young Kennedy had been spending a week of his summer vacation with the Wileys during the time his father, Joseph Kennedy, was the American ambassador to the Court of Saint James in London. Originally, Mrs Wiley had planned to give the altar to a church in Belgium, but by the time it was finished, war had broken out in Europe, and Belgium was occupied by the German Army. A priest urged her to send it to the Vatican.

Utterly charmed by this story, Mrs Kennedy departed the Pope with some assurance that something would be done for her sister. And, sure enough, in November 1962 her sister's marriage to

Michael Canfield was annulled, and Lee was married again to Prince Radziwill, this time in a church ceremony, in London on July 3, 1963, that was kept a total secret. To grant Mrs Kennedy's sister her annulment, the Sacra Rota compiled several hundred pages of Latin testimony to prove that at the time of her marriage Lee did not believe in its indissolubility. This was the legal hook found by the Sacra Rota to justify its decision while Pope John did his own special papal lobbying. The decision was never made public by the Vatican. Neither Mrs Kennedy nor her husband ever gave this information out to the press.

CHAPTER XII

Washington's View of the Vatican

CURIOUS TO find out just what the United States State Department had in its files about the Vatican, a representative from the apostolic delegate's office obtained over 1000 pages under the Freedom of Information Act, most of which were documents dealing with Giovanni Montini while he was a Vatican officer, later as Cardinal and Archbishop of Milan and then as Pope Paul VI in 1980. When the Vatican finally got the documents, there was general surprise as to how closely US embassy officials in Rome followed Vatican pronouncements and measured their effects.

Many of the papers were telegrams from American ambassadors such as John Volpe and Henry Cabot Lodge to the US Secretary of State. One early document showed that US officials ticketed Monsignor Montini more than a decade and a half before his election with a high probability of one day becoming Pope. One communication offered the opinion that Monsignor Domenico Tardini would probably make a better Pope inasmuch as he was 'more intelligent and able than Montini'.

Another thing about Montini that seemed to have bothered US Vatican observers stationed in Rome was his interaction, when he was Milan's archbishop, with that city's leftist political leaders. The American observers, worried about Montini's liberal tendencies, reported on his 'positive magnanimity toward . . . a leftward swing in Italian national politics'. When Monsignor Montini protested a reported death sentence for three anarchists in Barcelona, the US embassy in Madrid and the US embassy in Rome both opined this was an unprecedented interference in the affairs of another Catholic country.

At his election to the papacy in 1963, Washington was swamped with secret background material on Cardinal Montini, including interviews with the Vatican sources and Italian politicians of all stripes. From the US consul in Valencia, there was a report on Spain's reaction to Paul VI's election, including one about General Francisco Franco's close relative who 'had prayed and prayed that Montini would not be elected'. For most of Paul's reign, the released documents gave details on his verbatim speeches, his trips and his frequent meetings with foreign dignitaries.

In April 1973, the American ambassador in Rome expressed his concern that Pope Paul seemed to be turning his back on South Vietnam's President Nguyen Van Thieu, but then when the Pope gave favorable mention to Thieu in his next speech, the ambassador told the State Department, 'We may be responsible.' Each of the various US ambassadors stationed in Rome during Paul's pontificate were impressed with his flow of speeches and generally respectful of his ideas. Ambassador Lodge in a September 1973 note to his home office said that in a private audience he had had with Paul, the Pontiff believed that 'the youth in Panama cannot any longer tolerate' Washington dominating their country.

The Pope's openness to the Soviet Bloc countries was reported with some mixed feelings during the first part of his administration but later on this same openness provoked only casual commentaries. Of additional interest, perhaps, were the Pontiff's relations with Israel, particularly on the question of the internationalization of Jerusalem. The released documents also contained more than a hundred pages on Paul's 1968 birth control encyclical, *Humanae Vitae*, and much of the submitted materials dealt with the negative worldwide reactions. The Rome embassy at that time indicated its concern over the effect the encyclical would have on the Pope's credibility and influence on future issues, especially in traditionally Catholic countries.

Perhaps the one report that amused Vatican officials was that in which the remarks of President Jimmy Carter's mother were recorded after she had had a private papal audience in 1978. As reported by the US ambassador, Miss Lillian said: 'I just thought the Pope was the nicest, sweetest man, and I feel so holy. Anything I wanted blessed, he blessed for me. It was the most devout moment I ever spent, even in my own church.'

CHAPTER XIII

Fatima's Secret

GERTRUDE STEIN might have said that a secret is a secret is a secret. And the Vatican's expertise and partiality for secrets would bear her out. The bizarre secret of Fatima is a case in point. What makes the secret of Fatima — actually the third and last secret, which still has not been revealed — especially interesting is that Pope John XXIII was supposed to have made the contents of the third secret of Fatima known in 1960, while an expectant world waited with bated breath. So deeply shaken was John when he read it that he refused to divulge the contents. It is entirely possible that the contents of Secret Number Three may never come to light.

On May 13, 1917, in the tiny Portuguese village of Fatima, 70 miles (112 kilometres) northeast of Lisbon, three very young shepherds — 10-year-old Lucia Dos Santos and her cousins, Jacinta, and Francisco Marta, 9 (both of whom are now dead), saw the apparition of a tiny woman, together with an extremely bright flash, in a large pasture known as Cova da Iria. She said that she was from heaven (later the children were to report it was the Blessed Virgin Mary) and that she would appear one month later, on June 13, when a public miracle would take place so that everyone 'may believe'. Fifty spectators came to witness the phenomenon. Lucia carried on a conversation with an unseen person, after which the witnesses heard an explosion and saw a cloud rise from a tree.

A month later, on July 13, the three children saw a terrifying vision of hell and heard two prophecies — one that was revealed and one that was not. There was a crowd of 4500 witnesses. The prophecy said that the war would end but another would come in the year that Pope Pius XI would die (World War II began in 1939, the same year that Pius XI died). The prophecy added that when an unknown light was seen in the sky, it would be a sign from God saying that He would punish the world for its crimes through war, famine and the persecution of the Church. The children told the secret prophecy to Church authorities who sent it to the Vatican under seal. In the succeeding months the visions continued, and the turnout of people became larger and larger.

On October 13, more than 70,000 curiosity-seekers showed up in a pouring rain. Again the three children reported seeing the lady come down from a low cloud and then rise again. But something very strange happened on that day. The morning had been wet and dull, with a heavily overcast sky. Suddenly there was a rift in the clouds and a great expanse of blue was revealed. The sun came out, and then it seemed to tremble, to shake, to dance, to move back and forth. Now great beams of green, red, blue and violet light splashed and swept over the trees, rocks and earth. This astonishing spectacle went on for ten minutes as the multitude stood in awe. Many people sank on their knees in the mud, crying aloud for God to save them or sobbing out a prayer to Mary. After these solar fireworks, the sun zigzagged its way back into the sky, and then — as if one 'miracle' were not enough — the crowd discovered that whereas before they had been wet, their clothes were now quite dry. The ground now was also dry, no longer muddy.

After some initial opposition, the Bishop of Leiria accepted the children's vision as the appearance of the Virgin Mary. The building of a basilica was begun in 1929, and in 1953 it was consecrated. On May 13, 1967 (the 50th anniversary of the first vision), Pope Paul VI said Mass and prayed for peace in front of more than a million people. In the area today there are a number of hospitals to which vast numbers of sick people are brought for a cure. Although nearly a thousand 'cures' have been reported, the Church plays down this aspect of Fatima, but people continue to make pilgrimages twice a year; about a million people visit Fatima annually, rivaling Lourdes as a magnet for the faithful.

As for the third and last secret — now referred to as the famous Secret of Fatima — which was revealed to Lucia during the apparition on July 13, the Vatican decided to suppress its contents after it was read by Pope John. His secretary, Archbishop Loris Capovilla, said that the Pope wanted it concealed. Seven years later, in 1967, Cardinal Alfredo Ottaviani, head of the Holy Office under Pope Paul, said the Vatican would continue to keep it under wraps. At the time, Ottaviani would not confirm or deny that when Pope Pius XII learned what Sister Lucia had forecast, he fainted. Cardinal Ottaviani said that the secret was intended only for the Pope but that what was important for the public was the message of Fatima — and that was already known.

The Vatican will very likely never publish the secret. But inside the Vatican you can get a copy of the last secret from what could be called the Vatican's own equivalent of Russia's Samizdat press. It may not be acceptable as authentic, but several of the Vatican people carry a copy of the secret around. This is the text:

'A great punishment will fall on mankind . . . in the second half of the twentieth century. Satan will succeed in seducing the spirits of the great scientists who invent the arms with which it will be possible to destroy a large part of mankind in a few minutes. A great war will be unleashed in the second half of the twentieth century. Millions and millions of men will envy the dead. . . .'

If this is what Pius XII read and then fainted, he had good cause to. It would be no surprise if this is what John XXIII refused to divulge.

CHAPTER XIV

The Test Tube Baby

ON A quiet street in the northern outskirts of Moscow, well out of sight of Red Square and far from the shadows of the onion domes of the Kremlin, stands the Institute of Experimental Biology of the Academy of Sciences. Behind the walls lining Number 8 Baltiskaya Street biologists undertook what they had hoped to be the most fantastic biological breakthrough of the twentieth century.

The Soviet research team expected to be the first to produce a human being — one which had spent its full nine-month gestation period in a test tube. At one point in their research they had succeeded in keeping a fetus alive outside a human womb for as long as six months. This had been accomplished by sustaining the ovum of a woman in a special glass container filled with amniotic fluid, the liquid that human embryos grow in.

Just as the Kremlin successfully kept its work on the first Sputnik a state secret back in 1957, so too had an iron curtain of silence been wrapped around the test tube baby. But there had been a leak, nevertheless. The source was Dr Daniele Angelo Petrucci, an Italian doctor who had started the experiment several years earlier and had come in for an undue share of Vatican flak.

In his laboratory in Bologna, on Via Ruini 3, Dr Petrucci, a well-to-do surgeon, managed to keep one human embryo alive in a glass receptacle for 29 days before deciding to stop. A practicing Roman Catholic, Dr Petrucci did not want to go against the teachings of his Church after there were criticisms from Rome about his experiment. Following a conference with Vatican officials, Petrucci took up his pioneer work once more and kept another experimental baby, whose sex he determined as female, alive for fully 59 days. This one died as a result of a mistake. Dr Petrucci abandoned his project to give birth to a full-term baby in a tube, however, when the Vatican's semi-official newspaper, *L'Osservatore Romano*, condemned the work with the following comment: 'God surrounded the act of creation of a human being with the most supreme assistance of love, nature and conscience. It would be most monstrous to violate these conditions.'

This was in the Summer of 1961. In November of that year the Soviet Union — taking advantage of the Vatican's shortsightedness — decided to exploit Petrucci where the Vatican had foolishly let him down. He was invited to Moscow to talk with biologists about his experiment. Laying out the Red carpet, USSR scientists virtually adopted him, wined and dined him, picked his brain and sent him home with a medal after two months of conferences, discussions, meetings, panels, lectures and lab demonstrations at the Institute of Experimental Biology.

Just how did Dr Petrucci keep two human fetuses alive for 29 days and 59 days respectively? The answer to that was the same answer that applied to the work in Moscow, which was supervised by Dr Ivan Nikolaivitch Maiscki, director of the Institute, and carried out by Dr Pyotr Anokchine. For the latter, a brilliant biologist from Leningrad, the Russians were preparing a world propaganda buildup for the time when his new being — the world's first 'bionaut' — joined the human race.

The bionaut experiment began when Dr Petrucci, through surgery, had extracted the egg from a woman who could not have become pregnant because of a cancerous condition. He united this ovum with semen taken from a man who had believed himself sterile. Conception took place in a special glass container filled with the amniotic fluid removed from a pregnant woman especially for the test.

At the outset Dr Petrucci had more than 40 failures. All the eggs died within a few days after conception in the glass he used as a mother's womb. Then one day he hit upon an idea; he decided to use an ovum that according to the menstrual cycle was ready for fertilization. Through chemical and biochemical tests made on a patient, he was able to extract an ovum which that very day was ready for the spermatozoa. With the vacuum created in the small tray, the egg from the donor was then immersed in the amniotic fluid. Through tubes a supply of oxygen was pumped in, creating a perfect natural environment for uniting the male sperm with the female ovum.

This time Dr Petrucci's egg did not die after a few days. When the nucleus of the germ cell began to divide, subdivide and enlarge, Dr Petrucci knew he was at last on the right track. As the fetus took the shape of a baby in its early stages and started to develop legs (on the 29th day), Dr Petrucci killed it because of the criticism being leveled at him. One Italian newspaper, having dubbed Petrucci's fetus The Thing, claimed he was creating a Frankenstein monster. After the hullabaloo died down, the Bologna doctor quietly repeated the incredible trials and kept a fetus alive for 59 days. It had developed ears, eyes, a mouth, neck, reproductive organs, a heart and umbilical cord. By the seventh week Dr Petrucci could distinguish the eye formation of the embryo. On the 59th day, however, the heartbeat failed and the embryo died because the special nutritional transfusion plasma Petrucci had been feeding it proved no longer suitable. The Russians took over at the point where Petrucci left off.

The bearded Italian scientist, a specialist in tissues, made a strong plea to the Vatican for permission to continue experiments. He tried to convince a team of cardinals that he was not necessarily interested in creating human life outside of a human womb just for its own sake. Specifically his purpose with the experiments was to grow human tissues and glands which would not only be transplantable but acceptable by the body of an adult in need of such. Petrucci also told the Vatican that his tests had begun to show how to save the lives of countless unborn children. Convinced that observation of the living cell in a test tube had demonstrated some of the causes of miscarriage, he felt that one of the benefits of his experiment was that it might lead doctors to find ways and means to prevent miscarriage.

'One of my aims,' Dr Petrucci told me in a conversation shortly before he died unexpectedly of a heart attack at the age of 51 in October 1973, 'is to help women have babies, for I have been upset by the large number of women giving birth to stillborn children, especially at their first pregnancy. Thus my research was directed along humanitarian lines, guided by the Christian principles I have practiced since childhood. I love humankind. If a wife should lose a baby on which the hopes of herself and her husband have been centering, this is a human tragedy. That I should be denounced for my experiment, that the Vatican should interfere with my scientific research — this is a great personal blow, for I am a scientist dedicated to uncovering those mysteries of nature that God is prepared to reveal to us.'

The Vatican was not buying any of his views. It felt — and still feels — that children should be raised by parents and not by scientists.

CHAPTER XV

Why He May Have Been the Most Unpopular Pope . . .

DURING THE Holy Year in 1975, members of the Milan Flying Club — to honor Pope Paul VI whom they had admired and respected as a friend when he was the archbishop of their city — staged an unusual and rather spectacular ceremonial event. Holding a replica of the Madonna, which crowns the main spire of Milan's cathedral, *Il Duomo*, several members of the club parachuted into Saint Peter's Square. As they floated to the ground, the Milan Madonna cracked. On the way back to Milan the plane piloted by a World War II ace, crashed and everyone aboard was killed. Shocked as many people were, millions of Italians said they knew why the special event had been ill-fated and why the Madonna had cracked. The blame was put on Pope Paul because he was possessed of the 'evil eye'.

For Paul VI to have been tabbed with the evil eye, through no fault of his own, was bad luck for him, for the rumor spread all over Italy early in his reign and dogged him throughout his 15-year papacy. Unable to do anything about the Pontiff's alleged evil eye, the Vatican made no effort on the Italian mainland to clear Paul even though it was obviously a bum rap. At best, the Vatican had hoped that word of the pontifical evil eye would not spread to other parts of the world in which this superstition runs rampant, such as in France where it is known as the *mauvais oeil* and among the Arabs of the Middle East.

No matter where you go in Italy, you will find people using all kinds of amulets and talismans intended to divert the lethal glance of the evil eye (in Italian, *mal occhio*), which is believed to be so all powerful that it can bring on personal disasters, including death. Even Italians who scoff and claim not to believe in *mal occhio* often carry around some kind of charm. Among Italy's intelligentsia which says that it is all bunk, people jangle their keys because 'one never knows, one never knows. . . .' Benito Mussolini was one prominent Italian who insisted he did not believe in the evil eye, yet whenever he suspected that someone in his presence might have *mal occhio*, Il Duce would unabashedly put his hand into his pocket to tap his private parts for good luck, even during public appearances. It is known that the Italian dictator never trusted Pope Pius XII because he believed the Pontiff had the eye. Fortunately, the rest of the country did not share this view, as it did later on when Paul VI took over.

No less a person than Pius XII shared a similar view of the evil eye. When Montini was Archbishop of Milan, Pius XII would never look him straight in the eye whenever the two met. He also would not promote him to the rank of cardinal, even though Montini ruled over the largest, most important archdiocese in Italy with only the rank of monsignor (contrary to other archdioceses in Italy, such as Genoa, Venice, Florence and Palermo where each archbishop was a cardinal). Besides the factor of the evil eye, Pius XII just did not like Montini personally. But perhaps the more important reason for the discrimination against Montini was that the Pope was deeply upset that Montini, while working in the Vatican, had made overtures to Stalin after World War II to effect closer ties with the Soviet Union and its Communist Party. Strongly anti-Communist, Pius was quite angered by this unauthorized move when informed by Vatican spies as to what Montini had done, and he banished him to Milan, saying that 'as long as I am alive, I shall see to it that Montini will not be made a cardinal.' And, in fact, Monsignor Montini was never made a cardinal during Pius's reign. That came immediately after John XXIII replaced Pius in 1958 when, as one of his very first acts, he promoted Milan's archbishop to the rank of cardinal. John did not pay any attention to Montini's alleged evil eye.

The evil eye can be spotted easily, subscribing Italians explain, because it is something like the stare of a cat. If a person has the kind of eye that seems to penetrate when its possessor looks in your direction, then Italians know it is the evil eye. No one who has the eye has it by choice; it can be either congenital or acquired. To offset the eye, all Italians have their own preventive measures: some spit very fast or wear something blue; others jangle their keys or never look the person straight in the eye; still others (mostly the men) touch their private parts when confronted with the 'it'; another is to clench the fist, with the forefinger and the little finger sticking out, a loose equivalent of the British two-fingered gesture.

In Pope Paul's case, the superstition did his reign considerable harm in Italy. A series of disasters which preceded or immediately followed him throughout his travels strengthened the rumors. In 1967, for instance, an earthquake followed a Vatican announcement that the Pope would visit Turkey, and in 1970 a disastrous cyclone hit East Pakistan after the Pope decided to visit the Far East. Two other incidents, which got a lot of Italian newspaper space at the time, involved several top-ranking soccer teams who were received by Paul VI in a private audience; the teams subsequently lost very important matches, for which defeats the fans blamed the Pope. While Paul was in office, the somber bronze statue of Christ inside Saint Peter's Cathedral began to take on a bright shine on the inside of its thighs because Italians were rubbing the testicles to ward off the evil eye of the man who headed the Roman Catholic Church at the time.

Paul also added to his negative image when during his reign he demoted Saint Nicholas. In public opinion, a blunder! Saint Nicholas was held in low esteem by the Vatican, as were several other saints. Pope Paul demoted Saint Nicholas along with dozens of other saints by removing him from the Vatican's liturgical calendar of saints on the grounds there was no real proof he even existed.

Saint Nicholas (alias Santa Claus) has a world image as a jolly carrier of millions of dollars of toys to millions of sleeping children — which he does with Rififi-like sneakiness in his reindeer-drawn sleigh on Christmas Eve. But in Italy's lower Adriatic coastal city of Bari, where Saint Nicholas is the patron saint and where his bones are buried, he is venerated for other things having nothing to do with Yuletide. Known in other parts of the world as Kris Kringle, Père Noël, Sinterklaas and Father Christmas, Saint Nicholas, or in Italian, San Nicola, was the fourth-century bishop of Myra in Asia Minor, and his body, stolen from the Saracens, was brought to Bari in 1087 by Italian sailors. Exultant, the people of Bari proclaimed him as a saint and built a Romanesque basilica in the crowded old quarter of the city. His relics are buried in a crypt beneath the basilica where burns the single flame of a lamp in the form of a ship, fed by two separate containers of oil, one from Italy and one from Asia. The Barese people consider San Nicola the patron and protector of shipwrecked sailors and also the guardian saint of young girls without a dowry. In Bari the big day for Saint Nicholas does not come at Christmas, but during the month of May on the anniversary of the day the sailors came back with his body. To honor Saint Nicholas's anniversary, Bari's entire flag-decorated fishing fleet takes a symbolic coffin out to sea and brings it into port, amid feasting, ceremonies and street parades. No pope has ever attended this feast, nor given it his blessing — and no ranking cardinal from the Vatican has ever bothered to show up and beam an ecclesiastical approval, for Saint Nicholas has two strikes against him, as far as the Vatican is concerned — neither of which is his fault.

The first grievance the Vatican has against him is that both he and the Vatican were victims of one of the most subtle practical jokes in Church history. Around the altar where the 'holy bones' are buried and on the pavement in front there is an intricate design among which are some Arabic words. The Arab artists (commissioned for the work in the eleventh century), knowing that none of the Catholic officers could read Arabic calligraphy, pulled a fast one. Woven throughout what appeared to be a design was the creed of the Moslem religion, 'There is no God but God, and Mohammed is his prophet!' For centuries no one in the Vatican nor in Bari's church circles was aware of this. But eventually it got out, and because Bari's local priests did not want to ruin the exquisite floor or raise funds for the job, they decided to leave it there since few people would ever be aware of it. The Vatican disapproved of the decision but would offer no money to change the insulting pavement.

The second grievance concerns the saint's role as Santa Claus. How Saint Nicholas became Santa Claus all over the Western world is not easy to trace. Bari historians believe that the custom of giving children toys on December 6 (St Nicholas's birthday) started because he once wrought a miracle and brought three children slaughtered by an innkeeper back to life. The transformation of Saint Nicholas's name to Sant' Claus may have taken place in Holland where the Dutch apparently shortened the name to 'Sant' Claus'. Eventually this became Santa Claus.

After Pope Paul demoted Saint Nicholas, the Vatican's weekly newspaper took a swipe at him in an editorial saying he 'represents a monstrous substitution for the Christ Child and offends the faith', adding that the emphasis on toy-giving is an 'insidious form of de-Christianization'.

The downgrading of its indestructible patron saint came as a kind of hard knock for Bari. But the people of the city rallied to his cause and he continues to be revived. Sure, there is a Vatican, but if the folks in Bari have anything to say, there will always be a Saint Nicholas, too.

CHAPTER XVI

Was Pope John VIII a Woman?

In 1972 a British film called *Pope Joan* was released with Liv Ullman playing the lead role of the transvestite and supported by Olivia de Havilland, Trevor Howard and Franco Nero, with a script by John Briley, based on a story by Boccaccio. The picture was a distressingly pedestrian vehicle that became a dismal failure at the box office. It was to the Vatican's credit that the movie was ignored, for had they squawked about it, it would have brought on world publicity, and more distributors might have wanted to handle it. In January 1975 the Sofia (Bulgaria) Opera House put on a performance of a new opera by Viktor Stoyanov called *Pope Johanna*. It too was a dreadful flop.

Who was Pope Joan? Was she the person cited as Pope John VIII, who served for a period that lasted two years, five months and four days between the reign of Pope Leo IV (847–853) and Pope Benedict III (855–858)? Is it true that Vatican records once indicated a gap for this period — with no official explanation for this omission? Is it also true that officials changed their records of the date of the death of Pope Leo IX from the year 853 to 855 so that Benedict III's reign would appear to have started the same year that Leo died, leaving no room for a Pope John VIII/Pope Joan? To construct a coherent chronicle about the so-called Pope Joan would be a challenge as more than a thousand years have passed. It's worth taking a look at Joan, the she-Pope, nevertheless.

Known variously as Agnes, Gilberta or Johannes Angelicus, the person who was supposed to have been Pope John (sometimes called Papissa Joanna) is surrounded with doubt, a subject of old wives' tales which have been nourished by enemies of the Catholic Church and atheists. Not much is known about the early life of the she-Pope. Legend has it she was born in England and she was known to have traveled in the guise of a monk — first with her sickly father to many European destinations, and then with a monk called Frumentius, who was her lover. Since Joan constantly wore the garb of a monk, she and Frumentius had no trouble spending the nights together in monasteries — but during this time, she was getting wiser and wiser in ecclesiastical matters, as she enmeshed herself in scholarly studies.

In time, having shed Frumentius, she made her way to Rome, now determined to become Pope some day. Still passing herself off as a man, Joan became a notary of the Curia, delivered impressive, learned sermons and rose within the Vatican's hierarchy. She displayed great gifts as a politician and tactician, becoming Pope Leo's private secretary, and when Pope Leo died in 853 (or 855), Joan became the new Pontiff after an election that lasted fewer than four hours. Her reign was distinguished by the fact that she wrote three books, built five churches and ordained 14 bishops. She also took a lover, a 20-year-old youth who served in the capacity of her private attendant. The child that was born of this union grew up to become the Bishop of Ostia.

Joan was removed from office quite unexpectedly during a procession. While riding on a horse, the Pope fell to the ground with labor pains and gave birth prematurely to a healthy male child. The crowd of people watching the parade did not take kindly to the deception she had been practicing. Affixed to the tail of her horse with a rope around her neck and her hands tied behind her, she was forced to walk through the streets of Rome back to the exact place where the newborn babe had appeared among the folds of her pontifical vestment, there to be stoned to death within minutes. She was buried nearby without a tombstone. On that same spot several years later a statue, representing a woman, was erected by unknown persons, and it stayed there for many centuries until Pope Pius V (1566–1572) ordered it destroyed. The street on which Pope Joan was killed by the mob is always avoided by papal processions.

The story that a woman reigned as Pope between Leo IV and Benedict III has no foundation in fact. It is not known for sure where and how the hoax of the she-Pope began, but from about the thirteenth century it was a popular legend for at least 300 years, and not until the sixteenth century was the myth about Pope Joan exploded by a French Calvinist scholar named David Blondel. In his scholarly treatise entitled, *Éclaircissement familiar de la question: si une femme a été assise au siège papal de Rome*, published in 1647, Blondel described his painstaking detective work through papal records which clearly showed that Benedict III had become Pope immediately after the death of Leo IV in 855. Blondel traced the Pope Joan legend to a French religious writer of the thirteenth century, Stephen of Bourbon, who had based his tale on a legend that had been in circulation for a long time.

As late as 1600 a bust of Pope John VIII, with the Latin inscription Johannes VIII, femina ex Anglia, stood in a row of papal busts in

Siena's cathedral, and no none raised any objection to it or held it up to ridicule. The tenth-century pontifical history was never an issue with the masses — only with scholars who sought to find the origin of the Pope Joan story. In his monumental work, *The Rise and Fall of the Roman Empire* (which used to be on the Vatican's index of banned books), Edward Gibbon explained that the myth emerged with the influence of two sister prostitutes, Marozia and Theodora, noted for their wealth, beauty and political intrigues. 'The most strenuous of their lovers were rewarded with the Roman mitre, and their reign may have suggested to darker ages the fable of a female Pope', Gibbon wrote.

The matter of Pope Joan would have disappeared from the public prints except that a Greek novelist, Emmanual Royidis, put the legend into motion again with a novel published in 1886 called *Papissa Joanna*, which traced the history of the mysterious Pope John VIII. When Royidis's satire was banned and he was excommunicated by horrified Church fathers, the book became a best-seller, while translations into other European languages brought it to the attention of the rest of the world. The historic Joanna (if she ever existed) joined all other figures of Church folklore. After Royidis died in 1903, book sales subsided, but in 1920 a new edition of *Papisssa Joanna* came out in Athens and has been since then a perennial best-seller in Greece. Although the book was fiction, Royidis had written a preface in which he displayed considerable background of the era in which Pope Joan was supposed to have lived; the author also cited the mass of 'documentation' upon which the case for Pope Joan and her existence was based. Royidis firmly maintained, until the last day of his life, that he had fabricated very little about Pope Joan whose story, he said, was based on 'facts and events from unimpeachable sources and proved beyond discussion'.

Whether Pope Joan is history of legend, it is doubtful that any new meaningful evidence bearing on her existence will ever come to light. The legend lives on, however: in 1960 the eminent British novelist, Lawrence Durrell (author of *Justine* and several other novels and volumes of poetry and essays), made his own translation of Royidis's novel, and it became a fast-selling paperback. As the cover showed not Royidis's name but Durrell's prominently splashed against a woman pontiff sitting on Saint Peter's Throne, it gave the impression that Lawrence Durrell was the author rather than the translator.

'Pope John VIII is dead, long live Pope Joan!'

CHAPTER XVII

The Smallest City-State in the World

ON THE highest, most heavenly spot inside the State of Vatican City, where the breeze can sometimes get rather blowy, stands a structure known as 'The Tower of the Winds'. There is an elevator leading to the top floor which has been coverted into a penthouse apartment consisting of eight rooms and a terrace. This was one of the favorite places of Pope John XXIII, to which he often hied from his office in the Apostolic Palace 'on the other side of town' — and with a pair of binoculars would spend many a relaxing hour looking at what was happening on the streets of Rome. Considering the people of Rome his neighbors, Pope John liked to watch them do their thing, whether it was children playing on the sidewalks or housewives hanging out the weekly wash.

The Tower of the Winds, located near the West Wall, is today used by the Vatican as a private apartment for visiting dignitaries. While renovations were being made in the papal quarters, Pope John Paul II used it as his temporary office and personal quarters. Today's Polish Pope never goes there when he wants to unwind, nor does he make use of the Vatican gardens that John XXIII loved so much — they are never visited by the present Pontiff who has other preferences, usually sport, for whatever spare time may come up.

Although John Paul hardly ever ventures into the papal gardens, you indeed can. Among his early acts in office, His Holiness — blowing away some of the cobweb protocols of centuries — agreed that since he too would not be frequenting the gardens, they should continue to be accessible to pilgrims and other visitors. Thus the place from which Roman Catholicism's global affairs are run — one of the oddest specks on earth, less than one-seventh the size of New York's Central Park and not more than 15 acres (6.4 hectares) larger than Saint James Park in London — hitherto closed to the rest of the world, is now open to sightseers who can rubberneck all they want as they make the rounds under the wing of an official guide.

You are taken in a minibus through the Arch of the Bells, which is supervised by the grim-faced, halberd-bearing Swiss Guards, in striped uniforms with leg-of-mutton sleeves, and from there you are escorted mostly on foot to various quarters of Vatican City. It is an inimitable experience as you first go in and breathe the other-wordly atmosphere of a backstage that seems to be suspended between heaven and earth.

First stop is the Square of the First Roman Martyrs, where you are shown a marble disc sunk in the tiny square. On this spot stood an obelisk of Nero's Circus where thousands of Christians met death in combat with lions, tigers and other beasts. To the left, shaded by dark cypress trees, is a small burial ground known as the Teutonic Cemetery, which goes back to the year 799. Many prominent Germans and Swiss, who were connected with Vatican history, are buried here. Not generally known is that some of the land was brought from the hillside in Jerusalem where Christ died on the cross. The guide conducts you through the cemetery.

Your next stop — after passing through two arches — is Saint Martha Square, one of the Vatican's largest. Of the two buildings on the left, one is for office and apartments, while the other is a 300-bed 'hotel' run by nuns for the pilgrims. At the top of the square is the Vatican courthouse, and just beyond that, to the right, is Saint Stephen of the Abyssinians Church, the oldest church in Vatican City. Founded by monks in the sixth century, the church was used by Charlemagne when he worshipped in its crypt. Take a good look at its thick walls, for in the walls is a tomb with the body of a monk who died in 1740 at the age of 107.

Following the uphill road from the church, you come to the site of the Vatican's only industry, the making of mosaics. This is the Mosaic School, which is responsible for most of the mammoth mosaics found inside Saint Peter's. The laboratory, set up in the early part of the eighteenth century, perfected the delicate technique of stone-matching, and its supply of colored stones, kept in a long corridor lined with nearly 30,000 boxes, is the largest anywhere on earth. Some of the stones, colored by a formula no longer in existence, are over 200 years old; the blue ones and the red ones have yet to be duplicated. There is a showroom next to the workshop where some of the stones can be purchased and shipped to any corner of the globe.

Practically facing the mosaics lab is the rear of the Vatican railroad station serving what is doubtless the shortest railroad in the world, being measured in feet (2600 feet or nearly 800 meters) rather than miles. Erected by Mussolini as a gift and comprising one of Vatican City's curiosities, the candy-colored station (constructed in pink, green and yellow marble) was described by Pope Pius XI as 'the most beautiful station in the world'. The only pontiff ever to have used the

Vatican railroad was John XXIII in October 1962 when he and members of his staff made a trip to Loreto and Assisi to offer prayers for the Ecumenical Council. Freight trains arrive regularly, however, with tax-free goods, food and other necessities which are stored in the high-ceilinged waiting room. Incidentally, one of the walls of the station still shows shrapnel pockmarks from the bombing on November 6, 1943 — the only time Vatican City was hit during World War II.

The double-track spur, which connects with the tracks of the Italian state railway line, enters the pocket-sized domain through a pair of big iron gates that draw open slowly. Trains are drawn in and out by a small steam locomotive. Under an agreement signed in 1953, the Italian railway system must permit the Vatican the use of the main network and also provide royal coaches for the pontiff. Accordingly, Italy built several 'presidential coaches' complete with side balconies, kitchen and sleeping quarters. These are cleaned, polished and examined daily, ready for instant use — but the Vatican has no regular train schedule.

From Ethiopian Seminary Avenue, you arrive in Marconi Road where there is a yellow building that used to house the Vatican radio station, set up and run for many years by the father of radio, Guglielmo Marconi. (See Chapter XX.) At this point you get a glimpse of the hideaway tower apartment Pope John loved so much. The road flanking the Leonine Wall leads to what looks like a grass tennis court (and used to be) but is now the Vatican's 'airport', which John XXIII once referred to as 'our helicoptorum'. The landing plot was used by both President Eisenhower and President Johnson when they left Rome after a Vatican visit. Often overlooked is the fact that beneath the Vatican heliport are two subterranean reservoirs containing about 6000 cubic meters of drinking water piped in from nearby Lake Bracciano.

Overseeing every quarter of the city-state's 108.7 acres (44 hectares) is the titanic glowing dome of the mighty Saint Peter's Basilica which glorifies the spirit of Vatican City. Within the shadow of the colossal edifice, even MGM could not have conceived this one. Enraptured and mesmerized, don't overlook the Vatican Woods and Gardens, the oldest and most beautiful part of Vatican City, and manicured the year round by a greenfingered staff of 20. Indeed, it is a marvelous place to relax and meditate. Amid dozens of marble angels are towering trees, footpaths, flamboyant cannas ranged against green laurel hedges, cauliflower patches, plants rooted in huge ceramic pots and fountains of all shapes, some with lilies afloat in mossy pools. Especially noteworthy is the seventeenth-century Galleon

Fountain with each of its 16 cannon shooting water, as do some of the masts as well as the little boy on the prow who blows a spray through his horn.

To ensure an adequate water supply, Pius XI had 9300 irrigators installed, connected to 55 miles (88 kilometres) of pipelines. At the Pope's request, the irrigation system was equipped with some rather special gadgets — devices that can squirt jets of water at an unwary visitor. Whenever in a playful mood, Pius loved to drench the new cardinals whom he took for a walk along the pebbled pathways. Although the jets no longer work, the guide will point out some of the dry nozzles.

Continuing your guided tour of 'downtown Vatican City', you may notice that most of the people busy with their chores are not clergymen but laymen. These are the citizens and workers of Vatican City and they are the bakers, carpenters, gardeners, stenographers, bricklayers, painters, mechanics, street cleaners and firemen (all with their wives and families) who keep the Vatican City machinery functioning. It is interesting to note that citizens who live within the 17 square miles (44 square kilometres) that comprise the State of Vatican City and the handful of other Vatican citizens who live off the sacred enclave do not pay any income taxes to Italy — but they do contribute to the pontifical treasury an annual tax that is less than $5. Since there is no private ownership in the micro-metropolis, the residents have their quarters assigned to them. Citizens are not charged for electricity or telephone service; rents are also very low, usually about 4 per cent of income.

Since the early part of 1973, the 30 streets and squares all have street signs. This makes little difference to the mailman, for he knows the city and each of the residents very well. If you happen to hit the right time, you may be amazed to see the unique method of delivering a letter in some instances when the Vatican postman places an envelope into a basket that has been lowered from the top floor on a string and said basket is then hauled up.

The 'downtown' part of Vatican City, or the business district, is located to the right of Saint Peter's Square and can be reached by entering through the Saint Anne Gate, which is supervised by Swiss Guards wearing blue uniforms instead of the colorful, striped ones. The roadway from the busy Saint Anne Gate leads past the tiny parish church to the post office, the car pool and the garage, the press office, the offices of *L'Osservatore Romano*, the pharmacy and the supermarket. No one can enter or buy anything in the Vatican supermarket unless he has an identification card. Prices on each item are usually lower than in the rest of Rome and Italy. Whisky, for instance, is one-third cheaper than in the world outside, since no customs tax in imposed. Half of the shoppers in the market are civilians who live and work in the Vatican, and most of the rest are civilian friends of the Vatican whose families are historically close to the Church. The remainder of the shoppers are the clerics who are permitted to nudge their way up the queue to the cash register without having to wait their turn, if they are carrying only a few items.

At the apothecary across the street, there is not so much as a doorplate to identify it. Well-stocked with pharmaceuticals, the pharmacy does not sell barbecue charcoal or tennis balls (the way American drug stores do), but it does carry many products not available in Italian pharmacies such as Swiss saccharin and a German anti-herpes drug. Nearly 6000 prescriptions are filled each month. The shelves of the 'Pope's Drug Store', which is manned by trained pharmacists from Italy, Spain and Australia, do carry talcum powder, toothpaste and patent medicines — but notable omissions are women's cosmetics and perfume.

Located in the same building are the living quarters of the Brothers who staff the pharmacy and the outpatient clinic of the Vatican Health Service, which was set up in 1953. Vatican employees and pensioners who participate in the plan, to which they make a monthly contribution from their paycheck, receive free medical and dental care and prescription drugs without charges. Going back to the year 1277 when Pope Nicholas III named a 'Pontifical Herbologist' to supervise all the pharmacies of Rome and keep an eye on the Pope's health, the Vatican pharmacy must be the oldest drug store in the world — and it is one that most people do not even know exists.

A major curiosity for all visitors is the former Vatican prison, which because of lack of use, now serves mostly as a warehouse. More like hotel rooms than cells, the Vatican prison had two lockups with hot and cold running water and beds with soft mattresses. Through the bars a prisoner could look out at the stupendous vista of the dome of Saint Peter's, the Vatican gardens and a splashy fountain. Prisoners enjoyed heating (when needed) and tasty food (prepared by the same cook-nuns who made meals for the Swiss Guards). Other services to prisoners included a daily copy of *L'Osservatore Romano* (the Vatican daily), a deck of cards and a radio.

Only four inmates were known to have served time in the prison for a combined total of three weeks: one was a cleric, Monsignor E P Cippico, who had been convicted of money trafficking; another was a man caught stealing in Saint Peter's; another was a Swedish tourist who assaulted a Vatican priest, and another a tourist from Geneva who insulted a Swiss Guard. Today persons who commit crimes on Vatican soil are handed over to the Italian police, such as the Turk who attempted to assassinate John Paul in May 1981. (In September 1981 London's Independent Thames Television current affairs program, *TV Eye*, did a documentary in which an Italian journalist, Francesco D'Andrea, claimed that an unnamed senior Vatican official was quoted as saying the Vatican believed the Soviet KGB secret police were behind the attempted killing of the Pope. Prepared not to exclude the possibility of an international conspiracy behind the attack on John Paul, I checked this report with several of my own reliable sources and found the TV allegation to be without any foundation whatever.)

Not very far from the one-time Vatican prison is a converted palace called the Floreria, which is the junk shop of the Vatican — filled to the brim with all the things the Vatican does not need any more but does not want to throw away. In this Vatican attic, indeed a sacred warehouse, you find portable thrones no longer used, dinner services from the time the Vatican used to entertain, the busts of forgotten cardinals, an array of fans from Persia (they were waved over the pontiff's portable throne before the days of air-conditioning), some badly executed statues of the Virgin Mary, so many carpets that all count has been lost, gilded chairs for dignitaries, coaches adorned with gilded door handles and equipped with a single throne as the back seat, all the abandoned furniture of dead popes — such things as rickety bedside tables, wobbly stools, brass beds — all of them neatly labeled with the names of their past owners. There is also a large collection of very bad paintings — many of them gifts from all over the world to the papacy. Notable among these is a painting that hung in the famed Vatican museum for over a hundred years. Presented to Pope Pius IX by Queen Christine of Spain in 1850, the painting, *The Mystic Marriage of Saint Catherine*, was attributed by art experts to the seventeenth-century Spanish painter, Bartolomé Esteban Murillo. Not long ago the so-called Murillo masterpiece was found to be by a Vatican art expert a 'counterfeit beyond any doubt' and was dumped away in the Floreria. My guess is that if the Vatican ever wanted to rake in some easy money, it could sell much of the Floreria's pontifical paraphernalia.

CHAPTER XVIII

Christianity's Inner Sanctum

IN THE fall of 1978, the mini Republic of San Marino and the mini State of Vatican City tangled. It seems the postal authorities of each country were disputing who had the jurisdiction to print the work of sculptor Pericle Fazzini on a postage stamp. The piece in question, which graces the Vatican's general audience hall, was Fazzini's *Resurrection*, and San Marino had made plans to put out a special stamp in its honor. But the Vatican squawked. Threatening serious reprisal, papal watchdogs informed the republic in Italy's north near the Adriatic Coast that it had no right whatever to reproduce *Resurrection*.

There followed between the two Tom Thumb countries a series of secret diplomatic discussions — several of which were literally summit conferences in that they were held in the castle at the top of Mount Titano, 2300 feet (700 meters) above sea level. At the conclusion of the meetings, San Marino and Vatican City issued a joint communiqué stating that both sovereign nations had agreed that San Marino would substitute the Fazzini stamp with some commemorating 'popular Christmas symbols'. Vatican postal officials returned to their roost in Rome glowing. They had given the 'enemy' a good licking.

The Vatican post office dates to the fourteenth century when a pony-express system carried pontifical messages to all parts of Italy. Located just inside Saint Anne's Gate, the Vatican's main post office handles about two million letters a year, more than six million postcards and over 15,000 packages. Generally speaking, its PO is efficient and reliable — and many Romans have come to learn that if they go to the trouble of mailing a letter on Vatican ground, delivery will be faster and safer. The Vatican post office shows an annual profit, but this comes mainly from the sale of commemorative stamps and issues of Vatican coins and medals. Dealers, collectors and the general public usually buy out the stamps and the coins rapidly. In only one instance did the Vatican post office oversubscribe itself on the printing of a postage stamp; that was during the Holy Year in 1975 when nearly a million unsold Vatican stamps of Pope Paul VI were burned. In all cases of a new issue, the Vatican does not announce how many stamps are printed, but the number is limited to ensure the stamps a future value among philatelists.

As with every other country, even Vatican City has had its own postal rhubarb which activated alert collectors everywhere. A Vatican commemorative postcard became a hot item when it came out in the summer of 1981. For want of a better title to the story, let us call it 'The Mystery of the Pope's Amputated Arm' — the mystery remains unsolved to this day. In late June 1981 special commemorative postcards of Pope John Paul II went on sale in denominations of 150 lire and 200 lire in the two Vatican post office branches in saint Peter's Square (unlike the main post office which is not open to the public, these two stations are). Within an hour the Vatican had to withdraw the 200-lire card because it was discovered that the Pope had a 'missing arm' — his right one, which is the one he uses to impart the benediction. The right hand of John Paul, looking as though it had been cancelled out in printing, had been cleanly severed slightly above the wrist.

Since the Italian State Printing Institute does all the Holy See's postage stamp and postcard printing, both governments were thrown into confusion. With an investigation launched immediately, a swift check of the engraved plates did not reveal any damage at the point where the right hand should have been. No one came up with an answer, but there were suspicions — suspicions that perhaps the cards had been forged on another printing press and several batches of them were then slipped into the full cartons delivered to the Vatican. The guess is that the forgers then held on to the rest to sell them later to avid collectors in other parts of the world, while in Rome many people were busy doing their best to track down cards for themselves. Guesses among the residents of Vatican City were on everyone's lips. No one could come up with concrete evidence against any insider, so that was ruled out.

The residents of Vatican City number no more than 750, 95 per cent are male and fewer than half have Vatican citizenship. No one is born a Vatican citizen, but all cardinals are automatically citizens even if they live elsewhere. Vatican City does not have a residential section as such. More than 3000 people work at the Vatican where no private enterprise is permitted, and virtually nothing is privately owned. There are 50 palaces and office buildings all over the grounds, and many of these provide apartments for the folks who make Vatican City their home. The city-state has more telephones in proportion to its population than any other nation or city on earth. Living within the Vatican walls is hardly glamorous: the gates are closed at 11 pm, and the only form of commercial entertainment available is television. Since Vatican City is not run democratically (the Pope has final say on all matters), there are many regulations the people have to abide by (such as a ban on hanging out the laundry).

The main building in Vatican City is the Apostolic Palace. With more than 1400 rooms and nearly a thousand flights of stairs (overlooking 20 courtyards), the Apostolic Palace is a conglomeration of interlocked buildings built, for the most part, during the Renaissance. It is believed to be the world's largest palace, matched only by the Dalai Lama's palace in Tibet. The Pope has a 19-room apartment on the top floor facing Saint Peter's Square (on the right as you face the Basilica). His private office is commodious and its three windows are seldom curtained; when the sun is too bright, the inside shutters are drawn. The papal work chamber measure 60 by 40 feet (18 by 12 meters), the walls are panelled in blond wood and the floor is carpeted. About five feet (1.5 meters) from the door is the Pope's work desk. Whenever John Paul wants to make an appearance from his office, he will invariably go to the middle window which is draped in gold damask. On the lower floors are the apartments of the Cardinal Secretary of State and the rooms of many of the permanent papal staff.

Perhaps one of the most unusual rooms in the Apostolic Palace is a high-ceilinged chamber that is lined from floor to ceiling with steel filing cabinets, shelves and drawers from top to bottom. With its librarian's ladder standing like a sentinel, the room looks like the inside of a lawyer's library. Under an electric lamp in one corner of the world's most macabre library sits a priest who has one of the most unusual jobs anywhere, a job that very few people ever hear of. His work consists largely of sending tiny boxes and envelopes to all parts of the globe.

The drawers, cabinets, shelves, polythene bags and large, bulging envelopes are stuffed with the relics of early saints and martyrs, and these can be slivers of bone, ashes, bits of clothing and other saintly items associated in one way or another with the life and passion of Jesus Christ. Canon law requires that a relic must be enclosed in every altar of every Catholic Church or chapel. Because churches and chapels are inaugurated every month somewhere in the world, the priest-librarian is kept busy filling envelopes with pinches of dust or fragments of bone which are then mailed in registered letters.

The Vatican's attitude towards relics is a strange one — and its stance on the subject is simply that it prefers not to discuss it. Church officers are aware that most of the relics are not authentic, but there is a firm opinion in the Vatican — not excluding that of every pope who has ever presided, and including the present incumbent — that relics do the faithful good since it gives them inspiration when praying. Unimportant to the Vatican is whether its carefully kept records show that in various parts of Italy there are four ears belonging to Saint Procopius or nine breasts belonging to Saint Eulalia. Some of the relics are an embarrassment to the Vatican, such as the Holy Foreskin of Christ. This was removed from his body at the age of eight weeks when he was circumcised in the Temple and is preserved in a spherical crystal reliquary — on public display in a church in a small village 45 miles north of Rome. It might be mentioned that there is a rival foreskin to be found in Italy's Abruzzi region, but this one is not universally accepted, not even by the Vatican.

Though many of the relics have been the subject of acrimonious discussion by Vatican cardinals of the past, as to whether they are counterfeits or not, bishops, priests and other theologians continue to hold them in ecclesiastical esteem, not to mention the fact that they are given the greatest veneration by Italian worshippers. The Vatican classifies them as 'primary relics', 'secondary relics', 'tertiary relics' and so on. Even though hard-and-fast documentation is no longer possible, the Vatican generally does not discourage public attention to them.

One of the relics that draws worshippers is a nail allegedly used to crucify Christ. For this there is some evidence to support its authenticity but no positive proof. The nail, which is to be found in a ciruclar, glass-enclosed silver casket on display in Rome's Santa Croce in Gerusalemme Church, is about five inches (12.7 centimeters) long and tapers in its last quarter-inch to a blunt tip. Several other relics are housed in the same church: three wooden splinters from the Cross (kept in a gold and silver reliquary) and a fragment of the tobacco-colored, worm-eaten nameplate placed on top of the Cross on Pilate's orders with the Latin inscription, NAZARENVS RE. . . . Nearby in a metal frame that looks like a hand-mirror are two thorns from the crown placed on the head of Jesus. Ash-gray in color, the thorns are about an inch and a quarter (3 centimeters) long. No pope in history has ever visited this church, though it is virtually within walking distance of the Vatican.

Another relic in Rome that draws many of the faithful, but which a pope has yet to visit, is to be found on the Old Appian Way in a small church known as Quo Vadis. This is a cast of the footprints of Jesus, and the legend says that Peter, on his flight from Rome, having escaped from the Mamertine Prison, met Christ walking towards him on his way into the city and asked him: '*Domine, quo vadis?*' [Lord, whither goest Thou?]. The cobblestone that Christ stood on when he met Peter is the stone bearing the footprints.

Whenever movie director Luchino Visconti, whose family has had centuries of close ties with the Vatican (he himself as a small boy posed for a painting of the Christ Child, now on public display near Milan) was shooting a film, he would include a Christ relic in a scene, mostly to bring him good luck. In one film, for instance, he exhibited from the Church of Santa Prassede a section of the pillar to which Christ was bound and whipped (the remainder of the ancient column was brought to Rome in 1223 by Cardinal Giovanni Colonna from Jerusalem), and in another film Visconti showed a fragment from the table of The Last Supper which is above the tympanum of an altar inside the San Giovanni in Laterano Church in Rome.

Even though the Vatican keeps very good records of its relics everywhere in the world, it is not possible to count or even guess how many there are, in view of the fact that there are nearly 2000 saints in the Catholic calendar. The Vatican quickly destroyed the relics of one saint, not long ago, when Church archaeologists discovered that her ribs, unearthed over 200 years ago in a catacomb and preserved in the Vatican since then, were the bones of a large dog.

Inasmuch as there are, literally, hundreds of thorns taken from Christs's crown, the multiplicity of such relics everywhere remains for the Vatican a difficult question. What do you do when you know that there are three heads of Saint John the Baptist — one in Saint Mark's in Venice, another in Damascus and a third in Amiens, France — 28 thumbs and fingers belonging to Saint Dominic, two bodies of Saint Sylvester (one in Rome, the other near Modena), the body of Saint Luke in Venice and in Padua and more than 150 nails from the True Cross?

Many of the listings in the Vatican relics library, however, are single items for which some kind of authentication is provided in the files. These include, for example, the right arm and head of Saint John, the head of Saint Catherine of Siena, the full bodies of Saint Lucia, Saint Maximus, Saint Urio, Saint Felicity the Virgin and Saint Julian. Saint Julian himself brought a huge number of relics from Jerusalem, including a part of Saint Matthew's leg, a tooth from Saint Mark the Evangelist, the skull of Saint James the Less, the Holy Sponge which was offered to Christ's lips, some of the Virgin Mary's hair, a jar full of earth from Golgotha (soaked with the blood of Christ), and the jawbone of Saint Anthony, to mention some of the eminent ones. The jawbone lies in a bejewelled case in the Basilica of Saint Anthony, and what invariably astonishes visitors from abroad is how Italian worshippers behave in its presence: many people push and shove in order to kiss the case, rub their babies against it, caress it with their hands or rub lottery tickets over it.

This is not to mention, also, what these same Italians do in the small souvenir shop within the Saint Anthony Basilica. In almost reckless manner, worshippers from all over crowd into the supermarket-like shop and buy up effigies of Saint Anthony, plates with his picture on it, paperweights of him holding Jesus as a baby (when inverted, these produce a snowfall), candles blessed by the local bishop, candles blessed by the Pope, holy medals, rosaries and postcards with paintings of the saint. One such card, measuring three inches by two (7.5 by 5 centimeters), is a famous oil painting of Saint Anthony on the back of which is glued a shred of textile which, allegedly, was touched by the saint's tongue.

This last item is sold at a rather high price, and it demonstrates that apart from the element of veneration in relics in Italy, relics are also a good business in that country. This is especially true of any of the 30 major pilgrimage churches in Italy, of which Saint Anthony's is perhaps the most important. The Vatican, too, enjoys a healthy income from the relics it parcels out all over, for when a church requests a relic of ashes or bones, a sizable contribution of money is expected, the sum of which is left to the discretion of the pastor or bishop concerned. The umbilical cord of one saint (Saint Venerina), for instance, went for the astonishing sum of nearly $200,000 to a church in Calabria.

An item that is most often requested is a piece of wood from the True Cross, and such splinters or slivers are to be found in the multiple thousands not only in Italy but elsewhere. To borrow a quip from a maverick priest, who shall remain anonymous, there are enough pieces of wood from the Cross 'to build the Italian Navy!'

One conspicuous relic, viewed by millions of people each year, is the so-called Throne of Saint Peter, which in fact was one that the saint could never have used. This discovery was made in November 1968 after Pope Paul VI ordered that a Carbon-14 dating test be made on the wood used in the big wood-and-ivory chair. A seven-man team of scientists at Rome University examined the ancient throne, encased in bronze and placed above the altar of the cathedral in the apse of Saint Peter's. Sworn to secrecy, the scientists submitted their report to the Pope in which it was stated that the carbon tests showed that the wood dated from several centuries after the birth of Christ (Saint Peter was crucified in Rome either in AD 64 or 67). The Vatican has not pronounced on the matter. Three relics rest by the Throne: the lance that pierced Christ's side; wood from the True Cross; the veil used by Veronica to wipe the face of Christ.

Saint Peter's Basilica covers nearly 430,000 square feet (nearly

40,000 square meters), enough for a half dozen football fields — making it by far the largest church in Christendom. The marble-studded nave floor, by the way, has bronze lines embedded in it to demonstrate how much smaller certain other big churches in Europe are by comparison. Saint Peter's has nearly 500 columns, over 430 large statues, 40 separate altars and ten domes. No other church attracts so many people as does the basilica and more than ten million people a year visit. Just to maintain the church and Saint Peter's Square runs to approximately $2,000 a day. This does not include the unforeseen expenditures that mass visits can cause. Take the case of the Vatican's 800 black raincoats. . . .

On the doors of the basilica there are two conspicuous signs posted in five languages telling worshippers and tourists that they must be dressed properly in order to preserve an atmosphere of reverence. Women are not supposed to wear mini dresses, shorts or sleeveless dresses, and men, too, cannot go inside wearing shorts. Four ushers are in charge of enforcing the Vatican's fashion dictum, and almost daily they get into wrangles with some lightly clad visitors who strenuously object. One usher, after a fist fight with a German woman's escort, had to be hospitalized. Vatican administrators tried another tack: they decided to station a nun at the door to stem the tide of modern deshabillé from swamping the major temple of Roman Catholicism. That was during the summer of 1972, and Sister Fiorella did her job conscientiously. After three months of coping with more than 20,000 women wearing garb that was considered immodest, the hardy nun could not take the stress any more and had to withdraw. Now the Vatican came up with still another idea: 800 long, black plastic raincoats, acquired from a Milan firm for $2000, were lent free of charge to women in miniskirts or shorts and men in shorts. The Vatican thought it had solved the problem, except for one thing: the 800 black raincoats disappeared within a week. Filched as souvenirs. . . .

Saint Peter's has a way of drawing all kinds of questionable characters, some with inexplicable motives — like the crazed Hungarian refugee in May 1972 who attacked Michelangelo's *Pietà* statue (Mary holding her dying Son) with a hammer and made several chips on the masterpiece; he damaged the veil and face of the Madonna and smashed her hand. Other characters drawn to Vatican City may have ulterior motives, not to the Vatican's liking, as for instance the time 'Father Guido Sarducci' paid a call in 1981. He was an American comic-actor by the name of Don Novello who had created for NBC's comedy series, *Saturday Night Live*, a satirical personage called Father Guido Sarducci, who is supposed to be the gossip columnist for *L'Osservatore Romano*, a fact that has amused neither the Catholic hierarchy in America nor the Vatican. When the well-known television actor showed up at *L'Osservatore*'s new offices wearing his priestly black cape, a brimmed hat, pink glasses and cowboy boots, an outraged editor called in the Swiss Guards to arrest him and his photographer. Novello was accused of impersonating a priest and taking unauthorized photographs. Detained for nearly seven hours, 'Father Guido Sarducci' was escorted by four guards at spearpoint off the grounds and told in plain Latin that he was *persona non grata*.

Though he got some publicity, which was why he pulled the stunt, his cameraman, who had had his equipment impounded, failed to get shots of him being given the bum's rush by the colorful Swiss Guards, who are themselves another flashy item at Vatican City. Probably more color snapshots are taken of the Vatican's Swiss Guards than of any soldiers anywhere. But behind the spectacular uniforms and the aura of glamor that surrounds them, there's another story.

Twenty-one-year-old Kaspar Holzgang went down in Vatican history when he became the first soldier to desert the Pope's private army. Defying a tradition of four centuries, he went back to his home in the village of Rotkreuz in central Switzerland and told relatives that he quit because he found life in the Swiss Guards intolerable. Living conditions, he said, were medieval and the discipline was like something out of the Prussian army. Whenever you were imprisoned for a minor infringement, you were kept locked up in cells 'unfit for human beings', Holzgang complained, adding that the cells were tiny and had only a small barred hole for ventilation, besides which you were only allowed to the toilet three times in a 24-hour period.

Like other volunteer armies, the famed Swiss Guards — who fascinate tourists with their multi-colored sashed uniforms — are having a difficult time because they can't find enough recruits. The young men who join up and sign a contract to serve a two-year tour of duty hardly ever re-enlist. From time to time a few of the Swiss Guards go AWOL before they come back and take their punishment; nobody before or since Private Holzgang left in 1969 has deserted, however. The main problem is that all the Guards want out before the two years are up, and the word has got around Switzerland that being a soldier in the Pope's private army is not the glamorous job it seems to be. Among the Swiss Guards in Rome there is a maxim to the effect that once you have volunteered, the only thing to do is to stick it out.

What constitutes part of the recruiting problem is the fact that Switzerland has been enjoying a sound economy for along time now. Jobs are fairly easy to come by, and wages are rather higher, whereas pay for the Swiss Guards is quite low, the work is described as boring, and the discipline is apparently the toughest of any army anywhere. Private life is nearly impossible, since the hours are long and the men have to work on Sundays all the time. They are required to study in their spare time, and all must learn Italian, in addition to pursuing courses in technical or commercial studies to prepare them for the future. The Guards — all of whom have to be over six feet (1.8 meters) tall and between the ages of 18 and 25 — are not permitted to marry. Nor can they bring any women friends into the Vatican for social visits. Small wonder, then, that the maximum complement of a hundred men is usually never filled, from one year to another, remaining at around 50 or 60.

The Swiss Guards have the duty of watching the three main entrances to the Vatican and the palace at Castelgandolfo where the Pope spends most of the summer. Another place that is under 24-hour guard is the corridor just outside the papal apartments. There, whenever the Pope goes in or out, the Guard has to salute on bended knee. The soldiers are not allowed to carry automatic weapons, and must do their duty armed with seven-foot (two-meter) halberds, which is a combination of spear and battle axe. The Guards often complain that this is not the kind of equipment that could be used if there were a guerrilla-style terrorist attack in Saint Peter's or on the Apostolic Palace.

The Swiss Guards were founded by Pope Julius II, the so-called warrior Pope, who as a papal aide was so impressed by Swiss soldiery that in 1478 he got Pope Pius IV to sign an alliance with the Swiss cantons. When he became Pope himself, Julius II brought in 150 Swiss soldiers in January 1506, the year the first stone of the new Saint Peter's Basilica was laid, making them the oldest military corps in existence. Sworn to protect the life of the Pope at the risk of their own lives, the Swiss Guards narrowly escaped annihilation on the steps of Saint Peter's during the sack of Rome in May 1527 when a thousand German and Spanish soldiers stormed the Vatican. Three-quarters of the Swiss Guard complement was destroyed, altogether 147 men including the commanding officer (the invaders lost more than 800 soldiers), but the remaining 42 were able to protect Pope Clement VII and 13 of his cardinals as they fled along the Vatican ramparts into the impregnable Castel Sant'Angelo. After the 1527 slaughter, the Swiss Guards never again had to defend a pontiff, but on several occasions the Guards had to lay down their arms on the Pope's orders rather than face extermination. This was true in the case of Napoleon who invaded Rome and carried the Pope off to France. During World War II Pope Pius XII made the Guards store away their firearms (which Pope Paul VI abolished in 1970), and they patrolled the frontier between the State of Vatican City and Italy with their halberds, pikes or poignards while facing Nazi Germany's array of Panzer tanks that never once dared to cross the border without an order from Hitler. It was one of World War II's most curious sights to see the heavily armed, efficient Nazi troops stand by helplessly and sheepishly as a lonc Swiss Guard whom they considered a toy soldier patrolled up and down with his picturesque medieval uniform and hand weapon of bygone days.

Contrary to what travel books and tourist guides tell visitors about the resplendent Swiss Guard garb, it just is not true that the spectacular uniform of slashed bouffant sleeves, striped doublet and hose, all in gold, white, red, yellow and blue, was designed by Michelangelo or Raphael. Nothing could be further from the truth. Worn for the first time as recently as 1914, the apparel was designed by an unknown Vatican seamstress who surpassed herself when Pope Benedict XV asked her to create a ceremonial attire for soldiers. The bouffant sleeves, however, do go back to the middle of the sixteenth century and quite possibly were suggested by a Raphael painting from a design he copied that was at the time the style in France.

Like the Swiss Guards, everybody who works in Vatican City is terribly underpaid. If you ask an Italian who works for the Pope, he won't hesitate in nominating the Vatican as being the stingiest employer in Europe. Unharrassed by unions which are not allowed to exist, and not given to extravagance, the State of Vatican City lives in Rome bearing the image of a cheapskate. Be that as it may, the pontifical payroll which amounts to about $100 million a year, does indeed reflect a tendency toward parsimony.

Though the Vatican is a charitable institution (both in the receiving and the giving of charity), the papal wage scale has not kept up with the times. Even the Curia cardinals, the top-ranking and ruling officers of the Roman Catholic Church, who get the highest salaries of all Vatican personnel, receive meager pay envelopes at month's end. At the end of 1981, a cardinal on the Pope's immediate staff drew an income of $689 a month and an additional $100 housing allowance if he lived outside Vatican City. If a cardinal also headed a Congregation (a department or ministry in Vatican parlance), he would be allowed an extra $50. Thus some prelates earned a take-home envelope as high as $848 each month. A number of Vatican cardinals add to their incomes by discreetly selling their influence to Italians needing a favor from some official.

Unbelievably, the first raise in pay Vatican workers ever got in the postwar period came during the administration of John XXIII — and that happened only as a result of a chance meeting between the Pontiff and some of his garden workers while he was taking an afternoon stroll one day in 1959. When he found out, after some casual questioning, that sweepers in the Vatican gardens were receiving $1.60 for a day's work while the rest of Italy was making close to $10 a day, he exclaimed: 'What? No family with children can live on that. What has become of justice? Just wait . . . that's going to change!'

And in fact it did. As soon as John returned to his desk, he got the full facts about his staff's pay scale. On his order, a general review of all Vatican wages was made — and forthwith ruled an across-the-board salary increase. 'We cannot always require others to observe the Church's teaching on social justice if we do not apply it in our own domain,' the Pope told his administrators. 'The Church must take the lead in social justice by its own good example.'

Affecting some 3000 employees, the hike added an estimated $2.4 million a year to Vatican payroll expenses. Then in 1963, Pope Paul VI granted another raise of 20 per cent to the entire staff, increasing the Vatican's annual salary costs by another $1.44 million. In another unprecedented move, Pope Paul in December 1965 commanded that a special $160 bonus be paid to all Vatican staff to mark the successful end of the Ecumenical Council. The sum was over and above '*la tredicesima*', which is an annual extra month's pay that Italian law requires management to give each employee at year's end.

Popes at no time have shown much insight for labor relations. Pope Paul did install some system of regular rates of pay, a pension fund and facilities for granting loans as advances against salaries, after some formal complaints from a group of his staff reached him. In May 1970 Pope Paul granted a 10 per cent pay increase across the board to some 3000 employees and 900 pensioners. Burdened with high costs, in September of that year, the Pope disbanded all his armed and uniformed military units, except the Swiss Guards. The retrenchment of the pontifical military establishment, which affected more than 600 officers and men, came after a period of strained labor relations talks in the Vatican, stemming from a few weeks earlier when the blue-uniformed gendarmes had staged a four-day protest refusing to collect their monthly paychecks because of the Vatican's failure to backdate the May salary increase.

Years later when Vatican workers discussed the idea of a labor union with Pope John Paul II, he granted them only the right to form an association of lay employees that would not have any kind of permission to engage in collective bargaining with their employer; nor could they negotiate new work contracts. Within the Vatican one must remember that the Pope's powers are absolute. It is no wonder that on the wall of a street not very far from Vatican City there is a graffiti panel on which has been painted a warning — the words of which never fade because some disgruntled person every so often repaints them: 'Do not work at the Vatican — it is a false place!'

Laborers in the Vatican today earn about $400 a month but get monthly bonuses of about $20 for each dependent child (with no limit imposed as to the number of children). A Vatican journalist gets about $350 a month, while a staff typist draws $300, which is well below what their counterparts earn in the rest of Italy. As for a priest or nun — all of whom have taken poverty vows — income is well below that of the lowest-paid lay worker, but they get their room and board gratis, whether they live inside Vatican City or in one of Rome's religious houses. In addition, Italy pays all priests a monthly salary of about $90 a month, a regulation that stems from the 1929 Concordat. The Vatican does not pay overtime, but by tradition it gives out bonuses of about $380 per person upon the death of a pope and another upon the election of a new one. Italian citizens working at the Vatican are not required to pay income tax on their salaries, according to Italian law, but must pay an annual tax to the State of Vatican City — which, if you can believe this — comes to less than $5 per person.

One question that some people wonder about is the pontiff's salary. When a ranking cardinal wins an election to the Seat of Saint Peter, he earns, in effect, a promotion, but with a reduction in pay. Would anybody like to guess what the Pope's paycheck comes to? Almost incredible is the fact that the Holy Father himself receives not a penny in pay.

Perhaps the most curious fact about the State of Vatican City is the elongated piece of land that snuggles between it and Italy. The 1641 feet (5 kilometers) of territory belongs neither to Italy nor to the Vatican. Called '*La Terra di Nessuno*' (Nobody's Land), it is one of those geographical curiosities that somehow escapes attention. Even veteran travelers cannot usually claim to have been to an area which constitutes part of no nation.

Just how this piece of land touching the Vatican came to be unclaimed cannot be fully ascertained. One theory is that it resulted from a measuring error, and another theory is that the 1929 Lateran Pact between Italy and the Vatican simply overlooked it. Whatever the reason, it does not appear likely that Nobody's Land will ever be incorporated into Italy proper or become part of Vatican territory. Since the matter would become politically touchy today, officials of both countries prefer to leave it that way. And left it is — it has been completely deprived of any maintenance, and nobody, apparently, has gone there in years.

No Man's Land can be seen in plain view from afar. It comprises the Corridoio di Castello, the corridor built in the thirteenth century by Pope Nicholas III, which stretches from the Castel Sant'Angelo to the Vatican. During the Middle Ages the narrow link was used by the popes whenever they had to flee for their lives from the Vatican to the circular-shaped Castel Sant'Angelo, the former mausoleum of Emperor Hadrian which was converted into a fortress.

The last pontiff to have used the covered corridor, whose walls and windows are too narrow to allow two people to walk side by side, was Pope Clement VII on the morning of May 6, 1527. As the cut-throat mercenary armies of King Charles V zeroed in on the Vatican and the explosion of cannon was heard on the very steps of Saint Peter's, the Pope was persuaded to take flight along the vaulted hallway to Castel Sant'Angelo.

From the top of Castel Sant'Angelo I was able one day to go as far as the locked gate leading to the brick-paved corridor would allow. With its unwashed windows, the thick-walled, narrow-elevated tunnel, like a secret passage, has an air of great age hanging over it. At the other end of Nobody's Land, the part that terminates on Vatican soil, there is a tiny yard surrounded on three sides by an eight-foot (2.4-meter) wall, an iron picket fence and the imposing corridor walls. The Vatican post office adjoins one of the walls flanking this triangular courtyard. The small enclave is the only open part of La Terra di Nessuno and is often used as a car park.

Knowing what Vatican bureaucracy is like I made a well-researched attempt to get permission to visit La Terra di Nessuno (if only to have the distinction of being one of the few people to set foot in a real no-man's land). I failed. Though the Vatican has the only set of keys for the corridor, it does not have the authority to let anybody enter. Nor was the Italian government eager to make any waves with Vatican officialdom to intercede on my behalf. In one of the most thoroughly astonishing statements ever mouthed by a professional bureaucrat, I was told that his government would prefer not to engage itself in the maze of Vatican red tape.

Since Nobody's Land is kept under the Vatican's lock and key, without rhyme or reason, there was just no way to penetrate.

CHAPTER XIX

The Vatican's Spy Network

NOT EVEN the most knowledgeable Washington newsmen and experienced foreign correspondents covering the Soviet Union or the Eastern Bloc countries know how many secret agents are employed by the CIA or by the KGB. The most conservative guesses range from several thousand to upwards of ten thousand. Whatever the true figures are for either the CIA or the KGB, neither of them has as many secret agents in the field as the Vatican. Without doubt, the Vatican runs the world's most efficient and most elaborate spy system with agents in just about every country in the world and certainly in every capital city, no matter how small.

The Vatican's spies get their messages to and from Rome via many different channels, ranging from letter to word of mouth and from personal communication to the Pope to coded radio messages on Vatican Radio — which is the single largest radio network known (more extensive even than the BBC) and which broadcasts daily in more than 30 languages (see Chapter XX for more about Vatican Radio). The papal James Bonds, or pontifical 007s, came into being in 1910 under the rule of Pope Pius X and were put into full global operation during the administrations of Pope Benedict XV (1914–1922) and Pope Pius XI (1922–1939). The group of espionage agents came to be known by the Popes as *Sodalitium pianum*, and it includes every priest, nun, monk, brother or Catholic secular worker anywhere on earth. All of them understand that if he or she hears of anything or sees anything that the Vatican or the Pope should know about, they should communicate it to an immediate superior who will in turn get the crucial information to the closest diocese or archdiocese — from whence the said information will be swiftly communicated to Rome.

Just how quickly information gets to the Vatican is demonstrated by the case of the US Secretary of Labor James Mitchell: he had an audience with Pope Pius XII, and when talking later with some newsmen, Mitchell reported how astonished he was that the Pope knew some things about the United States — secrets of the White

House — that neither he nor anybody else was supposed to know. 'My God', exclaimed the flabbergasted Labor Secretary, 'he was already aware that the recession in the United States was technically over — and we just learned that ourselves only yesterday!'

The numerical extent of the Pope's world spy network can be calculated by citing official Catholic figures for 1981. There are nearly 260,000 diocesan priests, more than 120,000 regular priests, approximately 65,000 seminarians, over 210,000 male religious, and well over 950,000 nuns — not to mention an untold number of secular workers which runs to well over 2.5 million people. These professional Roman Catholics make up a part of the some 700 million Catholics from all parts of the globe. Since the Catholic Church is the most cohesive and most disciplined ecclesiastical organization of any, one that has a unique and extraordinary unity and continuity of command, the people who work for the Church believe in the institution, are not averse to its rules and observe its modus operandi. Faithful to the mysterious world that lives behind the heavy Bronze Doors, these people — most of whom have taken vows of obedience — are all recruits for the Vatican's secret service — 'God's Underground' — while carrying out their day-to-day jobs.

Though the largest number of Vatican spies are people who work at other jobs, and their informing is strictly a part-time activity that in most cases never bears fruit, the Vatican's intelligence service does indeed employ full-time persons whose job is just that — espionage at a professional level. One of the Vatican's best secret agents in recent years — a man who never got his name in the papers once — was Walter M Ciszek, a priest who worked inside the Soviet Union under the name of Vladimir Lipinski and who for many years outwitted the Moscow bears before he was finally convicted 'as a spy for the Vatican' and imprisoned for 23 years.

Like many another professional Vatican spy, Father Ciszek was trained for his specialized work in a Vatican-owned eighteenth-century building on Via Carlino Cattaneo in Rome. This building does not look like a spy center, nor are there any armed guards, electrified barbed-wire fences, or electronic security walls. In fact, under its official name — Collegio Russico (Russian Pontifical College, or Russicum) — the organization even has its telephone number listed in the Rome directory. The men who train in this strange school know that they will eventually be assigned to dangerous places.

Within the Russicum's huge classrooms and along its high corridors, the recruits — all of them ordained priests — are there to learn as much as they can about the Soviet Union and/or its Bloc countries: East Germany, Poland, Czechoslovakia, Hungary, Rumania and Bulgaria. Besides learning to speak each language like a native, as well as its dialects, the men saturate themselves with the history, economics, current events and politics of the country they are specializing in. Since the Vatican is not particularly interested in military intelligence, this thrust is not pursued. Other aspects of the Communist regimes, however, are of more interest. The Kremlin's distaste for the Russicum appeared in the first edition of the Great Soviet Encyclopedia, on page 352 of Volume 17, and in subsequent editions the same charge is leveled at the Russicum's Jesuits: '. . . perfidious and malicious enemies of all humanity desiring peace and progress . . . at the service of the most evil-minded forces of imperialistic reaction.'

Mostly of Russian, Polish, Czech and Hungarian background, the Russicum grads who carry out espionage duties for the Vatican behind the Iron Curtain do not steal secret documents, they never sabotage or destroy installations and they never kill. Theirs is nevertheless a hazardous assignment, for it involves the accumulation of information that is of special interest to the Vatican, and much of that often has to do with the state of the Church inside. In gathering this kind of information, a number of the Vatican's espionage agents have been killed while on duty. Vatican records show that Rev John Kellner was publicly hanged in the Ukraine, Rev Raphael Chomyn met a similar fate in Donetsky, Rev Peter Helwegen died in a prison camp in East Germany, and Rev Vendeline Javorka, after serving ten years in the Vorkuta prison camp, disappeared in his native Czechoslovakia and was declared officially dead by the Vatican.

Most of the Vatican's agents who go behind the Iron Curtain stay for about two years before they sneak back out. Operating completely as 'lone wolves' with no contact whatever with Rome or with any Catholic official elsewhere, the agent-priests sneak out when they think they have certain information that is of utmost importance, information that they would note dare transmit while on enemy soil. One such vital piece of information that was given to the Vatican during the Khruschev reign, months before it came to the attention of the United States or the Western press, was that the Soviet Union was undergoing a grain shortage, something that even most of its own subjects did not yet know. Western intelligence agencies had no way of getting the details of this important occurrence, but a spy-priest, working in the disguise of a farmhand in various parts of the USSR in the 1950s was able to pin down the facts, and after his escape, he returned to the Vatican and reported the burgeoning grain shortage to Pope John XXIII — who in turn tipped off US intelligence.

Another Vatican spy personally delivered to Pope Paul VI the incredible news that Russian grain had been contaminated with almost six times as much of the dangerous radioactive Strontium 90 as grain from other nations. The priest-agent, working as a farmhand in different parts of Russia, collected grain samples wherever he worked. Once back in the Vatican, priest-scientists tested the grain in their laboratory and found that Soviet grain had 23 units of Strontium 90 in comparison to a mere 4 units of Strontium 90 in American-grown grain. This information, too, was passed on to Washington, and it offered proof that the Soviets at that time still had not perfected a 'clean' nuclear bomb and that the Soviet bomb was still crude in comparison to the American weapon of similar size.

Although the Vatican does not have any one agent who could be dubbed 007 Jr, its top agent in the Communist camp is a bear-like Dutch priest with a Friar Tuck waistline who since 1964 had been a cause of vexation in each of the Bloc nations. At least until the end of 1981, the Red gendarmes have not been able to lay their hands on him, no matter how many times he sneaks in to help thousands of persecuted Catholic priests and laymen trapped in these oppressed nations. Despite being one of Communism's most feared enemies, he is relatively unknown in the United States and England, and because he is a man of a hundred disguises and has never been photographed, the Communists are not quite sure what the man really looks like. Necessarily, the Vatican keeps him away from any spotlight. His name is Father Werenfried van Straaten, and he heads the Vatican's Iron Curtain Church Relief with a complete lack of publicity. He is a good personal friend of the present Pope, dating back from the many times he was in Poland and helped the Archbishop of Cracow in one way or another.

The Bacon Priest, as he is affectionately known inside the Leonine Walls (more about the name later), is the one single man of the Vatican who meets the Reds head-on hundreds of times each year. Several years ago when one of the Bloc countries offered to 'sell' old priests to the Vatican for $2000 apiece, Father Werenfried swung into action. The country in question (which Padre Werenfried will not permit me to mention) needed dollars for international exchange and was willing to let 20 imprisoned prelates go free for cash on the nail. In a matter of no time, Padre Werenfried had the funds in hand and before the country in question could change its mind, as it indeed subsequently did, seven priests managed to get out.

A goodly part of Father Werenfried's budget, which he raises through contributions sent to the Iron Curtain Church Relief in response to a monthly newsletter that he edits and sends to his contacts all over the world, goes toward training priests and intellectuals in the free world so that they can be sneaked into slave countries in disguise. Most of these men are people who have previously been sneaked past the Red borders by Father Werenfried. Since they are trained by his organization for the priesthood, and since they already know the language of the country from which they escaped, they return to that country when any of the regimes crumble and the people need spiritual and clerical help to build up new churches. Padre Werenfried has trained more than 3000 such men, 800 of whom have already discreetly returned to Iron Curtain countries. In nearly all cases the new priests are accompanied by Padre Werenfried himself who has infinite ways to get in and out.

Rev Werenfried's modus operandi for his forays into the Communist countries would do justice to any secret agent or professional spy. He adopts a new name (with false passport), leaves his priestly robes behind and takes on one kind of disguise or another, whether as a farmer or a tourist or whatever. This is not to say that the padre is so good at these deceptions that he evades detection every single time. Once in West Berlin when his presence (in disguise) became known to the East German underground, an effort was made to kidnap him. He had ordered an automobile to pick him up, but when an auto did arrive, something instinctively told him not to get into that car. While he was deliberating about this, the car that was supposed to have fetched him arrived three minutes later.

Once behind the Iron Curtain, Padre Werenfried meets secret priests and bishops who are evading Communist detection by having been ordained not in a church but in furtive ten-minute ceremonies. Many of these meetings are in cellars or remote farm buildings. The men wear no robes; they work in the fields or in factories, acting as priests in their free hours. Some are betrayed, of course, but many manage to carry on year in and year out. Padre Werenfried helps these men as best he can by getting money to them, as well as books, food supplies, multiple slabs of bacon (hence his Vatican nickname) — in short, anything they need for their work, not excluding toys for children. The Bacon Priest keeps five large warehouses in different Western countries full of items ranging from shoes and clothing to smoked sausages and canned meats, which together with hundreds of other things (including typewriterss, for example) are delivered to some 70,000 different addresses in the Eastern Bloc.

Another unfinished project that the Dutch–Vatican spy has taken on is to solve the mystery of the 63,654 Italian soldiers who vanished in Russia during World War II. The Vatican has ample evidence that at least 20,000 are still alive. Although 23,000 of these men are accounted for as either dead or integrated in various frontier villages along the Arctic Circle, the fate of the other 40,000 has never been satisfactorily explained. What alerted the Vatican to the mystery of Italy's lost soldiers were some 'messages' that were sneaked out from behind the Iron Curtain and delivered to the Pope. One such message, scrawled in blue pencil on a piece of polished fir tree trunk which was included in a Russian shipment of timber to a sawmill at Conegliano, read: 'For 15 years I have been in Siberia. I am an Alpine soldier from the Carnia region. Please help me, Holy Father. Please!'

Another note was found attached to the leg of a black-plumed stilt plover, a bird migrating from Arctic Siberia to North Africa, which was shot down by a hunter in Sicily. On an eight-inch (20-centimeter) strip of paper was this communication in Italian: 'We have sent many messages but no hope. We have been working in mines as slaves. We are in the Polar Arctic. We are 300 Italian soldiers from Salara, Friuli, Verona, Padua, Rovigo. God is our hope of salvation.'

In a photograph of a recent Moscow Fair crowd at a food pavilion, which was published in several weekly picture magazines, a clear head shot of Private Nello Magnabosco, a truck driver of the Pasubio Division which left for the Russian front in 1941, was recognized by everyone in his home town of Chioggia. Magnabosco's brother tried for several years to get an entry visa for Russia — to no avail. He finally took his case to Cardinal Albino Luciani of Venice (later Pope John Paul I for 34 days) who passed it to Pope Paul — who turned the job over to Padre Werenfried.

Adding fuel to the fire, a delegation of Japanese officials reported on their return from the Soviet Union that at Vorkuta, Norijsk, Tajschet, Inta and Denigrad they had talked with many Italian prisoners. Credence was given to their statement when they documented their report by citing the names of Captain Paolo Ghira of Trieste, Corporal Gino Giorgi of Mantova, Sergeant Luigi Leardini of Verona and Captain Livio Corinaldi of Padua — all of whose letters to folks back home never reached their destinations. The Japanese gave the information to the papal nuncio in Tokyo and it was swiftly relayed to the Vatican Secretary of State.

As part of its Ostpolitik negotiations, the Vatican is keeping the issue of the missing Italian soldiers very much alive, but Moscow disclaims any Italian POWs and scoffs at the suggestion that many of

In 1970 movie director Vittorio de Sica made *Sunflower*, in which Sophia Loren played the part of an Italian housewife who traveled to the Soviet Union to track down her missing soldier husband (Marcello Mastroianni) after the war ended. When she eventually found him, he had settled down happily in a small Siberian town and had married a Russian woman who was the mother of his children.

the missing men are slaving in labor camps. Four different popes have now officially asked the Kremlin to state why the Soviets insist on holding these men for over 35 years when all POWs in all other countries have long since been sent home. As yet the papacy has received no answer. Maybe the Dutch-Vatican fireball will get one.

Werenfried van Straaten was born in the Netherlands in 1913 and became a student of classical languages at the University of Utrecht. He entered the Praemonstratensian Abbey of Tongerlo in Belgium and was ordained a priest in 1940. Twenty-four years later he founded the Iron Curtain Church Relief. In spite of the fact that God's partisans behind the Curtain are no richer or safer because of Padre Werenfried's help, the bishops, priests and seminarians who are doing God's service in those countries are prepared for any sacrifice and are determined to hold out to the bitter end. The Dutch cleric's visits to these persecuted fellow-Christians have shown him how much moral support and consolation have been gained from the Vatican's Iron Curtain Church Relief. What he saw on his very first sneak-visit was enough to spur on forever. He told me:

'I met my first bishop while visiting a cathedral in Yugoslavia. He looked like a peasant in his grandfather's wedding garments. His suit was worn out, too narrow in some places and too wide in others. There were patches on his trousers. He was the bishop, but he wore neither ring nor pectoral cross. His diocese contained many depopulated villages with burned-out houses and half-demolished churches.'

The bishop invited Padre Werenfried for a trip on the back of his ancient motorcycle to visit some churches. A few minutes later they were on their way, but now the bishop had changed his clothes. He wore a pair of yellow-brown corduroy trousers with wide black soldier's boots, a pullover, a Roman collar and a dark gray overcoat. No purple. They drove along unbelievably bad roads and visited the first church — which was no more than four walls without a roof. It was charred black. Mass was celebrated between the open walls on Sundays.

There happens to be a by-law in Yugoslavia that says a church may not be torn down as long as it is still in use, and for many years the priest had been trying to get permission to roof it in. Padre Werenfried, after his visit, decided to do something about that roof. Together with a cadre of workers, he sneaked back to Yugoslavia and by candlelight during the night, the roof was built, albeit feverishly against time. Later, back at the Vatican, through its secret system of communication Werenfried found out that regime officials were so angry at the overnight restoration of the roof that in retaliation they confiscated the parish priest's only bed. The Vatican took care of that emergency. Within a few days the Dutch priest–agent had sneaked a new bed to the cleric and threw in a dozen slabs of lean bacon.

Preceding Padre Werenfried's postwar activities, the Vatican used its independent status during the war and its freedom of communication with other countries on both sides to make it possible for the Pope's spy network to locate prisoners-of-war, missing soldiers and civilians of all countries. Organized in September 1939 and given the name, Vatican Information Office, the operation worked with a staff of nearly 900 men that, over a seven-year period, handled more than 10 million requests for information about missing persons. The Holy See was able to answer the majority of the inquiries regarding the whereabouts of missing families or family members, soldiers and civilians. The information about missing persons was gathered up by papal nuncios and apostolic delegates and their staffs in every country involved in the war — even as far away as Japan and Australia, by the facilities of Vatican Radio, and by couriers and postal services — not to mention clerical prisoners themselves who were able to get news out or bring news from the internment camps upon being released. The Vatican also obtained information through very delicate negotiations with governments at war, including the Soviet Union which gave satisfactory cooperation. Only Germany failed to cooperate: when the Pope petitioned Berlin at Christmas, 1939, for an official list of Polish prisoners-of-war, there was no response. From that time on, the Vatican never bothered the Nazis for any POW information and sought it out through its other contacts, mostly from well-placed spies within the Nazi hierarchy and from practicing Catholic priests in each of Germany's cities and towns where churches were still in operation.

Very little is known today about this particular Vatican operation which depleted the Holy See's coffers of untold millions of dollars. Having done an efficient job under difficult circumstances, the Vatican Information Office was an unheralded success which should have been given its rightful due. Its only failure came in 1940 when Pope Pius made a nearly successful attempt to act as the go-between to exchanging all prisoners-of-war. That it failed was due only to Adolf Hitler's unforeseen suspicion at the last hour. It is a long and complicated story that few people know about — but perhaps the Vatican will some day open up its archives on that noble near-triumph.

CHAPTER XX

Vatican Radio

THERE IS a favorite story that gets told in Rome every now and then about the time that one of Leonid Brezhnev's aides went into his Kremlin office with needle and thread and told him that he had come to sew the top button on his trousers. When asked by the Soviet chief how he had found out that the button was missing, the aide replied: 'I just heard it on Vatican Radio.'

All levity aside, the anecdote does point out the worldwide reputation Vatican Radio has earned for itself in the 50 years or so that it has been in operation, broadcasting 225 hours a week in 33 languages (including Esperanto) to a hundred countries by FM, shortwave and medium-wave. Without Vatican Radio, the Pope's spy system would probably not function so well. An estimated 80 million people listen to Vatican Radio, but it is virtually impossible to gauge the actual size of its worldwide audience. Not the least of these are the polyglot monitors and Vaticanologists inside the Kremlin and in other parts of the Soviet Union, as far away as Siberia, Sverdlovsk, Novosibirsk, Samarkanda and Karaganda where listening posts have been set up. From time to time Moscow has seen fit to jam Radio Vatican whenever news bulletins are being broadcast that the Kremlin has already embargoed. One clever deception Vatican Radio uses, which the Communists are now wise to, is to insert a particularly sensitive news item into just one foreign language broadcast that goes into Russia, while leaving it out of all the other newscasts of the day, in order to get the message past the monitors and avoid being jammed. This today still works some of the time — but in the past it worked every time.

The Soviet Union also keeps daily close tabs on Radio Vatican broadcasts that go into Bloc countries that are heavily populated with Roman Catholics — especially Poland, which the Vatican knows listens in in far higher numbers than any other Red nation, with the possible exception of Czechoslovakia. Neither the Czech regime nor the Polish regime has jamming equipment and both depend on Moscow to provide this 'service'. That Radio Vatican is listened to more comprehensively by oppressed peoples is borne out by the report given to Pope Paul VI by a Lithuanian priest who had spent ten years in a Siberian labor camp. He said that Lithuanian transmissions from Rome were listened to by the prisoner-workers over their hidden radios while on their knees 'as if it were a prayer' coming from Vatican City.

Run by Jesuit priests with modern equipment that includes the world's largest rotating antenna and a 500-kilowatt transmitter, Vatican Radio made its first broadcast in 1931 on equipment supplied by Guglielmo Marconi, inventor of wireless radio. In fact, it was Marconi's voice that emitted the first words ever broadcast over Radio Vatican when he introduced Pope Pius XI on February 12, 1931, who then said to his few hundred listeners: 'Using this admirable invention of Marconi, we can talk to all creatures and all men using the words of the Scriptures. Distant peoples, lend your ears. . . .' For several years after that Marconi lent his know-how and made improvements to Vatican Radio's setup which at the time was located inside the walls of Vatican City. Today the main transmitting center is situated 11 miles (nearly 18 kilometers) north of Rome in a compound ten times the size of Vatican City, though one antenna remains on Vatican grounds. Only once since Marconi inaugurated the station has it gone off the air, and that came about on December 19, 1979, when lightning silenced it for 18 hours.

Unknown to most people, even regular listeners, is the fact that during the early morning hours of eack weekday the office of the Vatican's Secretary of State broadcasts messages — many of them in code — to priests, nuncios, apostolic delegates and cardinals in all parts of the world. Each Church dignitary knows about what time to expect special announcements pertaining to him or his region. He also receives coded signals from the Vatican to remind him of the 'date' he has with his receiver. In contrast with other stations, Vatican Radio often communicates private messages that will not be understood by anyone but the papal representative for whom they are intended. One might, for example, hear something like this: 'Father Tizio, with reference to the information in your letter of the eighth of September, re the peasant woman who sees visions of the Virgin Mary, we have considered your suggestion, but suggest that *ad captandum vulgus*. . . .'

With a staff of more than 300 men and women, many of whom are multilingual non-Italians, Radio Vatican sends ot nearly 500 programs a week. These range from papal speeches and blessings to international newscasts and from jazz music to Masses. The Vatican hymn — written by French composer Charles Gounod — is played at least once a week. Technical religious discussions are kept to a minimum because Vatican Radio officers feel these are not easily understood and would bore most of its listeners. From the some 50,000 letters it gets from all parts of the world every year, Vatican Radio is able to guide itself as to what its audiences want.

One special feature Vatican Radio put on in September 1979 brought its biggest avalanche of mail in history. This was a show that involved an imaginary interview with the Virgin Mary during which she was questioned on what she thought of today's women libbers, the suicide deaths of Marilyn Monroe and Jean Seberg, world pollution, nuclear war, the holocaust in which six million Jews were massacred and the Palestinians' drive for a homeland of their own. Each of Mary's answers was taken from texts of the Gospels. Here is a sample from the script which was broadcast in Italian, Spanish, Polish, English, German, French, Portuguese and Esperanto:

Question: What do you think of the tragic death of film actress Jean Seberg who committed suicide like Marilyn Monroe?

Answer: Daughter, why have you treated us so? Behold, your Father and I have been looking for you anxiously. (From the Gospel according to Saint Luke)

Question: We are scared. The threat of nuclear war, pollution of the environment, the exhaustion of energy sources, terrorism, delinquency, corruption, torture. . . . Do you think the Lord will still have patience with this poor world gone astray?

Answer: His mercy is on those who fear him from generation to generation. (From the Gospel according to Saint Luke)

Question: Would you have ever thought of the holocaust of the people which gave birth to you?

Answer: He has scattered the proud in the imagination of their hearts. He has put down the mighty from their thrones, and exalted those of low degree. (From the Gospel according to Saint John)

Question: But where were you in those tragic moments of world history, which unfortunately continue to be repeated, as we see today in the sufferings of the Palestinians, Indochinese refugees and others?

Answer: Standing by the cross of Jesus was his mother. (From the Gospel according to Saint John)

Although the answers in the simulated interview were necessarily vague and rather cryptic, the program grabbed listeners everywhere.

Successes of that type, as with every medium of communication, are tempered by moments of great stress and near-catastrophe. Such was the case for Vatican Radio one year when the world awaited a special Easter message from Pius XII. Five minutes before he was to begin his live discourse in front of a mike in the Vatican Radio studio,

Pius XII (who suffered all his life from a hiccup affliction — a fact that for a long time was kept from public knowledge) suddenly developed a case of hiccups. With an international radio hook-up to millions of people tuned in from everywhere, the Pope could not seem to shake off this most tricky of ailments. As the secondhand of the studio clock raced towards the on-the-air deadline, staff members tried all kinds of devices to get the Pope to stop hiccupping — they spun him to the right nine times, covered his head with a paper bag, made him hold his breath, got him to drink some water from the far side of the glass and even tried to 'scare' him with a sudden movement. Someone even tried pounding his back, and someone else suggested pulling his tongue with a thumb and forefinger. But nothing worked. Yet a few seconds before the Pope was due to go on the air, the hiccups disappeared as mysteriously as they had come and the Pope delivered his words with not so much as a fluff.

Like every major news organization, Radio Vatican has ready prepared programs and tapes for the eventual death of Pope John Paul II. These are coded by the staff as Day X and would have been used in May 1981 when a Moslem Turkish gunman put three bullets into the Pontiff in Saint Peter's Square had the assassination attempt not failed. The Day X programs consist of a series of broadcasts that can run for several days (in each of 33 languages) and include speeches and statements made in public by the Polish Pontiff. There are also a large number of prepared scripts that Vatican Radio announcers can read from, after minor alterations have been made to fit the events surrounding the Pope's demise.

One of the geographical areas in which Vatican Radio is relatively weak is North America. It is not easy, if you live in the United States and Canada, to get any of the English-language programs because Vatican strategy is to penetrate atheist countries like the Communist states of Europe. People in mainland China, for instance, get better reception and more programs beamed to them, not only in English but in Mandarin Chinese and Esperanto. The Vatican believes that its Esperanto broadcasts, incidentally, are more valuable than most of the other languages with the exception of English; the papal authorities are convinced that English has become the world's most important international tongue and the most widespread second language in nearly all countries, having replaced French as the diplomatic language most used. French broadcasts into North Africa and the Middle East are still numerous, as is Spanish, which has the distinction of being the one language that is officially spoken in more countries (19 in all) than any other. Although Latin is the Holy See's official language, hardly any broadcasts are beamed out in that tongue.

General director of Vatican Radio is Rev Roberto Tucci who keeps in constant communication with the Vatican Secretary of State, Cardinal Agostino Casaroli. The latter supervises Vatican Radio quite closely, but he gives Father Tucci considerable leeway nevertheless. Though Rev Tucci does confer with John Paul II from time to time, he depends on Cardinal Casaroli to alert him on highly sensitive matters to make sure that a broadcast does not create problems for some Church officer under political or social pressures somewhere.

Father Tucci has admitted that his annual budget of nearly $4.5 million is really too small to do the thoroughly professional job he would like. Vatican Radio, despite its shoestring operation, is a successful mixture of professionalism and amateurism. So many of the staff announcers — quite a few of whom are priests and nuns — learn while on the job, but because they are dedicated in a common mission to spread the faith all over the world, and especially to the Communist and atheist world, they are truly a motivated group of people which learns fast and functions effectively. Though earning considerably less than what they could make in private radio broadcasting (in some cases the priests and nuns receive no pay whatever), the staff and its officials are most proud of the fact that on the occasion of Vatican Radio's 50th anniversary (on February 12, 1980) when John Paul II visited the radio's studios, he revealed to the assemblage that while he was a cleric in Crakow, Poland, both as a lowly priest and later as archbishop and cardinal, he rarely missed any of Vatican Radio's Polish broadcasts.

CHAPTER XXI

Hot Off the Press — The Vatican Daily

NOT LONG ago John Paul II discovered that the Vatican's semi-official daily newspaper, *L'Osservatore Romano*, had censored some of his own stylistic pearls from papal speeches. The Pope was quite miffed and let the paper's editors know that from that day forward he would personally supervise the editing and proofreading of his addresses before they appeared in the paper. He even went a bit further during 1981 and began to interfere with certain headlines that were to appear on the first page by rewriting them after they had been set in type. John Paul has particularly ruled out of the paper such statements that preface his speeches with: 'We present the following discourse from our illustrious and enlightened supreme pontiff, the Holy Father, as we have gathered it from his august lips.' The Pope also told intimates that he considered *L'Osservatore Romano* a dull newspaper and that its grayness should undergo changes, reaching towards heaven, so to speak, where there would be more light and less grayness.

The Pope is not alone in his opinion, for among virtually every journalist and editor in Italy, the professional feeling is that 'the Pope's newspaper' is without doubt one of the dullest newspapers of all time anywhere. It carries no sports reports, no crime stories, no financial news, few ads, no book reviews, no comic strips, no letters-to-the-editor column or 'people' notices, no regular columns, no scandals, and photographs almost never (unless it is one of the Pope). Furthermore, it often places an earth-shattering news item on an inside page while every other newspaper in the world has given it justifiable headline treatment on the first page (a case in point is the end of the Vietnam War, which appeared on page 4). As a matter of fact, *L'Osservatore* has even been known to publish a hot headline story several days after it has happened (as witness President Nixon's resignation which was reported two days later). In addition, the Vatican newspaper thinks nothing of running an article entirely in Latin — or in any one of 33 different languages, including Sanskrit, with no translation.

With an editorial staff of 30 writers and editors, only two of whom are priests (one of them, Rev Virgilio Levi, is the second-in-command as managing editor), and a printing staff of 60 employees, the eccentric *L'Osservatore Romano* has its offices in a two-storey building just inside the Vatican walls near the Saint Anne Gate. Since most of the copy is written with a pen, the sound of typewriters is rarely heard in the cloistered calm of the newsroom. Silence reigns in its many private offices (there is no large, open newsroom per se, as is found in many other newspaper buildings) which have old-fashioned furniture, high ceilings and walls adorned with religious paintings and crucifixes. The same is true of the dark corridors that connect the offices, many of which do not even have telephones. The *Osservatore* is a broadsheet size, eight-page evening paper that comes out five days a week but carries the date of the next day (it publishes no issue on Mondays). Since April 4, 1968, the Vatican has been publishing a tabloid weekly edition full of feature stories and papal speeches; these are issued in Italian, English, French, Spanish, Portuguese and German. Although the Vatican is secretive about its circulation figures, a printer inside the Vatican has revealed that the Sunday edition sells about 100,000 copies. Most of this is by mail subscription, since very few copies are purchased from newsstands in Rome, even though each newsstand gets two or three copies delivered each day by about 6 pm when the last edition of Italy's dailies go out. The paper operates at a loss of $2 million a year.

Yet *L'Osservatore Romano* is one of the world's most carefully read newspapers, circulating in over a hundred countries and wielding an influence well beyond its relatively small circulation of 60,000. Though banned in the USSR, seven copies are sent to the Kremlin each day (Josef Stalin took out the original subscriptions), and several copies are put on permanent file at the Lenin Library in Moscow. Copies of the paper go every day to heads of state in Peking, Washington, Senegal, London, Bonn, Paris and just about every capital in the world, not to mention such places as the Island of Hvar, the Republic of San Marino, Tibet, Alaska, Northern Ireland, Andorra and to the office of the *Daily Worker* in New York City. It is also one of the world's most quoted newspapers, for besides being carefully scanned by foreign correspondents stationed in Rome looking for quotes or nuggets, its views and opinions are frequently reprinted by other newspapers. *L'Osservatore* once printed a guest essay on boxing, for example, in which the writer expressed his disparaging view that the sport was 'mayhem'. Despite the fact that the essayist was reflecting only a personal opinion, many publications and the wire services picked up the story and reported that the Vatican was against boxing.

Later the editor threw up his hands in disgust and shook his head: 'We don't know if there is even any Vatican view about boxing. Nobody has ever told us about it.'

Founded in 1861 'to denounce and refute all calumnies against Rome and its pontificate', *L'Osservatore Romano* must go into the record books as the world's most unusual newspaper — noted more for what it omits than for what it publishes. Its staple diet is a mixture of papal speeches, Vatican documents, cultural articles, religious news from all over (mostly Catholic), feature stories with a strong Catholic angle, obituaries and 'news' articles that highlight the failure of totalitarian regimes to treat Catholic clergy humanely. One such example read as follows:

'The news agency, ANSA, quoting the Czech agency, CTK, reports that it has been publicly admitted for the first time that some Catholic priests were unjustly condemned during the Stalinist era. The daily newspaper, *Lidova Demokracie*, the organ of the Czech popular party, today quoted statements to that effect by representatives of the Secretariat for religious affairs.

'The officials stated that it is impossible to know how many priests had been tried and condemned during the years of Stalinism; but, they added, some of them had been granted an amnesty. Priests who had been freed under amnesty were required to engage in "productive work."'

L'Osservatore, open in its use of invective when it tackles Communism (which it describes as 'the unfeeling omnipotence of a materialistic state, without any ideal beyond this world, without religion and without God'), does not hesitate to take on totalitarian giants of other stripes. For instance, its feud with Benito Mussolini provided *L'Osservatore* not only with perhaps its finest moment but also increased its daily circulation to over 440,000 during World War II because it was the only paper in Italy that could print news reports, under the Mussolini dictatorship, from the Allied camp. What mostly raised Mussolini's hackles was that the editor, Count Giuseppe Dalla Torre (who ran the paper for more than 40 years, until he retired in 1961) steadfastly refused to call Mussolini by his pet title, Il Duce.

A blunt outspoken man, who wrote nearly all the hard-hitting editorials himself, Dalla Torre showed his contempt for Hitler when the Nazi leader went to Rome in May 1938 to meet Mussolini, a big news event at the time to which the world press gave flare coverage. Instead of running a news item on the Hitler–Mussolini summit conference in Rome, Dalla Torre used the editorial column of *L'Osservatore* to insult the two Fascist leaders: he pointed out that Pope Pius XI had left Rome for his summer villa at Castelgandolfo in the hills outside Rome because 'His Holiness finds the air in the hills preferable to that in Rome'.

For Mussolini — already enraged that he was never referred to as Il Duce — this was the insult supreme. He ordered Dalla Torre's arrest. While the pugnacious Count one day was walking across Saint Peter's Square, he crossed the white marble line on the pavement that marked the border of the sovereign State of Vatican City and Italy. Immediately two Fascist plainclothesmen accosted him and 'invited' him to go with them to the Questura, Rome's police headquarters, because he was under arrest. Nodding an agreement, Dalla Torre began walking with the two men making casual conversation and joking about the invitation — which threw both the cops off their guard. Dalla Torre then suddenly broke into a run, managed to cross back over the white border of the Vatican State before the policemen could stop him, turned around with only inches separating him from Italian soil and snarled at the two agents: 'Tell your Boss he knows where my office is and if he has anything to ask me, let him make an appointment with my secretary — and perhaps I will find time to see him!'

This kind of defiant behavior was not what Mussolini was used to in a country he was ruling with an iron thumb. The Big Jaw ordered Dalla Torre assassinated and assigned two of his Black Shirt hitmen to go after the cantankerous editor. Word from a Vatican spy in Mussolini's office swiftly got to the Pope who ordered his editor not to leave Vatican grounds until the war was over. Accordingly, Dalla Torre walked from his office to his one-room apartment inside the Vatican using a different route each day, just to make sure the gunmen did not take it upon themselves to violate international boundaries. Dalla Torre not only outlived Mussolini but he outlived Fascism in Italy, and Hitler, too.

Strangely enough, when the Allies liberated Rome in April 1944 and the Nazi troops that had been occupying the Eternal City fled to the north, Dalla Torre chose not to give this major event any kind of play. Instead, he ran an eight-column headlined story on page 1 that had nothing to do with the liberation — an important Church ruling that had been ratified by Pope Pius XII. The Rome liberation story got a few lines on the back page, and that issue is today a collector's item.

Another issue that has become a collector's item, worth over $100 on the open market, is the one with the front-page announcement in Latin on the election of Cardinal Albino Luciani of Venice on August 26, 1978, as Pope John Paul I, an issue that was put out in just 24 minutes. Overlooked by the *Osservatore* staff and the Vatican's translaters was the fact that the streamer headline: *HABEMUS PAPAM ALBINUM LUCIANI QUI SIBI NOMINEM IMPOSUIT IOANNEM PAULUM I* contained a non-existent Latin word. The error, amusingly enough, was found by the editor's high school son, who had just finished first-year Latin. Apologizing for not being an expert in Latin, he pointed out to his father that the word *nominem* did not exist at all in Latin and that the word *nomen* (which means name) should have been used.

Editor of *L'Osservatore* today is Valerio Volpini, who succeeded Raimondo Manzini, who in turn had followed Giuseppe Dalla Torre. Volpini had the distinction of being the only one of *L'Osservatore*'s nine chief editors to be sued for libel. He was found guilty in 1979 in an Italian court of accusing an editor of a Catholic biweekly publication of 'encouraging division with the Church' in an editorial entitled, 'Sower of Discontent'. Volpini was fined $299, but the court suspended the penalty because he had never been convicted of anything else. Pope Paul VI did not support Volpini during the trial because he had not seen the editorial before it was printed and because he personally found it unpalatable when he read his copy.

This raises the question of how official is anything that is printed in *L'Osservatore* and to what extent its editorials reflect what the Vatican or the Pope think on a given issue. Reporters who scour the newspaper looking for clues or hints sometimes make the mistake of misleading readers by not calling *L'Osservatore* 'the Vatican's semi-official daily', or by warning a reader that the opinion expressed, if not directly attributed to the Pope or an official Vatican spokesman, may or may not be what the Vatican is actually thinking. In spite of this, the government officials in over a hundred countries who get the paper look at it with a most careful eye in an attempt to read between the lines and understand its pronouncements on morality, religion, politics, inernational events and future Vatican policy on one issue or another.

Almost as if it serves a special mysterious purpose, the Vatican will not allow its daily newspaper to be called an official newspaper, though it is generally considered to be the voice of the Vatican — which, in some ways, it is, and, in some ways, it is not. The Vatican's only offical newspaper is the *Acta Apostolicae Sedis* which comes out four times a year and publishes Church documents, Vatican legislation and official information in Latin — which makes it the Vatican equivalent of *The Congressional Record*. The quarterly newspaper, with its world circulation (mostly distributed by airmail), is a fairly authoritative mirror of the Pope's views, serves as the most visible sword against the foes of the Roman Catholic Church and wields an influence well beyond its relatively small circulation. (Before the *Acta* was first published, the Vatican did indeed have an official newspaper called *Diario di Roma*, first printed in February 1829. Only one column wide, it had the distinction of being the smallest newpaper ever printed, measuring 2.7 inches by 4.3 inches (6.9 by 1.1 centimeters). In its masthead, it made mention of the fact that it was published *con privilegio pontificio* [with the Pope's permission], and the only extant copy of this mini-tabloid is now in Germany, on display in Aachen's Newspaper Museum.)

What is left out of *L'Osservatore Romano* is sometimes more significant than what is put in, as many a vaticanologist has found out. On the occasion of Pope Paul's *Humanae Vitae*, which forbade under threat of mortal sin the use of artificial birth control methods, *L'Osservatore* never reported or commented on the storm of protest his pronouncement had created among Catholics all over the world, especially those in the United States.

Aware of how closely *L'Osservatore* is looked at, the publisher (the Vatican, in other words) quite often gets uptight about what gets printed. Even the meagre ads come under scrutiny by Vatican administrators. Most of the advertisements come through an advertising agency, and they usually include banks, funeral parlors, books and similarly sedate subjects. Most other subjects are considered unsuitable, and from time to time ads that have appeared in the paper are suddenly invited to advertise elsewhere. A few years ago, for example, Johnson's Wax placed full-page ads on two different days: the ad on the back page showed a large blow-up of the front of Saint Peter's Basilica with the caption — 'Truly Splendid — the Basilica of Saint Peter's Recently Cleaned With Johnson's Wax Products.'

Though indeed Saint Peter's had actually been waxed with Johnson's Wax, the Vatican decided the ad was in bad taste because it showed the Basilica and because the Vatican had paid for the wax. The Vatican made it clear to the wax company that it could not prevent people from thinking it had accepted free wax and were effectively sponsoring the product.

CHAPTER XXII

What Are Vatican Astronomers Doing?

ANNOYED THAT the so-called Julian calendar, which had been devised in 45 BC, was 11 days out of kilter (thereby making the spring solstices occur some two weeks earlier), Pope Gregory XIII decided enough was enough. He therefore ordered the establishment of a Vatican astronomy laboratory in the mid-1500s to study the sun. The Pope reasoned that it would be a wonderful thing to work out a new calendar in line with the seasons. Accordingly, he placed the Tower of the Winds at the disposal of several papal appointees, Jesuits trained in astronomy, and work began. What is truly ironic about the procedure is that long before Galileo was to be accused of heresy (in 1632) for his theory that the earth revolved around the sun, the Vatican itself began compiling data along the same lines as Copernicus whose work Galileo took into account.

A slit was cut into the wall of what was then known at the Meridian Room, and the path of light around the earth was measured as it came through the hole: the sun would enter at noon on a precise north-south meridian line and thus when the shaft of light reached the furthest point north within the building, it was the longest day of the year — the summer solstice. From this information the Vatican astronomers compiled a new calendar for Pope Gregory and named it after him. In spite of the fact that the pontifical astronomers devoutly believed that the sun moved around the earth (the telescope had not yet been invented), they nevertheless made remarkably accurate calculations. The Gregorian Calendar, issued in 1582, which is the one used today in most of the world, errs by only one day in every 3323 years.

From that day forward the Vatican's astronomy program has continued with papal support, and Vatican interest in this field continues unabated to this day. It almost met a fatal blow in 1870 when the papal states fell under secular control during the struggle for Italy's unification; the new Italian government took over the Vatican's observatory. But, ten years later, Pope Leo III initiated another astronomy program and set up a new observatory. After the turn of the century, the observatory was moved to the Pope's summer residence in Castelgandolfo where there were no city lights (as in Rome) that would interfere with telescope vision. Today, the Vatican keeps seven full-time astronomers and four technicians at work studying, not heaven, but the heavens, with equipment that, admittedly, is a bit behind the times but nevertheless viable. Over the centuries the astronomy program has not met disapproval on the part of any pope, albeit that budget limitations from one pope to another often curtailed research in progress; there have been no cuts in appropriations on the part of John Paul II, however, who is an avid enthusiast about the stars.

The Vatican's main research projects deal with the structure of the Milky Way; a specific project under way is the spectra (light bands) of the stars. By using prisms to break the light into color groupings, the scientists can figure out the chemical composition of many stars. Another undertaking monitors the changing brightness of the stars by photoelectric means. A Vatican computer helps calculate the amount of light lost passing through the earth's atmosphere. To do a large part of their work, Vatican astronomers use a Schmidt telescope with a 38.5-inch (96-centimeter) diameter mirror and a 25-inch (63-centimeter) diameter thin lens in front of it to take the star pictures in which the spectrum of colors become separated.

One long-range project on which the Vatican cooperated with a number of countries went on from the 1890s through the 1920s. This was a worldwide observatory project to map the heavens, and the Vatican — which took on the responsibility for charting a designated segment of the sky — located more than 500,000 stars. The photos on which those charts are based are being used today to compare them with new sets of pictures that indicate how the stars have moved in the last 50 years. The Vatican observatory still exchanges information with many countries, including some of the Communist nations: it has a good rapport with China, but its exchanges of scientific data with the Soviet Union ceased in 1980. After John Paul II came into power, the Kremlin decided not to exchange any more astronomical information with a pope known to be hostile to its ideology. When word reached Rome about the Soviet refusal to cooperate, Vatican astronomers and technicians were quite disappointed. But Pope John Paul saved the day by meeting with the team of scientists and telling one of his favorite anecdotes about the Soviet Union space program.

'Moscow,' the Pontiff informed the staff, 'is besieged with requests on the part of Soviet citizens who want to join the space research team and become cosmonauts — because it is the only way they can get out of Russia.'

CHAPTER XXIII

The Exorcist at the Vatican

A 22-YEAR-OLD Roman woman, standing just over five feet (1.7 meters) in height and weighing no more than 105 pounds (7 ½ stone), collapsed one day inside Saint Peter's Basilica and began emitting rasping, baritone-like sounds and spouting full sentences and phrases in fluent Latin. When she finally became unconscious and fell to the church floor, five Swiss Guards came to her aid and it took all five of them to lift her limp body. Mystified, the soldiers could not understand why a little person of such fragile appearance had become so heavy when they were convinced that they could have lifted up an automobile with less effort.

Summoned from his second-floor office in the Apostolic Palace, Monsignor Corrado Balducci talked with 'Marcella' — as her case history came to be known in the Vatican archives — but he had to do it in the only language she could communicate in, Latin, which she knew so well that she frequently interrupted the priest to correct his grammatical mistakes. Monsignor Balducci was astonished at the number of fine points of Latin grammar she had at her command. But he was to become even more astonished when he learned that Marcella had never studied Latin, nor, for that matter, finished elementary school. Rather than place her in the care of a doctor, the Vatican called in Balducci because he was one of the Vatican's two clergymen directly authorized by the Holy Father to perform exorcism. Marcella was the victim of a demonic possession, and only an exorcist could give her the help she needed. In the some 25 years he has been a Vatican exorcist, Balducci believes that the case of Marcella was one of his most difficult because it took him eight months 'to banish ten demons from her body'.

Vatican records describe Marcella as sweet, with a light and gentle voice. Yet when she became possessed, the voice would become guttural and she would speak only in Latin — in spite of the fact that when she was in a normal state, the only language she knew was Italian, and a Roman dialect at that. During her possessions, as the Swiss Guards had discovered, she took on an inexplicable weight of more than a thousand pounds (over 71 stone). Another incredible aspect to her demonic possessions was her uncanny ability to know what was happening behind her back. Once when Marcella had been taken to Saint Peter's, Monsignor Balducci had positioned several priests behind the big pillars, unknown to her, with instructions to read the rituals at the same time. There was no possible way for Marcella to have known about those assisting exorcist priests, yet when they began reading sotto voce, Marcella screamed 'No! No!' and ran to each of the clerics behind the columns and one by one knocked the holy books from their hands.

At the end of eight months of exorcisms, Monsignor Balducci managed to rid the woman of all her demons except one; she reported that this demon called himself Lucifer and had assured her nothing would ever prompt him to leave her body. In desperation Balducci got Pope Pius XII to make an appearance in her presence, as the exorcist prayers were being chanted one day. When he walked into the chamber on tiptoe, as per instructions, she was screaming and struggling. Since her back was turned to him, she could not have seen him come in, yet she suddenly calmed down as if hit by a club. It was at this point that Marcella was completely exorcised. Today the woman is married, has several children and leads 'a peaceful, gentle life'. The case of Marcella has been filed away for good.

Another difficult exorcism handled by Balducci was the terrifying case of a 45-year-old nun working in the Vatican; she was found screaming in one of Saint Peter's chapels where she kept vomiting up thick pieces of glass and various kinds of nails. Balducci was assigned by Pope Paul VI in 1977 to handle the exorcism, an incident that went into the archives as 'the case of the levitating nun'. While lying on her bed, it would occasionally move and leave her suspended in mid-air. After a ten-day exorcism rite, however, the nun was finally brought back to normal and returned to her duties.

A third difficult case, now part of the Vatican's official exorcism file, was that of a 35-year-old man who was possessed by seven demons; each demon claimed to have been tormenting the man for ten years. Whenever any of these demons spoke, Father Balducci needed four men to restrain his 'patient' — not that he was medically ill by any means. His demons made him contort his facial features to resemble certain animals and his mouth imitate, almost precisely, the sounds that that animal would make. When his face stretched forward like that of a pig, the sound would be the oink-snort of a pig. The man would meow like a cat, or bray like a donkey — and in each case his face would take on the form of the animal. At other times he would squirm on the ground like a snake and hiss. Father Balducci's exorcism lasted approximately 58 hours, at the end of which all seven demons left the man's body simultaneously. The file on this man shows that when he was in a normal state, he could not do any animal imitations, except for the cat; neither could he pull faces successfully enough to imitate any animal. Moreover, he had no conscious awareness that he had ever done near-perfect animal imitations.

Another one of Father Balducci's cases, equally baffling, involved a Roman bank clerk, aged 23. The young woman showed supernatural powers and knew things that she had no possible way of knowing. She would shout and spit at sacred images, curl up on the ground and swear against the saints. Any time the monsignor made a benediction sign behind her back, she instantly jumped into the air higher than any human being normally can. On another occasion Father Balducci approached the girl behind her back with a religious relic in his arms, she did not see or hear him, but again she suddenly leapt involuntarily into the air. The exorcism rites took hold on the third day when the clock struck noon. She screamed with a frightening and terrifying howl, after which she crumpled to the ground as if dead. 'That howl was the departure of the devil', the woman's case history stated.

The Vatican's exorcism catalog of well-documented cases contains the details of a 14-year-old boy in Washington, DC (Douglass Deen) on which William Peter Blatty based his best-seller book, *The Exorcist*. The case of young Douglass, which was handled by a Jesuit priest from Saint Louis University, was not an instance of demonic possession but a simple case of poltergeist phenomena. The priest stayed with the boy constantly for two-and-a-half months, during which time the Jesuit went on what is known in Catholic doctrine as the black fast (water, bread and prayer) and lost 50 pounds (3½ stone) — and in May 1949 the ancient ritual brought on the hoped-for result. As with other cases in the Vatican files, Douglass during his possessions spoke rapid Latin, a language he had never studied and of which he knew nothing when in his normal state. The Jesuit priest, whose name must necessarily remain in the archives, largely because he had not obtained permission either from the Vatican or his archbishop to employ the solemn ritual, nevertheless made a full report to Rome on the more than 30 'performances' that were used to separate Douglass for good from the evil spirit. The Vatican is of the belief that the well-intentioned Jesuit, who was totally inexperienced, had bumbled the job, simple because he did it on his own without professional help from Rome.

Both Monsignor Balducci and Father Ventura explain an exorcism rite as a ritual that essentially involves a command from God for an evil one (the Devil, in most cases) to depart the body of a human being. The exorcism rites, as practiced by the Catholic Church today, were issued in 1614 by Pope Paul V in a document called *Rituale Romanum*, designed to formalize practices that had emerged since the early days of Christianity. Over the centuries the *Rituale Romanum* has retained its basic features placing special emphasis on the identification of diabolical possession, selection of the exorcist and the outlining of the texts (and the setting) to be used during the rituals. The only revision to this document came in 1952 which stressed that an exorcist must have a profound knowledge of the theory and practice of exorcism and that an older and wiser priest should be assigned to the task when it is a major exorcism.

As specified in the *Rituale Romanum*, the exorcism rites cover 23 printed pages and begin with a series of prayers, psalm readings and an initial command to the 'unclean spirit'. Gospel passages concerning possession are read; priest places his stole and his right hand on the possessed individual, and interspersed by the sign of the cross made on the person's forehead and chest, he utters the specific words of exorcism. Here is the text of one such passage:

'I adjure thee, thou old serpent, by the judge of the quick and the dead, by thy maker and the maker of the world, by him who has power to send thee to hell, that thou depart quickly from this servant of God, [Name of the possessed person], who returns to the bosom of the Church, with fear and the affliction of thy terror. I adjure thee again, not in my own infirmity, but by the virtue of the Holy Ghost, that thou depart from this servant of God, [Name], whom Almighty God hath made in His own image. Yield, therefore; yield, not to me but to the Ministry of Christ. For His power compels thee, He who subjugated thee to His cross. Tremble at His arm, He who led the souls to light after lamentations of hell had been subdued. May the body of man be a terror to thee, let the image of God be terrible to thee. Resist not, neither delay to flee this man [woman], since it has pleased Christ to dwell in his [her] body. And although thou knowest me to be a sinner, do not think me contemptible. For it is God who commands thee. The majesty of Christ commands thee. God the Father commands thee. God the Son commands thee. God the Holy Ghost commands thee. The sacred cross commands thee. The faith of the holy apostles Peter and Paul, and of all other saints, commands thee.'

Rituale Romanum advises an exorcist to add a variety of prayers like the Our Father, the Hail Mary and the Apostles' Creed, which should be repeated as often as possible for as long as the struggle permits. Since Latin is the language most often spewed out by a possessed person (whether he has ever studied that language or not), the exorcist should use Latin at all times, according to the theory that the evil spirit understands this language, since this is the language the victim is forced to speak.

Vatican exorcism experts, both in the past and today, have not yet worked out a definitive theory as to how exactly a person can be seized by a demonic force. In the Vatican's view, a possession is an internal seizure of one's psychomotor activities and displacement of personality, which makes it appear that another conscious ego (the Devil or an unclean spirit) is present. It is classified as demonic when the entity is distinctly malevolent, with pathologically aggressive or self-destructive tendencies.

In the 350 years that the Vatican has engaged in exorcism, it has never imposed a fee. So far as is known, no exorcism has ever been conducted in front of an audience or an outside spectator; even a pope is not allowed to watch. Several other rules and regulations were broken by the priest in the movie, *The Exorcist*; the Vatican does not condemn the film, however, because it made known to a wide public for the first time that God as a power is strong enough to overcome the Devil's influence. Even though the movie was factually inaccurate, the Vatican owns its own copy which it uses as a teaching device. One of the first things the new Polish Pope did was to watch the movie twice in one sitting.

CHAPTER XXIV

Pornography in the Vatican Library?

EVERY TIME the subject comes up, the Vatican makes a formal denial that its library maintains a pornography collection. When sex researcher Alfred Kinsey was putting together his two explosive reports, *Sexual Life of the Human Male* and *Sexual Life of the Human Female*, during which time his staff amassed what he believed to be the largest collection of erotica in existence, he told an interviewer once that he was pretty sure that the Vatican library had just as good a collection.

Although the Vatican library is not one of the biggest libraries, it is unrivaled in importance because its shelves and storerooms contain works on the Church that are not available anywhere else. With over a million books, more than 100,000 maps and engravings and nearly 100,000 manuscripts, the Vatican library is only open to accredited scholars who fill out forms explaining the nature of their research and which books or manuscripts will be needed. Most of the scholars admitted are priests or seminary students, but lay persons can gain admission under special circumstances.

Although the real founder of the Vatican library was Pope Nicholas V (1447–55), who ordered that the Vatican's scattered collection of manuscripts be assembled in one place, the probable date of the library goes back to Pope Martin V (1417–31) at the time of the return of the Popes from Avignon to Rome. When he brought the papal Curia back to Rome, he also brought the old library and the new purchases the Popes had made in France. Many of the manuscripts taken to Rome were, in fact, handwritten copies of books by priests; these were called *scriptores*, a word which the Vatican's priest–librarians still use.

The main entrance to the Vatican library is from the Belvedere Courtyard, the largest of Vatican City's many courtyards. Just inside the door is a white marble statue of Saint Hippolytus, a third-century work by an unknown sculptor. He was one of the first Christian scholars to catalog the canon of the Sacred Scriptures. The department nearest the door is the acquisitions department which, besides purchasing new books, also catalogues about 1500 magazines — most of them scholarly journals. Every new acquisition is stamped with the Vatican library seal on pages 1 and 41.

Since Pope Pius XI was himself a librarian, major innovations were made during his reign, all of which helped to modernize the Vatican library along American lines. A catalog system with duplicate cards from the Library of Congress in Washington, DC, a new ventilating system from the United States to keep the air from becoming too damp for book bindings, a modern lighting system from New York City and seven miles of steel shelves from Pennsylvania were all introduced into the Vatican Library after Pius XI took office. These were all items Pius had wanted to install when he was Cardinal Acchile Ratti, prefect of the Vatican library, but for which he found he could get no budget from Curia officials. Pius also sent four Vatican librarians to the Library of Congress, the Columbia University library and the University of Michigan library to work and study methods used there.

Pius XI once had a narrow escape from death in the Vatican library on December 22, 1931. Ten minutes after he had completed a business visit to the library, the roof of the room he had been in for a half hour crashed through the floor and on down to the basement. One person was killed (the priest with whom the Pope had been conferring), but very few of the books and manuscripts were damaged.

The main library collection is contained in five floors of stores. Whole blocks of the principal store room are locked behind heavy wire grilles which protect the library's greatest treasure — some 5000 incunabula (books printed before AD 1500). The some 100,000 manuscripts, most of which are in Latin, Greek, Syriac and other rare languages, are also kept in this section. The most priceless manuscript in the Vatican library is Cicero's *De Republica*, written on parchment and lost to the world until a library official found it in 1822. It is the oldest Latin manuscript known.

Although one has to get permission to consult any of the manuscripts, once admitted to the manuscript-consulting room, a scholar is left unsupervised. This room is a long, high-ceilinged hall lined with dark oak bookshelves and adorned with busts and paintings of former popes. Row upon row of long desks fill the center of the hall. Each place is assigned a number, and the person occupying the desk number is given a box of cards with the same number on them. Thus when he takes a book from the shelf, he places his number at that spot on the shelf so that if another scholar is by chance searching for the same volume and finds the position on the shelf empty, he will have no trouble finding the person who is using the book. Presiding over this system, which Pius XI put into operation, is an assistant librarian who sits at a desk on a dais. He not only keeps order, but answers questions or helps in locating a book.

Next door to the consulting room is the catalog room, a long, narrow chamber. In addition to its own properties, the Vatican also keeps a card catalog of ecclesiastical listings that are found in the catalogs of the United States Library of Congress, the British Museum, the French Bibliothèque Nationale and Germany's Gesamtkatalog. The Vatican library also maintains a number of small rooms that house the special collection of great European families who left their collections of books to the Vatican library on condition that they be kept intact.

The Vatican library also has a microfilm service. With the eventual goal of filming all the library's precious manuscripts page by page, this department is constantly at work filming manuscripts and developing the microfilm. Another job that seems endless is the restoration of old books. This is work that is done with many years' experience and with methods that are of the Vatican's own invention. With each book or manuscript, the parchment pages are separated and trimmed of their ragged edges. Each page is washed, dried and pressed much like a piece of laundry. On any given day one can see manuscript pages hanging across the room from a wire, much like a Monday-morning wash. If there are any holes in a page, new pieces of parchment, matched with microscopic precision, are laminated in such a way that the thickness of the original page is maintained. restored page is then covered with a sheer, almost invisible silk gauze which is then fused so that the restored page is stronger than when it was new. Paper manuscripts are patched with rice paper so skilfully as to avoid detection, except for a slight variation in color. The Vatican's 'manuscript hospital' is most proud of the time it restored 56 Coptic manuscripts which had been found buried in the sands of Upper Egypt. It took ten years of solid steady work to bring the faded sheets back to life.

The Vatican library also catalogs all of the some 4000 books that were listed in the Vatican's Index of Forbidden Books (*Index Librorum Prohibitorum*), which was abolished in 1966. The last such Index list in 508 pages came out in 1948, with a short supplement in 1964 that had 14 new names and included Alberto Moravia, Jean-Paul Sartre, Andre Gide, Simone de Beauvoir and Curzio Malaparte. The books are on the condemned list because they are considered heretical, dangerous to morals or offensive to pious ears. The last list contained the names of Hobbes, Hume, Locke, Kant, Montaigne, Montesquieu, Schopenhauer, Spinoza and Voltaire — but did not include writers such as Karl Marx, Boccaccio, Georg Hegel or Friedrich Nietzsche. But it did include the name of a forgotten seventeenth-century satirist, Gregorio Letti, who held some kind of record by earning 17 condemnations in 35 years.

Quite a few of the Index listings of forbidden books have forever baffled some Church executives, and these include Maurice Maeterlinck's *Life of the Bee*, Victor Hugo's *The Count of Monte Cristo* and *The Three Musketeers* (both of which Pope John XXIII checked out of the Vatican library and read with great pleasure), Oliver Goldsmith's *History of England*, Laurence Sterne's *Sentimental Journey Through France and Italy*, and Edward Gibbons's *Decline and Fall of the Roman Empire*. Since no reason was ever given for the anonymous bans, one can only wonder, too, why the Index listed such things as a 1664 treatise on the use of unguents for burns, an 1844 Swiss almanac, or a pamphlet on the museums of Italy. One mysterious listing is a 1701 English treatise by a John Wilkins which had the improbable title, *'Tis Probable There May be Another Habitable World in the Moon, With a Discourse Concerning the Possibility of Passage Thither*.

The Index was created in 1557 from an order given by Pope Paul IV, whose reign, of all popes, most embodied the Inquisition. He was reacting to the fact that literacy was becoming widespread among the faithful, as a result of the invention of movable type in 1452.

The Vatican library does indeed have many books that are classified as erotic, and some as pornographic. They are scattered all over the library in much the same way that some of them would be in a public library. As a browser I noticed three titles, none of which was in any special place on the shelves, other perhaps than alphabetical order: *A Scatalogical Anthology*, *A Narrative of Iniquities and Barbarities Practiced in Rome in the 19th Century*, and *The Perverted Peasant*. Authors for none of the books were cited.

Housed in the Vatican library is a small collection of manuscripts with illustrations of a man and woman with 'their particulars nude'. Whatever pornographic or erotic items the Vatican library may have, they are not classified in that way, nor are they kept in any special room or under lock and key. Any scholar who gets into the Library has access to any of the books on the open shelves, including the erotic ones if he locates them.

Perhaps more interesting than any of the elusive pornographic books is the library's brobdingnagian accumulation of letters from many of history's most important people, 236 of which were put on permanent display in May 1981 in the Vatican Museum. Most notable of these treasures is a petition from the court of King Henry

VIII of England after he had fallen in love with Anne Boleyn and wanted an heir by her, which meant he had to shed his wife, Catherine of Aragon. The 75 petitioners sent off a two-foot by three-foot (61 by 91 centimeter) parchment to Pope Clement VII which they bemedaled with 75 ribbons and 75 red wax seals. This is to be found among the miscellany of letters that include messages from Copernicus, Galileo, Erasmus, Napoleon, Voltaire, Rossini, Queen Christina of Sweden, Mary Queen of Scots, Genghis Khan's grandson and heir, and a letter from Pope Paul III to Michelangelo giving him free trips on the ferry across the Po River for life. There is also a charming correspondence between Queen Victoria and Pius IX, indicating what she thought of the some dozen of titles bestowed on the papacy. Queen Victoria, apparently not wanting to acknowledge any of the papal titles, began her letter with, 'Most Eminent Sir'. Obviously offended by this lack of respect, Pius in his reply addressed Victoria as 'The Most Serene and Powerful Victoria, Queen of the United Kingdom of Great Britain and Ireland and Other Regions, Illustrious Empress of India.'

The display is just a tiny sample of what the Vatican has, for there are millions of VIP letters in the archives. And this is the Vatican library's biggest uncompleted task today. To catalog and cross-reference them, the library's small staff would have to work several centuries more, even though over 300 years' work has already been done. The archivists tell you that one of their revered heroes, and at the same time most notable villain, is Cardinal Josephus Garampi who managed, while assigned to the library in the late eighteenth century, to catalog an awesome 1.5 million letters which he stored into 125 large folios. The illustrious cardinal goofed, however true, he arranged all the letters in alphabetical order but that was done according to their places of origin.

'It simply means, with all due respect to the good cardinal,' sighed a patient Vatican librarian assigned to the archives, who asked to remain anonymous, 'that in order to cross-index all his work, we just have to go through every one of those 1.5 million items again!'

CHAPTER XXV

Magnum Opus — The Vatican's New Latin Dictionary

TRULY, ONE of the historic moments in the history of Italy's Parliament came some years back when a member of the Chamber of Deputies, debating a current bill to suppress the instruction of Latin in Italian high schools, delivered a speech that lasted a fluent 15 minutes in a language no one present understood — Latin.

It was one of the few times that a Deputy of the Christian Democratic Party was not heckled by the Communists, simply because what the speaker had been saying was Greek to them. Unable to criticize something they found incomprehensible, the Reds decided to issue a formal objection to the use of Latin on the floor of Parliament. Nothing in the constitution, however, could veto the use of that ancient tongue in the Chamber. Further research indicated that the last time Latin had been spoken in Parliament was at the closing session of the Roman Senate when the Caesars had sung their swan aria.

Up until a short while ago in Italian schools, to the Vatican's great satisfaction, Latin had been a compulsory language — and a mastery of it was required to enter any of the country's universities. This is not to say that undergraduates would be capable of conversing in Latin — as witness what had transpired in Parliament when the politico delivered his linguistic bombshell.

As to whether Latin is a dead language, the controversy may go on *ad infinitum et ad nauseam*, but when you talk to a Wisconsin-born Carmelite priest in the Latinist section of the Vatican Secretariat of State, one Reginald Foster, he will tell you in no uncertain terms (in a modern language) that 'Latin is alive, Latin is necessary, and Latin is full of fun. Latin is concise, flexible, harmonious, full of majesty and dignity. And you can quote me *verbatim!*'

At the time of writing, Father Foster, who is XLIII years old and does not object if you call him by the Latinized version of his first name, Reginaldus, is in the throes of revitalizing the so-called dead language through the new edition of a Latin dictionary to be published by the Vatican Press. What bugs him most are certain words that have crept into the English language which almost seem to defy Latin translation. Foster has already conquered such words as television (*imaginum transmissio per electricas undas*), radar (*radioelectricum instrumentum monitorum*), atom bomb (*pryobolus atomicus*), tape recorder (*magnetophonium*), and central heating (*calefacientis aquae ductus*). Certain other new expressions, however, are really testing the priest's expertise, and he has made the Vatican understand why the dictionary's completion has been repeatedly delayed. The most difficult new word to confront is Watergate. 'Watergate!' roars Father Reginald. 'Forget it! No matter how hard any Latin scholar tries, that word will never be translated into Latin, or for that matter into any other language. Try defining Watergate, by the way, in a one-word synonym. See! It takes a few sentences before you begin to explain what it means.'

Petrodollars stumped the ecclesiastical lexicographer for a while, but then he came up with a temporary Latin equivalent — *numi americani petrolio comparati*. As yet unsure whether he will include it in the revised Latin dictionary, he wants to wait until he has had a chance to discuss it with the language experts with whom he maintains regular contact. His query list includes *gummi terebrata* (flat tire) and *cellula scansoria* (elevator).

Supplementing his regular work in the Vatican, where he has been assigned for the last 15 years, Father Foster serves as an editor of *Latinitas*, a Vatican quarterly review entirely in Latin (circulation: 1000 copies). Even the ads are in Latin — so that an advertisement for a toothbrush refers to a *peniculus dentarius* and a half-page display ad for a safety razor talks about *novacula ab inferendis vulneribus tuta*.

Having written his Ph.D. thesis on the letters of Cicero — all 827 of them written in Latin — the brown-cassocked, balding cleric with the boyish exuberance of a motivated scholar has worked up a lecture based on 500 of Cicero's most meaningful sentences which are pertinent in today's modern world.

'The letters are all human,' explains Father Reginald, with infectious fervor, 'and they could be used in an introductory course to teach Latin because unlike most teachers who make Latin a cut-and-dried subject, Cicero's lively way of saying things, especially his frequent use of humor, would keep any student attentive. One thing Cicero was not — he was not a windbag (windbag in Latin is *loquax*)'.

Father Foster has in his file a letter written by Sophia Loren to the Vatican Press in which she praises the language. The Italian actress, long before she became involved in divorce proceedings and therefore fell into disfavor with her Church, had enrolled in a Latin course in Rome as part of the education she never had during wartime Italy when she was a street waif in Naples. She became utterly fascinated with the language and can still read it easily. Father Foster has never seen her in a movie but is pleased to have her 'as a fan of Latin'. When the updated dictionary comes out, Miss Loren will get an autographed copy, despite her marital squabbles with Vatican brass.

For The Big Book, as it is known behind Vatican walls, some 10,000 new Latin words have so far been concocted to supplement the language's original 30,000 words. It is not known when the edition is expected to reach the bookstores, because Father Foster's work of inventing new terminology is necessarily slow. Because the Vatican thinks in centuries, it appreciates that a scholar will spend as long as three of four months working over a single word. Latin is the official language of the Holy See, and the Vatican believes that the new dictionary should be the final word.

'One word that I have already spent just too much time on — and it still gives me daily headaches — is "soul brother". You see, "soul" has a very special meaning in our religion. In addition, we run into the problem of not knowing whether to make it masculine, feminine or neuter since "brother" in this context could also refer to a woman.'

Because he is an American, Reginaldus has a keener ear for Stateside neologisms, which is one of the reasons why the Vatican wanted him rather than an Italian or a scholar from elsewhere. The Americanisms and American slang may take a little time before they become part and parcel of the British English spoken in other parts of the world. Father Foster is not uptight (*sollicitatur*) about newly minted American English and takes a cool attitude (*acceptum*) on novel interpretations of old words, euphemisms and the weasel phrases that emerge from Madison Avenue, the Pentagon, academia et al — which means that he faces challenges from words such as Amtrack, hard-core, fuzz, discotheque, stonewall, freak-out and gay to the male chauvinist pig of women's lib. Immersed in dative, accusative, ablative and vocative cases, not to mention the exacting world of the pluperfect subjunctive and the present indicative, the grammarian-priest has to ride choppy waters.

Padre Foster has had to draw the line somewhere, nevertheless — and these involve words that have been created by journalists and gossip columnists like Jack O'Brian and Liz Smith who, borrowing their cue from Walter Winchell, seek attention by being cute. Father Foster refuses to translate into Latin such words as 'saloonatic', 'tripewriter', 'schooligans', 'chutzpathic', 'millionheiress', 'blessed event' (that would include 'blessed hevent' and 'blessed shevent'), 'Ameritocracy', 'splitsville', 'trendency', 'apparatchik', and 'legislady'. Several newcomers that the priest will shun in the final draft of The Big Book, inasmuch as they are particularly obnoxious to Vatican thinking are: 'wife-swapping', 'Playboy bunny', 'deep throat', 'swinger', and the oft-cited headline, 'Hix Nix X Pix', which once appeared in *The Hollywood Reporter*. But, on the other hand, he has not yet ruled out certain journalistic gems which include 'The Big Apple', 'Capitol Hill', 'chow mein', 'Reaganomics', 'payola', 'Jesus freaks' and 'McCarthyism'.

Among the words not destined for translation into Latin and will go into The Big Book as written are WASP, LSD, veep, Uncle Tom, coke, pepsi, Big Mac, shalom, Old Glory, oneupmanship, Oscar, cat's meow, Nazi, macho, kitsch, Irish Mafia, Xerox, hero sandwich, hard-hats, Silent Majority, Girl Friday, Flower Power, Emmy awards, Berlin Wall and supercalifragilisticexpalidocious.

'That last word,' he comments, 'is formed from Latin roots, but I am 100 per cent against it because I'm not sure the word exists, not even as gobbledygook, besides which I cannot even pronounce it cleanly enough in one breath. Can you? So you can see that with incursions into our present-day language like that, English is Latin's most dangerous enemy and best friend. That's because English has given new life to what people call a dead language.'

When Pope Paul VI decided that the Latin Dictionary had to be updated, he was the first to reason that the job would have to go to an American. Pope John Paul II is of the same view, and so he made haste to reappoint the Milwaukee scholar, Foster, as editor-in-chief of the Latin Dictionary. Himself a linguistic buff — with slow but acceptable English — John Paul II possesses a fluency in Latin that is admirable. He had a chance to put it into practice on the occasion of his first chat with Father Foster. Curiosity on my part as to whether the Pope had made any mistakes in Latin at that time prompted the inevitable question.

'Well, er . . . not really,' hurriedly explained the priest. 'But if the Holy Father were perhaps a student in a classroom, he might want to bone up on his ablative a bit, since he would recognize that he might be a bit rusty. When he used the phrase, "in my fashion", it came out "mea moda", but he quickly made his own correction to "meo modo". That's the ablative case.'

Besides the Pope, Father Foster finds other people inside the Vatican, besides cardinals and bishops, who know enough Latin to converse. Surprisingly, a number of the Vatican's Swiss Guards personnel learned Latin back home and are eager to keep it up — so when Father Foster walks the streets of Vatican City, he is frequently accosted by one Swiss Guard or another in Latin. Recently, he was talking to a Swiss Guard with several semesters at Oxford behind him, and the soldier asked the cleric editor about the translation of line 209 of Book I of the Aeneid in which Vergil states: '*Spem vultu simulat, promit altum corde dolorem*.' The literal translation comes out: 'He simulates hope in his face, he presses down deep grief in his heart.' The two men agreed it had to be translated differently, but they both felt that it was a crying shame Vergil had to be translated at all.

Although frustrated by myriad idioms, Reginaldus Foster is convinced Latin should not maintain the *status quo*, since *ipso facto homo sapiens* will be using his *magnum opus* in a world where *tempus* must necessarily *fugit*.

CHAPTER XXVI

The Pope's Own Polish Jokes, His Ghost Writers And Those Letters

POLAND'S OWN Dennis the Menace, Little Piotr — age 6, going on 66 — has a high-powered ghost writer by the name of Karol Wojtyla, whose jokes make the Red regime in Warsaw volcano angr-r-r-y. Here are a few quip-lashes from Karol by way of Piotr:

- 'I know what will happen when Communism gets to the Sahara Desert. Judging from our own experience here, eventually there will be a shortage of sand. . . .'
- 'Communism is superior because it successfully copes with difficulties which do not exist in other systems. . . .'
- 'Warsaw says that by next year we will have an automobile for every five inhabitants — and a pair of shoes for every three feet. . . .'

These one-liners are quite simply wipe-outs that are uppercuts at Communism and make Party VIPs yell 'Foul!' And although the lines are delivered by Little Piotr, who is fictitious (as he does his thing all over Poland), the author is not fictitious. He is affectionately known in Poland as Karolek (Charlie) and throughout the rest of the world as the robust Pole who stepped into the Fisherman's Shoes when he changed his name, Vatican style, to Pope John Paul II. The Italians called him 'Papa Wojtyla' with various, unorthodox pronunciations, since his Polish name reminds many of the line of an eyechart.

Unlike his predecessors, the present incumbent of Saint Peter's Throne, unbeknown to his cheering public, is a goldmine of political stories and Polish jokes, according to his friends. They still remember Karolek Wojtyla when he was a factory worker who like his glass of wine and honey, either on or off the job, and could spin a real mean joke, with a punchline aimed at the sins and shins of the Reds. The jokes in question are not of the US breed, with their own, ethnic-denigrating flavor, but Polish jokes with an unparalleled political bite. Of these anti-Communist jokes, a member of the former Cracow cardinal's entourage and some of his personal friends told me that Karol Wojtyla created at least a half dozen a week during his term of office which would then take wing all over Poland. A prolific writer and also a playwright, Wojtyla is the author of four books and over 500 articles and essays. In 1960 his play, *The Jeweler's Shop*, a trilogy about marriage was published under the pseudonym of Andrzej Jawien, and in recent years the play was radio-broadcast in several countries.

Many of the Wojtyla/Jawien jokes crossed the borders of the other Soviet Bloc countries and were not only repeated clandestinely in Russia itself but also in such Eastern Bloc strongholds as Czechoslovakia, Hungary, East Germany, Rumania and Bulgaria, give or take a few modifications and name changes to fit local regimes. In Poland the principal carrier of Karolek's humor was invariably Little Piotr, through whom the present Pontiff found a most eloquent mouthpiece. As witness:

'Piotr is told by his teacher to compose an essay because it will be shown to the State School Commissar during an inspection tour. So Piotr writes: "I have a cute cat and it has three kittens. All of them are Communists." When the inspector comes a few days later, however, the lad's essay now reads: "I have a cute cat and it has three kittens. Two of them are Communists." Asked why he changed the story, Piotr replies: "Because one of the kittens opened its eyes this morning."'

The Pope's same small hero popped up in another yarn. Teacher asks Piotr: 'If one metric ton of coal costs 1000 zlotys and your father orders 3000 zlotys' worth of coal, how many metric tons will be delivered to your house?' Piotr's answer: 'Two and a half tons.' Told that this is not the correct answer, Piotr retorts: 'I know that. But what can we do? It always happens.'

And another bright comment from the little boy: teacher wants Piotr to describe Communism. 'It's five feet tall,' he says. How does he know that, the teacher asks. 'Well,' explains Piotr touching his neck, 'my father is six feet tall; he says he's had Communism up to here!'

Like nearly everyone else in his home country, the Catholic Church's first non-Italian Pontiff in 455 years was an avowed foe of Communism. And like everyone else he was fed up with State inefficiency, shabby products, too much bureaucracy, propaganda and government suppression of freedoms. And one of the few ways that Cardinal Wojtyla could fight back at Big Daddy in Warsaw was to keep the spirit of resistance alive with the political joke — satire reflecting the despair of his country. Using his creative talents and plenty of literary license, Karolek sought to push his country's stuffed shirts to the combustible point through jests written by him but dispersed by students in cafés over a glass of vodka or cup of coffee. It is not known whether John Paul the Second is still engaged in this kind of creative activity, but according to some knowledgeable admirers, he can still rattle off to Vatican intimates the kind of Polish joke that takes a swipe at Communism and its regimes.

Friends say that Karolek was always disposed towards critical comment on the totalitarian leadership of his country. In the grim days of World War II during the Nazi occupation, the man who was later to become Archbishop of Cracow won a place for himself among his people by organizing the underground Rhapsody Theatre in which he acted and for which he wrote anti-Hitler material. His slaps at the oppressive Third Reich rule were carefully honed, each word chosen for its maximum effect. After the Nazis were booted out and the Communists came in, Wojtyla never sold his soul to the Red Devil that strangled his country — and hence his jokes.

Another story believed to be the product of the fertile Karol Wojtyla brain, which circulated all over Poland while he was a cardinal there, goes like this: during a Sunday Mass, the presiding priest spots one worshipper who never kneels and he asks him why. The man explains he is Jewish. 'But, what is a person of the Jewish faith doing here, then?' asks the cleric. Responds the man from his pew: 'Because I'm against the government, too!'

That the Warsaw government failed to provide its citizens with enough meat for the family table was one of Wojtyla's frequent themes with his 'Polish jokes'. In one tale, an old woman asks her butcher if he has any steak, and he says No. 'Do you have any veal?' The answer is No again. 'Pork? Bacon? Ham? Sausages?' A bit miffed, the butcher tells her No, No, No, No — and after she walks out with her shopping basket still empty, the butcher turns to another customer and says, 'What a pest that old woman is — but what a memory!'

And another one: when Brezhnev pays a visit to Poland, the regime orders a 24-gun salute in his honor. After the shots have been fired, a little old lady approaches a policeman and asks why all the shooting. 'Dear Lady, we have Comrade Brezhnev visiting us today.' Replies the woman: 'What's wrong with you fellows? You fired all those rounds and missed him every time.'

Brezhnev figures in another one, coming apparently from the fruitful gray matter of our anonymous friend: one night a bloodcurdling scream is heard throughout the Kremlin from the Soviet First Secretary's apartment. A doctor rushes in and finds him white as a sheet and trembling. 'I had a terrible dream,' sobs Brezhnev. 'I dreamt that Red Square was full of Poles with their relatives from Cleveland and Chicago.'

'That's frightening,' says the doc, 'but after all it was only a dream.' 'Yes, but that's not all,' Brezhnev continues. 'They were all eating Kansas City steaks, Idaho potatoes and Boston Cream Pie.' 'That's not very patriotic,' the doctor shakes his head. 'But it's w-w-worse than that,' stutters Brezhnev. 'They were eating Kansas City steaks, the Idaho potatoes and the Boston Cream Pie with chopsticks.'

One of the most hilarious jokes heard in Poland concerns the archeological expedition that brought back a mummy from Egypt. When Warsaw University scientists could not determine the exact age, they called in the Secret Police. Three hours later the Secret Police emerged from the lab and said the mummy was exactly 3144 years old. The professors were amazed. They wanted to know how the answer was got. 'Simple', said the Secret Police. 'The mummy confessed.'

Laughter may be the best medicine, opines Norman Cousins, and Karolek's humor indeed represents a bitter pill for the Marxists. Rated top of the pope-ularity poll, Karolek's-kreations show a high degree of Polish polish.

Although John Paul is an accomplished and clever writer, today he needs the help of others when he is preparing speeches or encyclicals. The picture Vatican spokesmen paint is that of the Pope sitting long hours by himself at his desk, either very early in the morning or late into the night, searching the inner depths of his mind and soul for the right words, as he prepares his latest speech or his newest encyclical, which hundreds of millions of people all over the world will hear or read — and which will go down in Church history. This picture is not at all true. It might have been true in the past, with some of the popes of olden times, but the Pope today has ghost-writers. Since John Paul II prefers to write in Polish, he has surrounded himself with a team of Polish scholars who are sometimes, lovingly, referred to as 'the Polish Mafia'. The output of these men, who work closely with John Paul, is prodigious (the annual number of pages produced very often goes beyond the 4000 figure), and all of it must be translated from Polish into Italian (and not infrequently Latin). The job is handled by a team of Polish nuns, headed by Sister Celeste Zawadska and Sister Emilią Ehrlich, who have been in Rome for many years, long before John Paul came upon the scene. If translations into other languages are needed, the Italian text is used as the basis — but in any event, it all has to be scrutinized by Archbishop Giovanni Coppa of the Vatican Secretariat of State who, before he gives approval, has the manuscript looked over by various specialists who are expert in the affairs of specific countries. Often, Archbishop Coppa has to go back to the Pope for modifications.

Nearly all the Pope's ghost-writers accompanied him from Poland when he became Pontiff in 1978. The writers, all of whom are unknown to the outside world, are Monsignor Stanislaw Dziwisz of Cracow (who also serves as the Holy Father's private secretary), Monsignor Jozef Kowalczyk (who heads the Polish desk in the Secretariat of State), Monsignor Juliusz Paetz, Bishop Kazimierz Jan Majdanski, Monsignor Marian Jaworski and Dr Tadeusz Styczen. The last two scholars are not based in Rome and make frequent trips from Cracow and Lublin respectively whenever the Pope calls them.

The work of these men covers a very wide range of topics for specialist groups. Apart from encyclicals and his mini-lectures on the Book of Genesis which he delivers to his Wednesday audiences, the Pope usually has speeches prepared for various groups. These can be soccer teams, military chaplains, hairdressers, conservationists and so on. When addressing special-interest groups of this kind, the Pope barely has time to pre-read his short speech, so he depends entirely on his ghost-writers who, sharing John Paul's views of the state of the Church and all fundamental issues, can write effectively for him. The writers refer to newspaper clippings, memos, Vatican documents, the Bible, previous speeches and books from the Vatican library.

For important speeches, the Pope does work closely with his writers — sometimes right up to the last minute. All the speeches have to be written well in advance of the time they are to be delivered, a Vatican procedure that makes the routine quite cumbersome. In this way, changing developments in the world can have a bearing on what is said during a papal pronouncement — and this is why John Paul II has been known to change the text at the last minute or even while he is reading it. In Turin, for instance, the Pope left out at the last moment a line linking Marxism and terrorism. He did something similar at Fortaleza in Brazil where parts of his speech, prepared almost a month before, no longer seemed to have much relevance.

Apart from his writing, John Paul is the recipient of considerable reading matter in his mailbag. The postman not only cometh to the Vatican, but he delivereth his bundles in abundance every day of the week, including Sunday. The Vatican post office may be the only one in the world that works on Sunday — but that's because the Vatican works seven days a week.

The Pope — like a US president or a British queen — is flooded with correspondence from all kinds of people who discuss all sorts of subjects. There is one kind of mail that John Paul gets more of than either President Reagan or Queen Elizabeth II — and that is from children. Although these communications do not always reach the

Pope's desk, they are all read by Vatican staff. Few of these letters, however, receive answers, for the Vatican does not assign personnel to such a job. Most of the smallfry missives are eventually thrown out, but a goodly few are put into the files where they remain for an indefinite period. Here is a sample of what the Polish Pope has received in the last year or so from children:

'Dear Pope, you are different. The Popes before you like Paul the sixth and John the twenty-third were great Popes, and I liked hearing about them very much. But I like you the best. Do you think you could reform the world since your predecessors did not finish the task?' That came from a 14-year-old boy, as did this: 'Listen, Your Holiness: I want to ask you one thing — whether you can make me smarter and whether you can get me over this boring cold so that I don't have to blow my nose every second.'

The Pope's letters from children often show an awareness that Italy is living in troubled times with a crime wave, multiple kidnappings and acts of terrorism. Witness this letter which said in a scrawled handwriting from a girl who was eight years old: 'You who are the deputy of Jesus tell Jesus to put an end to purse-snatching, to put an end to wars and to put an end to all kidnappings because all these are sins.'

Another kid wrote, shortly after the May 1981 assassination attempt on John Paul's life: 'I saw you on the television before that bad man shot you. It must be a hard world for you to live in, exposed to danger that way. I know that Jesus will make you better soon. Spaghetti is good for the health, and if you eat it more often instead of Polish dishes, you will get better faster. Take my advice!'

'Dear Pope John Paul: What is it like when you die? Nobody will tell me. I just want to know, but I don't want to do it.'

'Dear Mr Pope, Sir, thank you for giving me eyes to see and ears to hear and breans [sic] to think and birds and dogs and cats and Debbie to play with. Church is all right but I don't like the music.'

In addition to letters, the kids even send telegrams to the Pope. Here is one His Holiness got not long ago: 'My dog died, and I loved him so. Can you fix it up that my dog can sleep next to God who can pet him until it is my turn to go to heaven?' Another telegram said: 'When I go to sleep at night, I have dreams. Sometimes my dreams are good but many times they frighten me. Please, can you have God send me better movies every night?'

What the secretarial staff of the Pontiff considers the funniest message yet is the one that came from a little girl in Boston who wrote: 'Holy Sir, my mother told me that when I was born, the stork brought me. Then when my brother was born, the stork also brought him.

Dear Pope, can you arrange it with God for my mother to have a normal birth next time?'

The little shavers don't play it for laughs, of course, but many of their missives to the Pontiff would outshine some of Neil Simon's cleverest. One of the very best letters was placed on the Pope's desk, and it has become some kind of classic. The young philosopher wrote: 'Dear Holy Father — would you please tell Our Lord that He made a mistake when He invented girls because their tongues never take a holiday.'

It is at Christmas, however, that the volume of kiddie mail to the Pope increases appreciably. In recent years some of the smallfry wanting gifts have taken to making telephone calls to the Vatican asking to talk to the Pope — they want the Pope to put in a good word for them with Santa Claus. One anonymous sprig laid his cards on the line and in some of the boldest lines yet communicated to a papal aide suggested that he tell the Pope to tell Santa Claus to bring cash in addition to toys. He explained that he was growing up and next year would probably not believe in Santa any more and he needed money to buy the presents himself, 'besides which I'm broke!'

Irreverence is often of no concern to children. Not long ago, one little addressed a letter to God c/o The Pope and opened his message with 'Here I am, O Jesus mine. I read your book. Next time you write a Bible, put a lot of zip in it.'

CHAPTER XXVII

One Author's Sparks With the Vatican

AFTER THE publication in January 1969 of my book, *The Vatican Empire*, the press officer of the publishers, Simon & Schuster, made arrangements for me to appear on some 40 television and radio talk shows and submit to intensive questioning both from the emcees, the co-guests (most of whom were invariably Jesuit priests or high-ranking officials from the nearest archdiocese) and from listeners who had read the book. These shows, several of which were coast-to-coast, the concurrent newspaper reviews, feature stories and news reports about the book, all helped contribute to *The Vatican Empire* reaching several of America's bestseller lists, including the most prestigious one of all, *The New York Times*. Despite seven printings and the impact the book was having in the United States and Canada (there were later to be foreign editions in French, German, Italian, Spanish, Portuguese and British English), the publicity people at Simon & Schuster were eager indeed to have the Vatican make a public pronouncement (for or against) about the book — the first one ever to address itself to the taboo subject of the Vatican's finances. I can remember vividly Fanette Cines, the S & S PR chief, saying: 'Nino, if you can somehow get the Vatican or the Pope to mention your book, good or bad, we'll sell a million copies, baby!' Easier said than done. Try as I might, it was not possible to convince Mrs Cines that the Vatican's wisdom on such matters was famed and the last thing it would ever do was to spur the sales of a book that had stuck in its craw by giving it a public comment. The Vatican, as was to be expected, remained silent.

Lifting the cloak of secrecy surrounding the Vatican's extensive business operations *The Vatican Empire* was a hard-hitting report that one would not expect to come from the typewriter of an American newspaperman raised in an Italian Catholic family which included several members of the clergy. However, it was not a swipe at the Roman Catholic Church, and nor did the author take the papacy to task. The book never speculated but instead objectively recounted the facts that were unearthed on Vatican involvement in, and control of, secular business. Penetrating the inner sanctum of the Vatican's high finances, it showed why the Vatican had become one of the greatest fiscal powers in the world during the period from about 1930 to the present.

Meanwhile, I had learned from my sources behind the Leonine Walls that *The Vatican Empire* had created quite a stir there. A dozen or so copies were circulating clandestinely from one person to another, having more impact than any author could even dream of. One report came that Pope John XXIII had read the book. From a cardinal I met one day at a press conference there came a gratifying comment. He said (paraphrased): 'It is good this book was written, for we know of these things, but we who are with the Church are not able to speak out so frankly and tell our people what they should know. It is good that you, a layman, and a Roman Catholic, are able to do so.'

Later, when Simon & Schuster's paperback division, Pocket Books Inc, made ready to publish the low-priced edition, a new PR chief, Barbara Hendra, took up the cudgels for the publicity workout — but, lo and behold, she was happily upstaged by the Vatican itself. Having until then ignored the book completely, it now unexpectedly broke its silence.

In July 1970, about 18 months after *The Vatican Empire* had appeared, *L'Osservatore Romano* did something it had never done in its 115-year history: it devoted a column and a half on page one (and another half column on page two) to its finances, saying that *The Vatican Empire* was a 'fantastic exaggeration'. In approximately 1800 words of caustic refutation, the Vatican said it had felt the need to clarify some of the published allegations. *L'Osservatore* discussed an article that had appeared in French in the Swiss daily, *La Tribune de Lausanne*, which had run a book review on the French edition, *L'Or du Vatican*. The reviewer of the book had also included some data of his own — and since they were bits of information that could not stand up under scrutiny, the Vatican cited these for refutation, allowing the public and the press (which gave the *Osservatore* article worldwide coverage) to infer that I had published this information. The inference included statements that the Vatican had speculated in German marks, that the Vatican had owned shares in the Lancia automobile company and that the Vatican had a working capital of nearly $13 billion. No such things were even mentioned in *The Vatican Empire*. Thus, instead of coming to grips with the profusion of data cited in *The Vatican Empire*, *L'Osservatore Romano* built up a case against me by the

The British edition of my book was re-titled *The Vatican's Wealth*, and published by David Bruce & Watson, London.

hoary propaganda trick of inference and misquotes. The Vatican had commented on some things that were not in the book but never refuted anything that was in the book.

Besieged by correspondents all over Europe who telephoned me in Vienna, I issued a prepared statement for print and for radio/TV journalists which said: 'Until such time as the Vatican makes public the totality of its finances and its investments, in an official annual report signed by His Holiness, I stand by every fact stated in my book, particularly since the information was accumulated by me during a ten-year period of quietly spying on the Vatican's ramified fiscal operations, which have hitherto been cloaked in secrecy. I stake my reputation of six years as a university professor in the United States and 28 years as a journalist (13 of them here in Europe as a correspondent specializing in economic affairs) that my book contains no "fantastic exaggerations" and deals only in straight facts. Rather than *L'Osservatore* engaging in derogatory terminology, let the Vatican refute my information with its own hard facts, for which the world is waiting, after centuries of papal silence.'

The New York Times, commenting on the unusual denial made by the Vatican which was reported in nearly every newspaper in the Western world, said that *L'Osservatore* had raised more questions than it had answered. It added that the Vatican's mouthpiece had scarcely contributed to clarifying the issue by having boiled the argument down to semantics. *The Times* concluded its editorial by saying that the *Osservatore* article demonstrated that no matter how rich or poor the Vatican was, 'there is plenty of evidence that its canny businessmen are doing their best to make it richer.' To all the statements and observations by leading newspapers and by myself, the Vatican issued not one word more — neither of defense nor refutation. And it has remained once again silent on *The Vatican Empire* ever since — and also on the sequel that I wrote on the finances of the American Catholic Church, *Vatican, USA*.

A bit miffed that I had been libeled by *L'Osservatore Romano* (I was not contemplating any kind of libel suit, however) on the basis of a mistake a Swiss reporter had made in a newspaper article about me and wanting to point this out in a by-lined article or letter-to-the-editor in the *Osservatore*, I petitioned the managing editor of the newspaper who granted me an audience in his office. He treated me kindly, and in a fatherly manner suggested that perhaps I had sinned in using my God-given talent as a writer and journalist in a manner most inappropriate. When I asked to be allowed to prepare a 1000-word article (or letter) for his pages, he told me this would never be possible as I had become *persona non grata* with the Vatican.

My other brush with Vatican officialdom came while I was researching *The Vatican Empire*. When the finished manuscript was submitted to my editor at Simon & Schuster, it contained a chapter — a really hot potato — on a Vatican-owned drug company that was producing and marketing birth control pills. This chapter was removed. Although I tried to get it back into the book as the publisher kept putting out extra editions in hardback and again into the paperback, my efforts went for nil. As much as Simon & Schuster had the courage to be the first house ever to publish the startling details on the finances of the Vatican, its editors opted for leaving this particular chapter out of the book, despite the fact that I had at my disposal thorough documentation on the subject. This decision was made late in 1968 a short while after Pope Paul VI had condemned the use of contraception in his historic *Humanae Vitae* encyclical — a document that threw many of the world's Roman Catholics into confusion and controversy. Disclosure at that time to the effect that a papal pharmaceutical house was selling oral birth control capsules would have been topical, to say the least.

When my second book, *Vatican, USA*, came out, however, Simon & Schuster permitted two paragraphs on the subject to be included as part of a chapter but not as a separate chapter. During the promotional tour that took me from coast to coast to appear in some 75 radio and TV talk shows over a two-month period, many of the emcees and listeners who telephoned, somewhat startled at the revelation, asked specific questions about the Vatican's birth control pill. The reaction behind Vatican Walls, on the other hand, was more drastic: the Pope ordered that the company be divested of any financial interest on the part of the Vatican.

For sale in every Italian pharmacy, the Vatican's oral anti-baby pill (as the Italians usually call it) was packaged in a harmless-looking, little white box and called Luteolas. It was manufactured and distributed by the Istituto Farmacologico Serono, and Prince Giulio Pacelli was chairman of the Serono board of directors. Prince Giulio was a nephew of Pope Pius XII, who before he became Pontiff was Eugenio Pacelli.

Italian laws prohibit the selling of birth control pills, and yet they are openly available in every Italian drugstore. Ordinarily the Pill cannot be purchased by a customer unless she has a doctor's prescription, but in perhaps more than half of Italy's pharmacies, the Pill can be easily bought without any medical authorization. How the Vatican drug company and eight other companies got around the Italian law was quite cleverly done: the boxes of each brand, including the Vatican's product, did not indicate on the front, back or sides what was contained inside. Nor did the boxes explain what the contents were supposed to do for a woman who took them. Inside each box, however, there was a sheet of technical explanation, which to most Italians was incomprehensible. Once translated into everyday language, the sheet merely stated that the capsules were to be used by patients who had a need to regulate the menstrual cycle. It also made a point (but in the most difficult polysyllabic terminology that covered both manufacturer and dealer, should there ever be any legal action) that the contents of the package could not be used to prevent pregnancies.

Since Italy's laws made it illegal to sell such a product, the Serono company abided by the law. It registered the formula for the Pill with the Ministry of Health — but included in the formula one ingredient that was harmless and had no effect whatever on the other ingredients. This made the capsules, legally, another kind of pill but not the Pill. Here is how it worked with the Vatican Pill: the Serono pharmaceutical house had registered Luteolas with the government and received a Ministry of Health Registration Number 20984. The following formula was recorded: *3-beta, 17-beta diacetossi-17-alfa etinil-4-estrene mg 1 17-alfa etinil-estradiolo-3 metil etere mg 0.1 Eccipiente (amido lattosio, stearato di magnesio) q.b. a meg 100.*

99,999 people out of every 100,000 who read that will not make sense of it, but a trained pharmacist would know that the part in the above formula that reads, *amido lattosio, stearato di magnesio*, is an insert substance that has nothing to do with the chemical ingredients that keep a woman sterile.

What makes the contraceptive pill situation in Italy even more farcical is that most Italian citizens belong to some kind of government-sponsored medical aid program, and women who use the Pill under a doctor's care 'to cure feminine ailments' get their money back from the state treasury. So you have the situation where one Italian law prohibits the sale of the Pill and another Italian law reimburses the many women who buy it.

As for the Serono company, most Italians did not know it was backed by Vatican money. Pope Paul himself did not know it — or more likely, had not given it any thought. There is one clue for any journalist seeking to determine whether a given company is a Vatican-owned or a Vatican-controlled company: the Vatican has a policy that whenever any of its capital is heavily invested in a business enterprise of any kind, it places one of its agents — or 'men of trust' — either on the board of directors or within the upper echelons of the administration itself. These 'men of trust' come from families that are either directly related to high-ranking Vatican officials in the past —

often with a pope himself — or from families that have had a long and intimate association with the Vatican. Most often these families have members who hold titles that have been issued to them by the Vatican, such as prince, duke, count or baron, but have no real royal connection with Italy's past kings or queens. There are some 25 so-called Vatican families whose names are fairly well known.

Such was the case with the Istituto Farmacologico Serono. The Vatican 'man of trust' was Prince Giulio Pacelli whom I interviewed while I was writing assignment articles on Italy's economy for the *New York Herald Tribune* and its daughter operation in Paris, now called the *International Herald Tribune*. Before I saw Prince Giulio I wanted to make absolutely certain that Serono was indeed a Vatican company, even though the presence of Prince Giulio in the company was significant. It was never said who backed Serono, although it seemed many people knew anyway, but I wanted to hear it for myself from Serono staff.

What I did was to station myself one morning across the street from the Serono plant, located on Rome's busy Via Casilina 125, on the corner of Via del Pigneto, and waited until the coffee-break when dozens of the company's workers flooded into the coffee bar. As the workers filed in and yelled whether they wanted an espresso or a cappuccino, I was already parked at the bar with a cappuccino. In no time, I was surrounded with as many targets for my question as I needed. But my question was not, 'Is that a Vatican company across the street?' because I felt that that would arouse suspicion. Instead, I opened a conversation with an Italian man, not a difficult thing to do in Italy since Italians are probably the most sociable people anywhere in Europe and enjoy talking to an American — especially if he has fluent Italian. When I thought I had established rapport, I asked: 'How do you like working for the Pope?' This approach, I suspected, would not be thought suspicious. Anyway, I got my answer because several other Italians quickly joined the conversation: I was told in strong terms that working for the Pope was not profitable because he was a cheapskate and did not pay his workers well. All the men lamented that if they could find a job in another company that was not owned by the Vatican, they would do so immediately because they had families to support and were finding it difficult to make ends meet in inflationary Italy on their meager papal pay. I had confirmation — Serono was indeed a Vatican company.

The next target was Prince Giulio himself, the Vatican 'man of trust'. On the pretext that I was preparing a piece for the *Herald Tribune* on Italy's pharmaceutical industry with favorable references to the Serono company (a piece that indeed appeared in print under my by-line), my plan was to establish a good rapport with Prince Giulio, accumulate all current Serono data and history from him and eventually to ask him bluntly what about Luteolas, the birth control Pill, and Pope Paul's encyclical making the use of artificial contraception impossible for Roman Catholics?

Receiving me in his plush office, board chairman Pacelli spent nearly an hour giving me a statistical rundown of his company's several hundred products, of which one, ironically, was a product called Pergonal that increased fertility. He told me that the company had a payroll of 250 people who worked in a modern, automated plant measuring 8550 square meters (92,031 square feet or 10,226 square yards), had a capitalization of $1.4 million, showed a net profit of $172,000 the previous year and employed a laboratory staff that undertook research projects in the pharmaceutical sciences. When the interview had reached its professional conclusion, I gathered up my notes and papers and put them into my briefcase, getting ready to make my departure, though I had not yet posed by blockbuster question. In his most charming manner, the prince walked me to the door, and while I had my hand on the knob thanking him for his time and courtesies, I said: 'Oh, sir, I just remembered — I have still one more question to ask, if you don't mind.' He nodded graciously and waited. How did he justify a Vatican company manufacturing and selling a birth control pill called Luteolas when the Pope himself had spoken out against such products?

He blanched. The prince was taken aback but quickly managed to regain his composure. He asked me to come back into the office, and closed the door. Obviously annoyed at my indiscretion, but with a fixed smile nonetheless, Pacelli said that Luteolas was not a birth control pill. In the most complex words he could muster, with an avalanche of tautology, he said that Luteolas was a product to assist the medical profession in helping women who were having gynecological difficulties and who therefore needed to effectuate controls on their menstrual cycles so as to keep themselves in healthy regularity. There was, he said, no proof, statistical or otherwise, that Luteolas was an oral birth control capsule. Yet, he added a bit nervously, '. . . but you're not going to put *that* in the *Herald Tribune*?' I assured him it would not appear in the *Herald Tribune* (which it did not), but I never promised him that it would not appear in a book.

I did not tell Prince Giulio that before we met I had gone into 12 different pharmacies in various parts of Rome to ask about Luteolas. My modus operandi was to hold up the white box of Luteolas pills and ask for what reason did customers buy the product I was holding up. The answers I got from each of the 12 pharmacists was that 'she does not want to become pregnant' or 'she doesn't want to have a baby' or 'she needs it to remain sterile'. One assistant even went so far as to explain that the Luteolas pills, if taken once a day, would block pregnancies in more than 99 per cent of cases: he took the trouble to show me that the sheet inside the box was a menstrual chart explaining what a woman needed to know about her so-called fertile periods. Though I had not had Luteolas analyzed in a laboratory, I felt secure in the knowledge that, contrary to Prince Giulio's statement, it was indeed an anti-baby pill

Later I learned from a friend of my wife, a woman in her thirties, that she was taking Luteolas regularly. When I told her that the product was manufactured by a Vatican-owned drug company, she giggled and said, 'Well, if that's so, then Luteolas could turn out to be a very embarrassing situation for Pope Paul.' It did.

CHAPTER XXVIII

Quo Vadis, Johannes Paulus?

STILL MAKING the rounds long after his death are some anecdotes about Pope John XXIII that remain perennial favorites. One such story is the time his relatives, soon after his coronation in 1958, visited the Apostolic Palace for the first time. A papal audience is an impressive experience for most people, and John's folks were no exception. Having walked timidly through the golden halls, past the omnipresent Swiss Guards, they dropped to their knees and bowed their heads when they saw John dressed in his splendiferous pontifical white robes.

'Forget all that!' said John. 'What are you afraid of? It's only me!'

Adored, cherished, revered, admired, respected and hailed as a saint, Pope John was a pope among popes. He was a 'soft and good soul', and his rustic, paternal ways enchanted people. I recall the day when, for the first time in Vatican history, Pope John invited members of Rome's Foreign Press Club and their wives to a press reception in one of his chambers. Cynical though many foreign correspondents are, Pope John so charmed everybody that day that we could not help being impressed by this utterly *simpatico* human being. I remember vividly what my colleague, Irving R Levine — then Rome correspondent for NBC — whispered with a sheepish grin on his face: 'Nino, you know I'm Jewish, but this is one guy who could get me to change religions!' John was that kind of man.

Although a Pope may be idolized and worshipped by pious people all over the globe, inside the Vatican he is regarded more as a man than as a saintly being. His tiara can also be a crown of thorns, for behind the big Bronze Doors the office of the papacy is not without its enemies who daily surround the Pontiff. Inside the Vatican the man who holds the official titles of Bishop of Rome, Successor of the Prince of Apostles, Supreme Pontiff of the Universal Church, Servant of the Servants of God, Patriarch of the West, Primate of Italy, Archbishop and Metropolitan of the Roman Province, and Sovereign of the State of Vatican City and the unofficial titles of Rector of the World Upon Earth, the Vicar of Christ on Earth, Father of Princes and Kings, and

Pontifex Maximus is simply called *Il Papa*, a title that comes from *pater patrum*, a Latin phrase meaning father of fathers. The Italians themselves, both inside and outside the Vatican, usually call a pope by his family name — Pius XII was Papa Pacelli, John XXIII was Papa Roncalli, Paul VI was Papa Montini and John Paul II is Papa Wojtyla. No single pope in recent times has been such a draw, away from his immediate domain, as has the Pole who sits today on Peter's Chair. His public appearances both at home and abroad have attracted the biggest crowds of Catholics and non-Catholics alike in the history of the papacy. His charismatic appeal, even among the millions of people who owe him no spiritual allegiance, has made many a reporter search for new adjectives to do him justice.

When John Paul II was elected Pope and achieved instant renown, he also lost something, however. He lost his original name, he lost most of the civil ties that bound him to the country of his birth, but, most important, he lost his freedom (Pius X pointing at the Swiss Guards standing sentry once whispered to an old friend, 'There are my jailers!'). Like every other pontiff before him, John Paul found that his daily life is regulated by tradition, often to the most minute detail, and that the Curial cardinals around him run things, even though in public they may drop to their knees and bow their heads. Though judged by world opinion, while using God as the source of his authority, John Paul takes orders from his colleagues in the Curia in carrying out his complex job. Although he is one of the world's few absolute rulers, he is on the other hand one of the few absolute rulers who is ruled. Vatican propaganda from time to time conveys an image of the man who presently wears the tiara as being his own boss. John Paul is beholden to the big frogs in the Vatican pond, however, who exert a firm control upon him, while he furthers a public image of himself as a free and open pope. As the Pope he can never forget that his actions are fraught with eternal consequences for himself and his flock.

The Pope finds himself in the tricky position, moreover, of not being personally well-liked among the heavyweights in the Vatican's central government. For one thing the old Curia oligarchy is unhappy about the Pontiff's special emphasis on Polish issues and his retinue of Polish assistants. The conservative cardinals look with an unhallowed eye at Papa Wojtyla for favoring audiences with Polish pilgrims, for speaking frequently about Poland and Polish problems and for having remained a Pole, first and foremost. The Curial bigwigs resent him for this, but they recognize that hundreds of millions of faithful rate Karol Wojtyla top in any popularity poll.

Since the hub of John Paul's administration is the Curia and since its powerful Italian factions are doctrinaire in their defense of ancient bastions, the Pope is forced into a commitment toward the ecclesiastical institution of which he is the titular head. This means that, as far as vital internal Church matters are concerned, John Paul is being forced to direct Catholicism along conservative lines, undertaking, as it were, certain inquisitorial actions. It is no longer a question of whether John Paul as Pontiff is the guarantor of freedom and openness in the Catholic Church, for he is cracking down hard on the secularizing tendencies among the clergy and especially among the Jesuits. Whereas Paul VI dealt favorably with more than 95 per cent of the 33,000 requests by priests for laicization, John Paul II had not absolved a single priest from his vows up until the end of 1981.

Ever since he took office, John Paul has been on a collision course with certain scholars and theologians in Holland, the United States and Germany. Foremost among these is Rev Hans Küng who was stripped of his authority to teach Roman Catholic seminarians at the University of Tübingen in West Germany after a series of interrogations — or what his followers termed inquisition-like actions by the Pope. John Paul told Küng that however brilliant and well-intentioned he was, he did not speak with the official voice of the Roman Catholic Church.

Author of numerous books on the issue of papal infallibility, celibacy, Church structures, the virginity of Mary, historical aspects of Jesus Christ and intellectual freedom within the Church ranks, the beleaguered, progressive Swiss theologian, after the Pope's 1979 decree, told several thousand cheering supporters that he was deeply ashamed of the Church. Vowing to fight the Holy See's decision, Professor Küng wondered whether 'the darling of the masses and the superstar of the media was truly free from the closed authoritarianism as exemplified by the Church's biggest failure, Pius XII'. He rebuked Papa Wojtyla for approving 'the inquisitorial proceedings against other streams in contemporary Catholic theology — this in spite of his call for human rights outside the Church'. Küng said he seriously doubted whether this Pope from a country with a totalitarian regime would ever bring democracy to the Catholic Church, in spite of the fact that history's first Polish Pontiff is a committed, active enemy of Communism and other totalitarian regimes.

Central to Father Küng's statement is the charge that the Church has failed to act on the reforms authorized in 1965 with Paul VI's promulgation of the decrees of Vatican Council II. For this Küng blames the Curia outright. His understanding of Vatican politics is as complete as his grasp of Catholic dogma, for he lived several years within the Vatican walls (at the Germanicum College where he was ordained in 1954, following which he went on to graduate studies in London, Amsterdam, Berlin, Madrid and the Sorbonne in Paris, winning his doctorate at the age of 29).

Perhaps the reason that Vatican hardliners fear a man like Küng is that his books are easy to read and his speeches eschew polysyllabic double-talk in favor of everyday language. The Vatican is apprehensive that people will understand what he is getting at — and, if so, sooner or later that his deadly pen and nimble tongue could snowball the Küng controversy into a mass movement. Simply put, what Küng wants is Church affairs brought out into the open, brought out to the millions who support the religion; and Küng has the guts and the skill to wrangle with the 'absolutists of the Church — the Curia', which he calls the worst bureaucracy on Planet Three.

Küngian prose, delivered with optimum effect by the nattily dressed professor show an undisputed knack for bringing his message to roost: 'Can the Holy Ghost come down for just one bum decision and then fly away again?' or 'How can the man sitting on Peter's Chair worry about such things as papal infallibility when kids can't even learn the Apostles' Creed?' or 'I'm not itching for a fight — I am itching and I am fighting!' or 'Power politics in the Vatican masks itself as spiritual service!'

Given the supreme scholarship of the renegade, which he has been displaying in the classroom since 1960, and his fluency in German, Italian, French, English, Spanish, Dutch, Latin, Greek and Hebrew, the polemical prof is an intellectual giant, a formidable adversary whose name is *verboten* in the Vatican. It is known that of all his bon mots, one of Father Küng's rebellious comments particularly outraged John Paul the most. He was fit to be tied when he read the following: 'Of course the solution to the Church's problem,' Küng had said with sarcasm, 'is that we could get a new Pope. We had three in one year once. . . .'

The Küng case does not stand alone. Another articulate scholar, suspected of heresy and interrogated for his ideas on the immaculate conception, the divinity of Jesus, the infallibility of the Pope and the organizational foundation of the Church, is Rev Edward Schillebeeckx, whose book *Jesus, An Experiment in Christology*, is known to have made John Paul irate. Rev Schillebeeckx, professor of theology at the Catholic University of Nijmegen in Holland, was summoned to Rome to defend himself on nine points of alleged deviation from Church dogma. Father Schillebeeckx is on record as saying that he remains 'within the Catholic dogma and faith' but that there are differences of interpretation between him and his conservative critics. As complex as it is thorough, any attempt at summary of

Schillebeeckx's thesis (which shows exactly what early Christianity understood about the affirmation that 'Jesus is the son of man, the Son of God, the Lord') runs the risk of oversimplification, and cannot therefore be discussed here.

Of the panel of four cardinals, three were allotted three points each of the nine that Schillebeeckx has espoused to research and prepare for fully. Schillebeeckx, however, had to face the commission alone. Schillebeeckx had asked to be accompanied by Professor Bas Van Jersel, the dean of the theological department of the Nijmegen University, but the request was turned down. Professor Van Jersel was allowed, however, to sit in the next room where from time to time Schillebeeckx could consult him when given permission. Only during several coffee breaks and during lunch was Dean Van Jersel allowed to join the commission of cardinals, but no discussion on any of the nine doctrinal points at issue was permitted, nor were any questions allowed to be put by the visiting dean. The findings of the four cardinal members were sent for evaluation to the ten cardinals who are the permanent members of the Congregation for the Doctrine of the Faith (formerly known as the Holy Office), and their report, together with still another report from a second Schillebeeckx interrogation in 1980 was handed over to John Paul for review.

Although there are rebellious priests in several other parts of the world who bug the Vatican with challenging ideas, the United States has an inordinately large number of dissenters who are toe to toe with Pope John Paul. They run the gamut from scholarly Jesuits to lowly nuns in the convents who, drowned out by the deafening ovations to the first non-Italian Pontiff in modern times, are nonetheless raising questions about the papacy today and sniping at the Polish incumbent. At the forefront are three warriors who are jousting with the giants of the Church and getting, incidentally, press recognition for themselves — Rev Anthony Kosnik, co-author of *Human Sexuality: New Directions in American Catholic Thought*, Rev Charles Curran, author of *Issues in Sexual and Medical Ethics* and *Transition and Tradition in Moral Theology*, and Rev John J McNeill, author of *The Church and the Homosexual*. (See Chapters XXIX, XXX and XXXI for a more detailed treatment of some current, controversial issues plaguing the Church.)

Each of these men has raised howls from the pages of the Vatican's *L'Osservatore Romano*, a paper that Hans Küng has compared to *Pravda*. These highly vocal liberals, among others, are unanimous in their view that priests and laymen should be able to participate in the nomination of bishops and thereby bring a sense of involvement to the Church. They also believe it is one thing for Pope John Paul to win the hearts and imagination of the world by his personal magnetism, but it is another matter to apply repressive measures against the Church's best minds and Catholicism's most articulate communicators — especially since none of these people want to relinquish the cloth. Believing that the Church's crisis is one of credibility, consensus and alienation, these dissenting Americans, however independent they may be of Vatican officialdom, maintain that John Paul's aversion to discussion within the ranks is contrary to the spirit of 'collegiality', which was one of the chief fruits of the Second Vatican Council.

The Curia's stand on religious matters, as supported and carried out by John Paul II and which many Catholics consider a stain on his pontificate, continues to add oil to the papal fires.

When Professor Küng took his crusade on a lecture tour of the United States in 1963, Vatican bloodhounds dogged him from city to city; he was prohibited from speaking at the Catholic University of America; he was barred from setting foot in the archdiocese of Los Angeles; he was banned at a number of other American institutions, both Catholic and secular, as a result of commands from Rome to the local bishops, who then pressurized municipal or school officials not to let Küng speak. Father Küng did, however, manage to give a lecture to theological scholars at Georgetown University in Washington, DC.

It was on one of his trips to the United States not long ago that Küng delivered one of his most profound thoughts to subdued listeners. Immaculately dressed, the compelling orator — ever seeking to upend the hierarchal pyramid of the Church — said: 'The Curia would like to burn me at the stake as a heretic, but the twentieth century has given me a stay of execution. The Lord never gave His permission for the kind of Church government we've been getting since the third century AD when our Church left the hands of Jesus Christ.'

CHAPTER XXIX

Celibacy and *The Priest's Wife*

WHILE SHOOTING *The Priest's Wife*, a controversial 1970 film dealing with celibacy in the church and starring Sophia Loren and Marcello Mastroianni, movie director Dino Risi could not get Vatican permission to shoot a scene in any church in northern Italy. Risi headed instead for the nearby hills of Padua where he thought he would be certain to find a parish priest who had not yet heard of the film. Risi, a medical doctor and a trained psychiatrist before he took to making movies, found a perfect church in a remote wine village which was apparently still living in the sixteenth century. Or so he thought.

Risi figured he would soften up the local pastor with a large donation to the church's meager building fund, do the scene and get out of town as fast as he could before the Vatican caught up with him. To do the scene, Risi needed the pastor's permission since the sacristan could not by himself authorize it. The priest, however, not be located anywhere. The priest was away — getting married!

In *The Priest's Wife*, the issue of celibacy was subjected to deft cinematic satire. Playing the part of a Catholic clergyman, Mastroianni falls in love with a miniskirted pop singer (Loren) while counseling her about her attempted suicide. Because the priest feels his religion so deeply, he is unable to resign from the Church, nor is he able to live a lie. Both Loren and Mastroianni gave interviews to the press at the time (including separate conversations with this writer) in which they took a public stand in favor of priests not being forced to practice celibacy. Loren felt a priest should get married 'because only by being married and having a family of his own, can he understand other people's problems'; Mastroianni, indifferent to whether he was inviting excommunication by making the film, felt that when priests say they want to get married, it is not only for sexual reasons 'because they all have girl friends on the sly anyway'.

To stop the production, and later the distribution, of *The Priest's Wife*, the Vatican pulled out the big cannon. Carlo Ponti, the producer and Loren's husband — and himself an old hand at making films that irritated the Vatican — was ready, however, for such onslaughts. Soon after the film crew started work in Padua, Vatican officers paid an unexpected call on Risi, accompanied by Padua's police chief and two *carabinieri* (Italian state policemen). They made no move to stop the filming, and however much it appeared that the visitors were there to intimidate the Ponti crew, the leader of the group said they were merely interested in watching how movies were made. A likely story, thought Risi — but he decided he would be one jump ahead of his unannounced visitors and pre-empt any legal campaign on the Vatican's part.

The scene to be shot had to have a church building in the background, and as luck would have it, Risi had scheduled a clinch-and-kiss scene between Mastroianni (in his priestly garb) and Loren (in her miniskirt and tight, low-cut sweater). It was not the kind of scene designed to make conservative Church officials particularly joyous.

Risi rose to the occasion. Unknown to his distinguished visitors, he set up another camera around the corner of the church where he positioned Miss Loren (also hidden). The clerics watched stonily as 'Father' Mastroianni rushed out of the church, after finishing Mass, to trot along the side of the building. Nothing wrong or objectionable with the scene — and this is what the visitors saw done six times, take after take after take. After one of the takes, however, Mastroianni slipped unobtrusively around the corner where the second camera and the nubile Neapolitan were out of view. The two went into a clinch and the befrocked 'priest' gave her a masterful lover's kiss while cupping his hands on her buttocks. The trick worked, and the clerics went away none the wiser.

In making the film, producer Ponti was not above baiting Pope Paul VI by irking him at a personal level. Ponti hired the Pope's former cook, Armando Carzanita, who worked for Paul when he was Cardinal Montini in Milan. When the Pope heard that his one-time chef was playing the role of a cook in the movie, he registered 'grieved astonishment'. There was no doubt in his mind that Ponti and Loren, having been labeled by the Vatican as public sinners after their Mexican proxy marriage (while Ponti was in the eyes of the church still married to another woman) and having been forced to take out French citizenship to avoid bigamy charges, were making the movie for revenge. The producer and his superstar wife, on the other hand, maintained that they were making the film as a social document which they believed would have an impact on public opinion and the issue of celibacy.

As it turned out, *The Priest's Wife* was a lemon and did badly at the box office. It had no impact on the controversy of celibacy, which is still a Number One issue inside the Vatican. Should priests of the Roman Catholic order be allowed to marry is a dilemma that a committee of cardinals, convened secretly in April 1970 inside the Vatican, took up for discussion. Whatever disagreements may have existed among the princes of the Church, suffice it to say that shortly after, Pope Paul made the Church's stand quite clear when he declared publicly: 'Where preparation for the priesthood takes in an atmosphere of prayer, charity and self-humiliation, the problem of celibacy does not even arise. Young men find it more than natural to consecrate themselves to Christ in a full and total way.' The answer, Pope Paul felt, did not lie in relaxing the Latin Rite law on celibacy. The present Pope shares this view and is pursuing the same hard line on the 1600-year-old celibacy discipline. Indeed, John Paul II has decided to stake his papal authority on the issue of whether priests should marry.

From the way John Paul's opponents are lining up, both clergy and laity, the Pontiff has his hands full. The Vatican knows full well that some half a million priests, including members of the male-only religious orders, share a majority opinion that they should be allowed to marry. One reliable figure from the United States that reached the Pope's desk not long ago was that more than 60 per cent of America's priests feel that priests should be permitted to have a wife and that if such permission were granted, as many as 31 per cent would probably marry. The report also stated that nearly all of the priests in the survey wanted to remain priests.

Another survey on priests in Holland on the subject of celibacy, found that more than 95 per cent disapproved of compulsory celibacy and 81 per cent were strong in their view that married men should be able to become priests. Interestingly, 62 per cent of the respondents expressed the view that celibacy had been, in their own case, extremely beneficial. The report on behalf of the Dutch Catholic Church reminded the Vatican that during the first centuries of the Church, bishops were often married men and that Saint Paul, in his First Epistle recommended that a bishop be 'the husband of one wife'. Of special interest is that celibacy, which is entirely without scriptural warrant, was not generally enforced in the Catholic Church until more than a thousand years after the time of Christ.

Not to be confused is the difference between the vow of celibacy and the vow of chastity. As defined by Canon Law, the latter means the abstention from sexual relations, and the former the abstention from marriage. The vow of celibacy is not broken, according to Canon Law, if a priest, monk or nun engages in sexual relations. As far as the Church is concerned, the difference between the two is that forgiveness for sexual relations can be obtained by making an honest declaration in the confessional, whereas absolution for any priest who marries can only come from the Pope who, if he gave the absolution, would impose a penalty, which would probably mean the priest having to leave his wife.

What reason does the Vatican give for refusing the right of marriage to its ordained workers? Apart from theological considerations, the Vatican views marriage for priests as a danger: a married priest has a wife to love as well as his Church. He has a to meet as well as his Pope's demands, and sometimes the two may not be compatible. He has something outside the Church to occupy him, to distract him, to claim some of his time, energy, affection and passion. Above all, a married priest has an anchor outside the Church and is less likely continually to tolerate papal authoritarianism than an unmarried one. All this applies with greater force if his wife is a non-Catholic. Finally, it is felt that married priests would sap the power of the Catholic Church and drain its lifeblood, and that, by permitting marriage, the Vatican would cause its power to be diminished.

As for why priests should have the right to wed, here follows an excerpt from a letter sent to John Paul II not long ago from a British priest who announced his decision to marry a 27-year-old Malaysian woman who is a non-denominational Christian:

'We Roman Catholic priests wish to marry for one or more of many mundane reasons. A priest is in love; he wants the company of a woman; he wants to love a finite being in a finite way. Your Holiness may say that the Church and Heaven are home enough for him, but the priest is no longer satisfied with these words. He wants an earthly home in which he can withdraw physically, mentally and emotionally from the divine stamping ground; he wants a chance to be human himself, to feel earthy human passions and to indulge them. He wants to be an ordinary father as well as a spiritual one; he wants to have children, to be part of a human family and not just part of a heavenly one. He wants to experience for himself the hundred and one problems of living which he has previously experienced only vicariously in the confessional box. True, if I marry, I may also be moving away from the authoritarian control of the allegedly divine ecclesiastical power structure, but if you surrender some complete power over a man, it is better for the Church to have half power over him than none at all. The malaise that currently afflicts our Church is that we have government without the consent of the governed. . . .'

In his 1979 declaration to priests, John Paul urged them to keep their commitment to celibacy and 'not ask to be released from their vows'. John Paul made it clear that dispensations to abandon the priesthood would not easily be granted. It comes as no surprise, therefore, to discover that there are well over a thousand applications a year from ordained members of the Church who want to get married. These applications for laicization remain virtually unattended on John Paul's desk.

During the 1963–1978 pontificate of Paul VI, Vatican procedures were somewhat liberalized, and several thousand priests were released from their vows. Compare that with the years between 1914 and 1963, when about 800 priests petitioned the Vatican for laicization and only 300 or so were granted.

CHAPTER XXX

Women As Priests

It Is no secret that the Vatican is a man's world.

It is also no secret that women want to be included. But Pope John Paul II has firm views on the matter, and senior members of the Church agree that women 'should stay in their place'. This was the message the Pope imparted in October 1979 when he was greeted by Sister Theresa Kane, then president of the Leadership Conference of Women Religious, in the Shrine of the Immaculate Conception in Washington, DC. Sister Theresa requested that all Church ministries be opened to women.

Sister Theresa told John Paul, essentially that Catholicism cannot be complete unless women participate fully in the Church, since they really are a gift to mankind. She believes that although women today are not part of the institutional Church system, they have nevertheless influenced it in an unofficial, informal way — 'but we have not done it in a rational, systematic way as being full members of the Church the same as men are'.

The Pope also has reports — most of them from the United States — that Roman Catholic women are carrying out liturgies for clandestine groups of worshippers that are similar to the official Catholic Mass, in which they break bread and share wine in the name of Jesus. These liturgies are taking place in homes, apartments, mother houses and conference halls in such cities as New York, Washington, Philadelphia, Boston and Chicago. Because they are unofficial, an accurate count of the female 'clerics' and the participants is not possible, but the Vatican is aware that the numbers are increasing.

Beyond the fact that John Paul II and Paul VI both made it clear that women cannot be ordained into the priesthood, the Vatican prefers to consider the case a closed issue, ignoring whatever evidence comes in. Such evidence includes the recent discovery by a woman archeologist who reported that she took photographs of ancient mosaics, frescoes and inscriptions showing that there were female priests and bishops in the early Christian Church. Photographs taken by Professor Dorothy Irvin of the College of Saint Catherine in Saint Paul, Minnesota, show a fourth-century fresco in a Roman catacomb depicting seven women celebrating a eucharist, a fourth-century catacomb fresco in which a woman is being ordained by a bishop, numerous frescoes of women dressed in liturgical vestments and striking attitudes of liturgical leadership, and tombstone inscriptions of women bishops. Professor Irvin, who earned her doctorate in Old Testament and Ancient Near Eastern archeology from West Germany's Tubingen University, took the pictures for Tubingen's Archaeological Institute. Copies of these photos have been given to the Vatican in the hope that they would undermine papal arguments against women's ordination, on the grounds that it contradicts Church tradition of centuries past.

Of most significance, however, is the letter John Paul has from a woman who was 'called to the priesthood'. This document, which the Pope is ignoring for the present, is known to have outraged him. It is printed below with a few minor deletions:

'I am a woman. This is the story of my calling to the priesthood, ordination and first year as a priest in a Roman Catholic community in a large city on the east coast of the United States.

'But my story really began in my earliest years in school when I felt a deep desire — a call? — to celebrate the liturgy, the sacraments and the life of a priest. Some laughed good-naturedly when I expressed my hopes in my elementary school years. Some smiled in high school, wondered in college and doubted when I left for the seminary. Some sincerely believed then I had gone off the "deep end". Eventually I received my master of divinity degree. Five years later I was ordained.

'I wish I had the freedom to share with you my name, those of my friends, the location of our community with its core of several dozen worshippers. But I fear retaliation against us if I did.

'After graduating from the seminary I returned to my home diocese where I have lived for more than 30 years — a city where progress in theology and liturgy is not trusted and where women's participation in liturgy is not enthusiastically encouraged. . . . It became increasingly difficult for me to worship in my home diocese — and then one of those surprises of the Holy Spirit, one of those chance meetings, changed my life. I found there was a community worshipping in the Roman Catholic tradition with legally and validly ordained Roman Catholic priests, but where liturgies were planned by its members and participation and input by all were expected and accepted.

'I was told that the diocese does not recognize this community as a parish and even considers it illegal. In studying the community's history, I discovered that many of the reasons they were considered illegal a decade ago have now become common practice in the Church — for example, communion in the hand, women lectors, communion under both forms. Then I remembered learning that prophets are often run out of town. I decided to attend a liturgy and I experienced the pilgrim. I found tolerance, acceptance and love.

'The first time I talked with a priest from the community he apologized to me that the official Church was moving so slowly about women. I did not have to defend myself or apoligize for wanting to be ordained.

'Then came summer. Our pilgrim church meets in a beautiful grove in summers. We have an agreement that if it rains we meet at our inside location, some distance away. One thing about pilgrims, though: they come from all directions. One Sunday it happened. Wine, musicians and priests were inside. Bread, music papers, liturgy planner and most of the pilgrims were outside. After some time we decided to proceed. I saw the planner start walking toward me. Oh no! "Will you lead us?" he asked. I remembered reading that in the early Church, the one in whose home the celebration was held was the leader. "It's okay, you have the training." Oh, why didn't it rain where I lived?

'The community agreed and together we prayed the eucharist. It was a moving experience for many as we all gathered around the altar and together recited the words of consecration. Later in the day the priest celebrant heard what happened and he, along with the lay leaders, insisted I had been called.

'The next time he celebrated I could not believe the theme was liberation. He told me he had to respond to the Spirit within him and around him. He said he could not celebrate the eucharist on liberation when women are oppressed and we had the power to begin to heal the brokenness. He said he wanted me to come forward and celebrate with him. I just put my head down. But I heard clapping and people saying my name with "Go ahead!" At the altar the smiling priest with a twinkle in his eye said! "You have been called now. Any other ceremony will only affirm what has already happened."

'Almost a year of serious and prayerful deliberation followed that day. In the spring we had a summary meeting. Can and should the community call a person, a woman, to full liturgical ministry? There was no hiding the negative: who were we to ordain someone? This was going too far. It would cause loss of ties to the larger Church and a loss of members, some of whom were in this community from the very beginning and were not fearful, non-risk-takers, but this was too much. But then the "pros". It would right a wrong; justice demands it; it would express a clear idea of our view of personhood in ministry; we must return to our roots of speaking and acting prophetically while going forward to Vatican III. After grueling yet sensitive sharing, the vote was overwhelmingly, while not unanimously, Yes. I felt as if I were floating. We hugged and kissed and cried. Even those who could no longer worship with us came to me amidst their tears to make sure I would not take it personally.

'The assembled pilgrims prayed in thanksgiving that we were enabled to participate in a great deed. One prayed in thanksgiving that her son would grow up thinking it was normal for a woman to celebrate the eucharist. Still, I'm afraid. Is it really right? Did it do more harm than good to our community? Was it sinful presumption to have thought we should do this? Can an ordained minister be a secret? Would I cause scandal and disappointment to those in the larger Church who found out? Who am I to celebrate the eucharist?

'The year since then has made a difference. My questions still outweigh the answers. Am I a priest just for our community? And it is hard to be an open person and hide special things from people I love. Yet I believe I had been ordained validly. Those who said they had to leave never did return. The others believe and so do I. I have baptized, celebrated a second holy communion. I celebrate Mass regularly for our community — about once a month.

'At Christmas I volunteered to stay in the background. But the planner and the priest said that the community ordained me and we cannot go backward. Some people became believers that night.

'On my anniversary this year we celebrated our collective courage. In preparing my homily all my fears disappeared. I remembered about *chronos* and *kairos* (Greek words). *Chronos* is calibrated measured time, *kairos* is the reign of God. Our community anticipated the *kairos* by accepting the challenge to make the *not yet* an *already*, making the reign of God real in our day.

'Ordination of women will come to the larger Church. We stepped beyond time because for us "now is the acceptable time, now is the day of salvation." [*Signed*]

'PS: Please believe I thought it would be different. I would have been so much more comfortable. I was a scrupulous kid from a conservative diocese — but I realize most change in the Church occurred this way.'

CHAPTER XXXI

Homosexuality and the Church

IN AN article published by *Tempo* magazine, an Italian weekly, French writer Roger Peyrefitte — himself a declared homosexual — accused Pope Paul VI of being gay and of breaking Church rules with his sex life. Peyrefitte, the author of a 1950 book called *Saint Peter's Keys* (about alleged sexual misbehavior by Vatican prelates), claimed in his article, published in April 1976, that when Pope Paul was still Monsignor Giovanni Montini and archbishop of Milan, he had a boyfriend who was a movie actor (unnamed by Peyrefitte). Peyrefitte misfired on that one, for it was no secret in inner Church circles that Monsignor Montini had a girlfriend — not a boyfriend — before he became Pope in 1963.

Coming to his defense and extremely angered by Peyrefitte's allegations, Pope Paul — then 78 years old — addressed a crowd of about 20,000 persons in Saint Peter's Square a few days later, and without mentioning the French writer by name, said: 'We know that our Cardinal Vicar and the Italian Bishop's Conference have urged you to pray for our humble person, who has been made the target of scorn and horrible and slanderous insinuations by a certain press lacking dutiful regard for honesty and truth. We thank you all for these demonstrations of faithful piety and moral sensibility.'

Up until a short time ago, the Roman Catholic Church's policy on homosexuality among its priests, was one of 'see no evil, hear no evil'. In January 1976, in a public pronouncement on homosexuality, the Vatican referred to gay acts as 'intrinsically disordered'. The Vatican's blanket proscription against homosexuality is based on four references in the Bible, the most direct of these being a passage from the Book of Leviticus which says: 'If a man also lieth with mankind, as he lieth with a woman, both of them shall have committed an abomination: they shall sure be put to death; their blood shall be upon them.' The other passages are in Paul's letter to the Romans 1:18–32 and in I Corinthians 6:9–10 (Jesus does not mention homosexuality at all), and in Genesis 19:1–26 (the Sodom and Gomorrah story) from which the term 'sodomy' originates.

In its 21-page document, approved by Pope Paul, the Vatican advocated a more tolerant attitude towards homosexuals but harshly denounced homosexual conduct. the document, entitled a 'Declaration of Certain Questions Concerning Sexual Ethics', was published by the Vatican's Sacred Congregation for the Doctrine of the Faith (formerly the Holy Office), the highest authority after the Pope on questions of doctrine. Referring to a letter of Pope Leo IX written in 1054, the declaration stated that 'homosexuals must certainly be treated with understanding and sustained in the hope of overcoming their personal difficulties and their inability to fit into society. The culpability will be judged with prudence'. It continued: 'But no pastoral method can be employed which would give moral justification to these acts on the ground that they woud be consonant with the condition of such people. For according to the objective moral order, homosexual relations are acts which lack an essential and indispensable finality.'

The gay movement, which has gathered momentum mostly in the United States, has brought additional problems to the Roman Catholic Church, for it has known for a long time that a large number, although still a minority, of its priests are homosexuals or latent homosexuals. One such priest has assumed prominence — this is Father John J McNeill, a leader who advocates a liberalized attitude toward homosexuality on the part of the Church and who was one of the founders of Dignity, an organization for Catholic homosexual men and women. When Dignity held its first annual convention in Hollywood, California, Father McNeill was the chief speaker. Almost 200 priests attended the conference which featured a series of workshops on the relationship of the homosexual to the Catholic Church. Father Tom Oddo, who was selected as executive director of Dignity at the convention, sent a letter to every Catholic bishop and to the Vatican as one of his first duties, in which he said: 'The first mandate I have from the Dignity convention is to forward to the officers of our Church an affirmation and appeal which states our loyalty to the Church and requests the Church to meet the needs we have as gay Catholics for increased acceptance by the whole Church, bishops, priests and laity.'

In his address, Father McNeill summarized the essential points from his book, *The Church and the Homosexual*, which the Vatican had urged him not to publish. It also asked him to stop writing and lecturing on the subject until his teachings could be investigated. After two years of review, permission was granted to publish the book provided the Church's permission (*imprimi potest*) be removed from the title page. In the book, the Jesuit priest contended that homosexuality can be morally good and should be measured by the same standards of love as heterosexuality. He also argued that negative views toward homosexuality had been fostered by a misunderstanding of certain biblical texts and that the Vatican's directive had a chilling effect on the faithful's vision of the gay world. Father McNeill went on to say that the Church's attitude toward homosexuality was 'another example of structural social injustice', adding that the Church's policy was for the homosexual to become heterosexual or to observe total abstinence from all sexual expression.

No one really knows how many homosexual priests and homosexual monks and nuns there are, but this embarrassing skeleton in the Church's closet wants to come out into the open while the Vatican tries to keep its foot against the door. Essentially, bishops and religious superiors refuse to admit that a substantial number of priests, brothers and nuns are gay. Yet disturbing reports keep reaching the Vatican, both from clerics and lay sociologists. The gist of these reports, which are never commented on, state that (1) one gay priest reported that half of his ordination class was gay; (2) two Catholic counselors reported to the Vatican that from 30 to 50 per cent of priests and monks were at least latent homosexuals; (3) it is difficult to estimate the number of homosexual clerics because celibacy has prevented many from discovering their true sexual orientation; (4) another report showed that there are, proportionately, as many gay priests within the Church as there are gay persons in the general population; (5) as more and more priests are discovering and learning to be comfortable with their homosexuality, they are thinking seriously of coming out in their parishes, dioceses and religious communities but are afraid of the consequences their superiors would set into motion.

Seminaries today, acting on the Vatican's stand on homosexuality, will not accept a person who publicly acknowledges his homosexuality. This is what happened to a gay schoolteacher in his mid-twenties when he applied for admission to a religious community. Although he passed the psychological tests with honors and promised he would remain celibate because he wanted to, he made the mistake of thinking that honesty was a virtue in the Church and therefore made an admission to the order's officers that he was gay. He was rejected outright. He has brought his appeal directly to the Pope's desk, but John Paul II has not been able to countenance homosexuality in the Church or priests who want to come out of the closet.

The Pope also has on his desk a report from Holland, put out by the Catholic Council for Church & Society in the Netherlands, an official agency of the Dutch hierarchy. Not considered by any stretch of the imagination as a Church organization set to pick up the cudgels for the gay movement, the Council entitled its report, 'Homosexual People in Society' and called for the focus to be taken away from excessive sexual corruption and, instead, to an awareness that 'every human being is created by God in God's uniqueness and is loved by God . . . the ground and essence of the equality of all people, no matter what their individual differences.'

In the United States, where the gay movement is strongest and where there are about 4 million homosexuals and lesbians among the Catholic population (who are in turn a part of a much bigger gay minority), the National Conference of Catholic Bishops in 1973 issued a guide to confessor-priests on the question of homosexuality. It acknowledged arguments put forward by gays about orientation and the need for stable relationships. It went on to say: 'To these relatively new arguments the confessor should respond with firmness, showing how erroneous is the idea that each person has the right to variety in sexual expression contingent upon his sexual orientation.'

The current status quo is an uneasy one for the Vatican. Slow to concede that there is such a thing as a general gay lifestyle, the Vatican is unable to decide how Catholic parishioners would react when they discover their priest is gay or how Catholic parents would react when they learn that their kid's teacher is a professed homosexual. But the Vatican must be certain of one thing — that the gays are not going to go away.

Perhaps to offset any suspicion that John Paul II was gay or to block any eventual rumors to that effect — as happened to Paul VI — the Vatican, taking a hint from the way many governments do things from time to time, decided to 'leak' a story about Karol Wojtyla's love life before he became a priest. As a 14-year-old boy Karol developed a sentimental attachment to a Polish girl who later became a star actress in Cracow's Stary Theater. The girl was identified as Halina Krolikiewicz Kwiatkowska, now in her early 60s, by the Italian newsweekly magazine, *Panorama*, which said that the two maintained their relationship from 1934 until she married someone else in 1945. A year later Karol Wojtyla was ordained a priest.

Halina and Karol were both active in the Polish underground and were often seen together on dates. Young Wojtyla infuriated his soccer teammates because he devoted more time to Halina than he did to his soccer game. The two were also active together in semi-professional theater productions. Whether the twosome ever became engaged cannot be ascertained, especially since Mrs Kwiatkowska (now divorced from her husband who was a Polish scriptwriter) told a reporter that the only 'love' between her and John Paul II was 'a love of poetry' and 'a love for freedom'.

After the Vatican leak had spread to all parts of the world, a Vatican spokesman stepped in and denied the printed reports. He said: 'In connection to the questions posed by some journalists and reports that have been reprinted by several publications, I have been authorized to confirm that these reports are only rumors deprived of any foundation.'

CHAPTER XXXII

Taboo Art Works

FROM HIS office in the thirteenth-century Palazzio Vecchio, Piero Bargellini, the mayor of Florence, peering out of his window at the rising flood waters mixed with crude oil, grease, mud and excrement that swirled around the ankles of the enormous reproduction of Michelangelo's David in the historic Pizza della Signoria, sweated as he desperately tried to get a phonecall through to the director of the nearby Uffizi Palace, the most important Renaissance museum in the world.

Outside, the November 1966 flood tossed cars about like toys and ripped apart thousands of homes, stores and buildings, while it engulfed the hundreds of priceless statues, frescoes, canvases, books and manuscripts in Florence. Before the height of the Arno River flood, when contact with the outside was still possible, Mayor Bargellini had received from the Vatican a high priority phonecall. Concerned as it was about Florence's valuable art treasures, the Vatican was apparently equally concerned about Florence's other art treasures, the hidden art works of special interest and concern to the Pope and Vatican officialdom that were stored in the cellar of the Uffizi — and concerned that they would suddenly come out into the open. Though the mayor was fewer than 50 yards (45 meters) away from the Uffizi, he could not get a wire through — nor could he go to the Uffizi in person since the gushing waters in the square had already isolated his headquarters, preventing any outside mission even if that mission was of prime importance to the Vatican.

Both the Vatican and Mayor Bargellini could have rested easy, for Dr Maria Becherucci, the chief conservator of the Uffizi, had already gone into action. Working feverishly as the water filled the cellars and flooded the ground floor, Professor Becherucci and her small staff managed to evacuate the lower rooms where the museum's archives, works in restoration, photographic negatives and 'other' art had been placed in permanent storage. It was this other art that was of vital concern to the Vatican.

Although the famed Uffizi Palace has 42 rooms upstairs crammed with masterpieces (all of which were in fact saved), Florentine and Vatican officials gave a quiet sigh of relief that the city's 'other' art, kept under lock and key by order of the Italian government (acting on a Vatican request), had not been washed out of storage into the open. It would not do at all for anyone to glimpse this 'other' art, masterpieces by great artists that the public was not supposed to look at. Even more threatening was that photographers might take pictures before the art works were finally hidden away again, to enjoy a seclusion it had already enjoyed for centuries.

Some experts estimate that Italy's 'other' art masterpieces are worth about $40 million. Although the sale of the creations could doubtless balance either Italy's budget or the Vatican's budget, there is not the slightest chance that they will ever be put up for sale or auction. It is safe to say — barring another calamity like the Arno overflow — that these art works will never see the light of day. These are works that have been classified by the Vatican, and at Vatican behest legally classified by the Italian government, as 'unfit for human observation' — in spite of the fact that many of them were produced by masters such as Michelangelo, Raphael, Da Vinci, Titian and Tintoretto. Although Italy's guide books never list which painters and sculptors went 'too far' with what subjects, the taboo masterpieces depict scenes with a sexual element, and invariably involve certain of Christendom's most revered heroes and heroines.

'That sex should be mixed with art should not come as any special surprise,' Dr Fausto Bonato, one of Italy's top art critics told me. 'Artists, after all, are human beings who combine talent with a compulsion for presenting the world as they recognize it. Since artists share as many quirks as the rest of mankind, it would be indeed strange, if they did not from time to time devote themselves to depicting some of the more erotic aspects of life.'

What the Vatican is particularly uptight about is the realism with which Renaissance painters captured certain biblical scenes concerning the torture of Christ and the saints and apostles. Most of these have had to be withdrawn permanently, under Vatican pressure and lobbying — as have various sadistic portrayals of Christ being flogged, Saint Cecilia having a stiletto plunged into her breast and Saint Sebastian suffering martyrdom as he stands affixed to a column with his body and private parts punctured with arrows. (A number of Saint Sebastian paintings are on public exhibit, but none show his genitalia wounded with an arrow.)

Italy's Renaissance period produced an impressive lineup of great masters who were to produce their share of works that have remained for the most part unseen by the public. One of the best of these is a collection of pagan frescoes that the great painter Raphael and his most gifted pupils did for Cardinal Bernardo Bibbiena's bathroom on the third floor of the Vatican in 1516. Rarely mentioned in Vatican artbooks because so few people have seen them, the forbidden frescoes are of mythological themes which show the Goddess Venus, Cupid and Adonis. One of the panels — which appears not to have been done by Raphael himself and which pays scarce homage to Christianity — is a seduction study of Vulcan and Pallas in which the former, clearly intent on what he is doing, is stroking the covered genitalia of the latter, to her surprise but not to her objection. These paintings were made at the request of Cardinal Bibbiena after his apartment had been damaged by fire. The cardinal, known and admired at the time of Pope Julius for some risqué plays he had written, made his own choice as to what the fresco panels should portray, and Raphael — who was then engaged to Cardinal Bibbiena's great-niece, Maria (who died before they could marry) — carried out the commission. Although access to the Bibbiena bathroom is always officially discouraged, the great Bernard Berenson, the respected art historian who lived most of his life in Florence, once saw the prohibited Raphaels and described them as true masterpieces of Renaissance art. Privately, he bemoaned the fact that the world would never be able to see them, but he did not condemn the Vatican for keeping them under wraps.

When Michelangelo's Last Judgment was first unveiled in the Sistine Chapel in 1551, Pope Paul IV did not like what he saw, especially the most conspicuous genitalia on some of the figures. He would have preferred to have had the entire fresco completely covered up on a permanent basis but was prevailed upon to come up with a compromise. Accordingly, he commissioned painter Daniele de Volterra to put clothes on many of Michelangelo's nude figures, a fact that earned for him the amusing sobriquet, *Il Braghettone* — the breeches-maker.

The Vatican, which has long evidenced displeasure at any nudes depicting important female personages in its history, keeps padlocked a fifteenth-century painting by an anonymous artist which describes the legend of a saint known as Liberata. She is unclad, but she sports a beard which, according to the legend, a miracle enabled her to grow so that her sex was masked and her virginity preserved.

Cruelty to women in art is not found in profusion, but of the few examples in existence, Italy itself and the Vatican, too, believe them to be indelicate and repugnant to the senses. One famous frieze of a Greek warrior in combat grabbing an Amazon by the hair preparatory to plunging his blade into her chest has for years been able to public view after Church officials had it banned. A similar fate befell a statue called *Dying Amazon*, who with her bared right breast pierced, is lying prostrate after she has fallen wounded in battle. For years this statue was kept hidden, and soon after it was finally put on display at the University of Rome, it was put back into storage as a result of Vatican pressure.

Perhaps the most well-known statue of a nude — which has been covered, uncovered, covered again and uncovered yet again — is the one greeting visitors who enter the front hall of Rome's princely Borghese Gallery. This is the statue of Napoleon's favorite sister, Pauline Bonaparte. Pauline in her state of *puris naturalibus* so upset the Nazis occupying Rome that they ordered it covered with a tarpaulin during the war. This was not, however, the first time, for Napoleon's younger sister had remained sheltered under a bedsheet and hidden in the basement, at Vatican insistence, 'prudently concealed from the knowledge of the vulgar', until 1902 when the Italian government bought the Borghese art collection for museum purposes.

The history of this statue goes back to 1809 when Pauline went to the studio of Italy's great Neoclassic sculptor Antonio Canova, whose gifted hands had a way of turning marble into warm human flesh, and explained she had something ambitious in mind. What she wanted was a full-length study of herself coiffed and dressed as 'Venus Triumphant', reclining on a couch and holding an apple, as a symbol of love, between the thumb and forefinger of her left hand. Canova agreed. With no qualms about posing in the nude, Pauline refused to substitute a professional model during the long sittings. When the work was first exhibited, it created a scandal even in those uninhibited times. The Church squawked — and squawked loudly. Her husband was of the same view, while his staid family flipped their royal wigs at the life-like statue. As soon as Pauline went back to France, the family hid the marble figure in the cellar, with Vatican officials giving their full approval.

Another common erotic theme is the Twelve Labors of Hercules. Florence's Palazzo Vecchio has a series of statues by Vincenzo de Rossi depicting the Great Man in various poses which show not only his strength but his masculine prowess. Two of the statues lining the huge concert salon of the Palazzo are particularly noteworthy for their erotic message — *Hercules Punishing Queen Hippolyte* and *Hercules and Diomedes*. In the latter statue, of the two strong men wrestling, the upside-down Diomedes seems to have Hercules at a tentative disadvantage in a grip you never see in jujitsu manuals. For years the Vatican has sought, unsuccessfully, to get these two particular items stored out of sight. The Vatican scored a victory, however, regarding another of De Rossi's sketches, in which he conceived Hercules' *Thirteenth Labor*. The sketch was never made into a statue, and it shows Hercules about to have intercourse with a voluptuous woman. Scattered around are about a dozen obviously spent females and another dozen waiting their turn.

The issue of obscenity in art is still a highly controversial one. Whether nudity can be considered sinful is something on which neither the artists themselves, the general public nor government officials have ever been quite clear. The Vatican, however, is convinced it knows; it has set its own standards and zealously seeks to maintain these standards, succeeding in getting its way, at least in Italy, more often than not. Consider the case of a rarely mentioned work by Michelangelo: it is a canvas of the Greek Queen Leda engaged in coitus with a big white bird; chances are good that no one alive will ever have a chance to see this masterpiece, as long as the Vatican has its way. This is the case, too, with the multiple number of paintings and statues which show Jesus naked. As can be determined, not one of these works is visible anywhere in Italy because of the Vatican's feelings on the subject. Another subject that is not allowed, thanks to Vatican intervention, is any art work which depicts a naked or nearly naked Jesus on the Cross — especially if the figure is not that of a man but of a woman. There are at least 50 such works.

Dr Fausto Bonato, commenting on Vatican interference in art, has this to say: 'Agreed, that no nude, however abstract, should fail to arouse in the spectator some vestige of erotic feeling, even if it be only the faintest shadow. If it does not do so, it is bad art and false morals. The desire to grab and be united with another human body is so fundamental a part of our nature that our judgment of what is known as "pure form" is inevitably influenced by it; and one of the difficulties of the nude as a subject for art is that these instincts cannot lie hidden, as they do for example in our enjoyment of a piece of pottery. Even so, the amount of erotic content which a work of art can hold is very high. The Vatican fails to understand this. . . .'

CHAPTER XXXIII

The Subject Of Christ

CONTRARY TO what the millions of Roman Catholics throughout the world might believe about Christ and the Vatican, the subject of Christ in the Vatican is not a popular one. There is even an inept joke about Christ inside Vatican City to the effect that if He ever came back to Earth and paid a call on the Vatican, he would be thrown out.

By and large, the subject of Christ is avoided in the Vatican. And if there were some new information to be made public about Christ, the Vatican would apparently be the last to make the announcement. There are currently seven such items that the Vatican is wrestling with but it will probably not be making any comment.

1 Was Christ already dead when taken down from the Cross? Although the Catholic religion and the other Christian religions steadfastly maintain that Jesus died on the Cross, the Vatican has in its possession a report which suggests, with some scientific evidence, that Christ was still alive when taken from the Cross. While he was still breathing, the report states, His body was wrapped in a sheet and placed in the Holy Sepulcher. The International Foundation for the Holy Shroud of Zurich has told the Vatican that blood stains on the cloth used to wrap the body contradict Gospel reports 'because a dead body would not have bled to the extent that the blood stains on the Shroud indicate'.

The Foundation maintains that the stains show that although Christ had apparently stopped breathing on the Cross, His heart was still beating. If the heart had stopped beating, the bleeding would also have stopped and there would be no stains from fresh blood on the Shroud 'because dead people do not bleed'. Having spent approximately $150,000 investigating the cause of Christ's death, the Swiss organization disagrees with the generally held conclusions that the Roman centurion's spear brought on the death of Christ. The Vatican has been told that the spear that entered the body at a 29-degree angle did not cut into the heart but penetrated the lung instead. The heart was still beating when Christ was entombed. If it is true that Christ was alive when brought down from the Cross, the Resurrection therefore never took place since Jesus might have been alive when he walked out of the tomb.

2 What was the medical cause of Christ's death on the Cross?

A distinguished French medical doctor on the surgical staff of the Saint Joseph Hospital in Paris, Dr I Barbet, took a special interest in the details of Jesus's death on the Cross and over a period of 20 years studied photographs of the Shroud in Turin's Cathedral showing the four nail holes, the flagellation cuts, the thorn marks from the crown, the spear wound and the sweat and dirt stains. In a private report to the Vatican, Dr Barbet — a devout Roman Catholic — said: 'Christ apparently died of suffocation while crucified. He was unable, after a short while, to breathe in because His lungs had become so inflated with air that He could not exhale. The respiratory mechanism having reached full capacity intake and being powerless to let this air out, Christ died of suffocation.'

The report goes on to explain the phenomenon. A person hanged by his hands or wrists suffers from a certain kind of anatomical stricture. The muscles of his arms and his trunk undergo contraction during the first stage. Shortly thereafter, the breathing mechanism becomes restricted. The two sets of muscles that control the intake and the exhalation of air contract to a point where they no longer can function properly. Because the 'inhaling muscles' are stronger than the 'exhaling muscles', and therefore break down more slowly, the lungs take in more air than can be expelled. After the exhaling muscles cease functioning completely, the inhaling muscles still function partly. Eventually, the victim has so much air in his system that respiration is impossible. This is what happened to Christ on the Cross, Dr Barbet stated, who added that the nails holding up Christ's arms were not hammered into His palms but into the wrists. The evidence shows that the delicate bones in Jesus's palms would never have been strong enough to hold His Body on the Cross.

3 How tall was Jesus Christ?

To this question one of Italy's top sculptors and a distinguished expert on anatomy, Professor Lorenzo Ferri, devoted some 40 years of his life in dedicated scientific research which he turned over to the Vatican. Confident that he had come by the correct answer, Professor Ferri believed that most historians, as well as the Vatican, were wrong on a few counts, including Jesus's physical size. Although of the Semitic race, Jesus was quite unlike His fellows who tended to be slight of build and short of stature; therefore, among His people, Christ was a giant in more ways than one. In his statement to the Vatican, the septuagenarian researcher claimed that the Man of Nazareth who was crucified at Golgotha stood at 6 feet 1 inch (1.8 meters) and was sturdily built. The basis of Ferri's contention was the Shroud in Turin. Working from photographic enlargements of small sections of the stained piece of material, Ferri was able to transfer the imprints on the cloth to a large strip of transparent plastic. From the plastic imprints he fashioned a wooden piece of sculpture which showed the face and body of Christ with the myriad wounds, cuts, lash marks and abrasions. Together with his knowledge of anatomy and sculpture, and the clues he got from staging the crucifixion in his studio with a live model, Ferri's scientific calculations determined that Jesus was over six feet tall.

'The Biblical version of Christ's death on the Cross is substantially correct,' Professor Ferri reported to the Vatican. 'However, we discovered some other things. Jesus's arms were pierced by a nail driven through the wrist and the other by a spike driven through the hand. A nail was driven through one of His feet twice. Christ's shoulder was dislocated when one of His executioners yanked His left arm.' Ferri made two other discoveries that negate previous theories. Christ's right foot had two holes in it, which led the professor to deduce that a spike had been hammered through it and then pulled out so that another spike could be hammered through both feet at the same time. As for the flagellation, Ferri advised the Vatican that Christ must have been flogged by a cat-of-three-tails and not by ordinary whips.

His report continues: 'The thickness of the blood stains also indicates beyond any doubt that Christ did not hang only from the spikes. There had to have been a support of some sort, either some kind of wooden shelf under his feet or a wooden bar at the crotch. My studio stagings show over and over again that Christ would have suffocated to death because the lungs, under the weight of His own body, would not have been able to take in any air within two minutes.'

Ferri concluded: 'My study, to which I have devoted 40 years of my life, is about the body of a man that has been taken down from a cross after a certain period of crucifixion. I cannot say from my studies if the Shroud is authentic or not — but if the Shroud is indeed authentic, then the man whose crucified body I have studied for all these years is Jesus Christ.'

4 Did Christ die of a ruptured heart?

This is another medical report on Christ's death that keeps the Vatican in a dilemma. Way back in 1847 an English physician proposed a theory on Christ's death to the effect that He died of a ruptured heart. Not until late in 1978 did the Vatican receive a report from one of its own scholars, Rev Giuseppe Toscano (a doctor), that the Englishman's theory was correct. Father Toscano, basing his theory on Gospel accounts of the death of Jesus and on accounts of what happened earlier in the Garden of Gethsemane, reported that the accounts coincide with what is known as an ischemic infarction. This is a spasm of a heart artery when a person is under great stress, as Christ was on the Cross, resulting in a weakening of a part of the heart from a loss of oxygen.

Father Toscano also stated that when a victim of crucifixion dies, the muscles become rigid from lack of oxygen; neck muscles become stiff and cannot bend. 'But Saint Luke says Christ cried out in a great voice and then I understand His head slumped forward and He died. If Christ had died from asphyxiation, His head could not have moved from the rigid upright position.' He added that Christ suffered a heart attack during the night, because, as the Gospels noted, Christ sweated profusely, suffered from a great fear of dying, and hardly spoke. This description is typical of a person who has had an ischemic infarction. Its victims have a sense of impending death and usually find it too painful to speak.

In his report to the Vatican, Father Toscano said that Christ's anguished cry at the moment of death, and the fact that his head pitched forward comprise 'the perfect description of a heart rupture'. Christ's agony 'was so fatiguing that under the pressure his heart ruptured at the weak point caused by the ischemic infarction'. The priest goes on to say that after a Roman centurion pierced Christ's side with a lance, blood and water came out. 'What happened was that in the some three hours after he died, blood from the ruptured heart had flowed into the heart cavity; the red and white corpuscles had been deposited on the bottom while the plasma floated above it. Plasma looks very much like water. Thus when the spear pierced the heart cavity, it looked as if blood and water were coming out, and this is why the Gospel made this description.'

5 On which day of the week did Christ die?

Thursday, not Friday. The Vatican is sitting on a report from an emeritus professor of physics at the University of Tennessee, Dr Roger Rusk, who using a computer, deduced that Christ died on

April 6, AD 30. The deduction would mean that Jesus lay in the tomb three whole days, as He had foreseen, instead of the 36 hours supposed in Church tradition. Dr Rusk says, however, that the movements of the moon did not provide the occasion for it at that time.

In making his assessments, Rusk used tables of new and full moons from 1001 BC to AD 1651, calculated on a complex computer in use at the Princeton Institute of Advanced Studies. These new tables provided the first exact sequence of new moons by which dates were set by Judaism in the time of Christ. The Jews lived by a lunar calendar. Since Jesus died on an afternoon before the sunset beginning of Passover, just what day it was hinges on when Passover started that year and that, in turn, depends on the time of the new moon. In the deductions Professor Rusk noted that Passover begins on the fourteenth day of the Jewish month of Nissan, the start of which is determined by the spring new moon. The new tables show that Nissan 14 came on Thursday only in the year AD 30 in the general span of years when the Crucifixion could have occurred.

6 Which language did Christ speak?

For several decades the Vatican has been toying with the idea of making an official announcement that the language Christ used was not Hebrew but Aramaic. No Catholic Church anywhere has ever given a service in Aramaic — though the Vatican's semi-official daily newspaper occasionally runs an essay in Aramaic. One issue of the Sunday magazine section not long ago described the dialogue between Jesus and Governor Pontius Pilate and said that while Pilate questioned Jesus mostly in Latin, though posing several questions in Greek, too, Jesus replied in Aramaic through the aid of an interpreter.

The mother tongue of Jesus and His disciples, Aramaic was also the language used to preach the Sermon on the Mount. The Old Testament books of Daniel and Ezra were written originally in Aramaic, as was the New Testament Gospel of Saint Matthew. Other portions of the Old Testament (for example, Jeremias, Esther, Tobias and Judith) were written in Aramaic. Today the only place in the world where Aramaic is still heard is in a small Syrian settlement of about a thousand people living in the hills outside Damascus.

Vatican linguists are of the view that Aramaic is not particularly beautiful to listen to. It has a large number of guttural sounds, sentences are usually long and repetitious, emphatic word endings replace the definite article, and there are no possessive pronouns. In spite of this, an Aramaic sentence often requires many more words when translated into another language — for instance, 'Our Father, which art in heaven', is said in two Aramaic words, *Abhinu shebbashamayim.*

Related to Phoenician, Hebrew, Arabic and Assyro-Babylonian, Aramaic is a Semitic language. In Jesus's time it was the popular idiom of Palestine. Although Jews of the first century read the Scriptures in Hebrew, they always used Aramaic to converse with friends and business associates. The language flourished from about 700 BC to AD 700, and was first spoken in Arama (now Syria). It gradually replaced Phoenician and Hebrew in the Middle East, as the language spread by traders and diplomats. After the seventh century, when Islam's armies swept out of the Arabian desert and conquered a world that spread from India to Spain, Arabic became the popular speech and the Aramaic faded away.

Papal philologists will point out that Aramaic is not a dialect of Hebrew, even though Aramaic employs the same alphabet symbols used for Hebrew. Phonetically, Aramaic is different in that it favours the 'a' vowel and certain consonants. Vatican scholars are convinced that Christ also knew some Hebrew which he learned from His mother. Mary taught Him the Old Testament stories in Hebrew. There is also some evidence that Christ had a smattering of Greek. Jesus was apparently familiar with the Septuagint Old Testament, the pre-Christian Greek version of those books.

Whatever language Jesus used in His time, millions have known the meaning of his words, for He spoke in a voice that will be heard forever by people of all languages.

7 Did Jesus have any siblings?

Without any doubt the prime subject to be avoided inside the Vatican is anything that even hints at the possibility that Christ had a brother or sister or that there were other children in the family of Joseph and Mary. The question of whether Jesus was an only child is one that popes and priests, in the past and today, never refer to in public; yet the Scriptures give sufficient evidence that Jesus did indeed have four brothers and at least two sisters, all of whom were born after Him . Only the brothers are named by Matthew (13:54–56) — also by Mark (6:3) — and they are listed as James, Joseph, Simon and Jude. Jesus's sisters are not cited by name anywhere but are mentioned by Mark (6:3) in the plural. Two of the books of the New Testament were written by Jude and James, and the latter became the leader of the church in Jerusalem and presided at the Jerusalem Council (Acts 15:13, 19). Catholic clerics do not give recognition to Psalm 69 in which Christ says: 'I am become a stranger unto my brethren, and an alien unto my mother's children.' Scholars who have researched this subject make it clear that the Vatican went beyond the Scriptures and established a doctrine to safeguard the purity of Mary. The doctrine of the Immaculate Conception was set forth by Pope Pius IX in his papal bull of December 8, 1854, *Ineffabilus Deus*, which reads as follows:

'We declare, pronounce and define that the Most Blessed Virgin Mary, at the first instant of her conception, was preserved immaculate from all stain of original sin, by the singular grace and privilege of the Omnipotent God, in virtue of the merits of Jesus Christ, the Saviour of mankind, and that this doctrine was revealed by God, and therefore must be believed firmly and constantly by all the faithful.'

Parallel with the doctrine that Mary was born without sin, there developed a Vatican stand that gave Mary the attribute of impeccability, that she did not commit sin at any time during her life. Augustine, considered the leading theologian of the ancient Church, opposed the idea of immaculate conception, as did Thomas Aquinas, another great teacher of the Church, who subscribed to the belief that while Christ did not contract original sin, 'the blessed Virgin did contract original sin but was cleansed therefrom before her birth'. So strong was Aquinas's opposition to the hypothesis that it became a point of honor throughout the Dominical Order to oppose the premise as theologically untenable. The Franciscans, however, supported the idea, as did the Jesuits later on, who made it one of their special theses. When the bickering between the Dominicans and the Franciscans became so fraught that it threatened to alienate the two orders and the ecclesiastic barometer had begun to show its low opinion of the Church, Pope Sixtus IV stepped into the controversy in the fifteenth century and, without deciding the issue in favor of one side or the other, forbade further discussion on the subject.

CHAPTER XXXIV

Vatican Politics Make Strange Bad Fellows

POLITICS MAKE strange bedfellows — but international politics, as played by the Vatican, make even stranger bad fellows. Pope John Paul II's visit to Poland is a case in point. Himself an open enemy of Communist, the former Cardinal Karol Wojtyla visited Cracow in June 1979, as well as other places in Poland, not so much as a former citizen who was homesick but as the leader of Roman Catholicism's millions, of whom about 50 million live in Eastern Europe. It is not known whether the first Polish Pope in history visited his native land for political reasons or on account of unfinished Church business to be conducted with the government in Warsaw.

Whatever his motives, John Paul II's visit was approved neither by Poland's leaders nor by Moscow. After his first request to be present for the feast of Saint Stanislaw had been refused, the regime of Edward Gierek proved more cordial and extended him a 'warm invitation' — but not before Warsaw had consulted Moscow over the problem of how to handle this eminent guest. Brezhnev and his colleagues reckoned that Poland would be the loser both ways: if it blocked the Pope's visit, Poland's image would be tarnished (this was well before Solidarity came to the forefront of attention); if it admitted the Pope, Poland's image would still be tarnished. By admitting him, however, Poland would be hurt less, since most Poles would welcome the Pope.

As it was, Warsaw resisted the Pontiff's intentions to visit to Poland in mid-May, 1979, when John Paul sought to attend the 900th anniversary of the death of Saint Stanislaw, the patron saint of Poland who, as Stanislaw Szczepanowski, was beheaded because he opposed the totalitarian rule of King Boleslav the Bold. Stanislaw is considered by the Polish people to stand for the rights of man, but the Communist leaders do not share such respect for him. They have always labeled him as a 'Polish traitor' on the grounds that he betrayed his people by soliciting help from a German emperor.

On two previous occasions Warsaw turned down visas for Pope Paul VI (who, incidentally, spoke fluent Polish, as a result of the years he had served in Warsaw as the Vatican's nuncio). In 1966 and then again in 1976, Paul VI was refused permission to enter Poland, because party bosses were apprehensive that a papal visit would bring out the populace in such overwhelming proportions that the national regime and Communism in general would have sustained a good kick in the shins. Having succeeded in blocking one pontiff twice, Warsaw tried it again in 1979 and managed to keep the Pole in the Vatican away from Poland on the dates he originally wanted — May 13, 14 and 15, 1979. Warsaw had hoped that John Paul the Second, once rebuffed, would not even try to visit Poland at a later date, but well-practiced in the art of defying a totalitarian state, he knew all the chess moves. And by moving a few bishops he got the jump on Warsaw.

Behind the Polish visit was John Paul's determination to continue his predecessor's so-called *Ostpolitik*, which the Holy See had been pursuing already for 15 years or so. Headed by the then 'Papal Kissinger', Archbishop Agostino Casaroli, now a cardinal and the Vatican's Secretary of State, the Holy See's *Ostpolitik*, essentially, had been seeking to establish a *modus operandi* between the extreme points of view of Communism and the social and political views at the other end of the spectrum held by the Catholic Church. This meant that the Vatican had been observing a policy of playing down the points of disagreement and playing up the points of agreement between the diverse philosophies. Some observers might have called this an 'accommodation', while some would call it 'competitive co-existence'.

Although popes have for a thousand years followed policies that smacked of 'thinking in centuries', the man currently occupying the Throne of Saint Peter shows no such tendency, and, in fact, while he was the Cracow archbishop, he sometimes became critical of the Vatican on this score. More down to earth on social issues than most recent popes, John Paul talked with Polish officialdom on matters that were close to his heart while he served in Cracow: the Holy Father wanted the Gierek regime to give legal recognition to the Church, to guarantee employment equality for believers, to put an end to atheist teaching in the schools and to give the Church permission to broadcast daily and publish a newspaper. Though a dialogue was begun, the Vatican talks were stalled when Solidarity moved in.

Prime Minister Gierek was painfully aware that the Church was the only opposition party in Poland, albeit it did not call itself a political party and maintained its ecclesiastical image at all times. On several occasions the Church supported various of Warsaw's social measures, thereby , ironically saving Gierek's neck. This strange working relationship in which Communism and Catholicism could never fundamentally agree and yet 'cooperated' with each other, may sometimes be incomprehensible to foreigners. Although he despised Catholicism, Gierek needed the Church's support and reluctantly solicited its help from time to time while he was prime minister, and the Church responded in exchange for small concessions.

Since 93 per cent of the 33 million Poles were baptized in the Catholic Church, Premier Wojciech Jaruzelski running Poland today does not have an easy job dealing with the clergy, especially when one of them is a charismatic 'trouble-maker' such as Cracow's last cardinal. When Wojtyla was elevated to the papacy late in 1978, the big shots in Warsaw were frankly glad to get rid of him. The last thing the regime expected was the Pope's return.

CHAPTER XXXV

Halo With Horns — The Vatican and the Mafia

LONG CONSIDERED something the archeologist dragged in with his shovel, the largest island in the Mediterranean (once a kingdom in its own right) is 10,027 square miles (25,965 square kilometers) of inferiority complex. Glance at the map and take a look at this schizophrenic seagirt speck, noted for its dubious reputation of exporting gangsters to the United States, and you will note that the toe of the Italian Boot seems to be giving it a good swift kick. Such is Sicily.

Sicily is a world and a way of life apart from anything. It is the backwash of the Mediterranean where people live stagnation lives. In this human morass the Vatican has a formidable stake, that is part of its checkerboard of international interests, a fact that ofttimes enables the clergy to become the strange bedmate of the Mafia. In Sicily it is the Mafia which has final approval on who will be put up for office on the Christian Democratic ticket. This is not to imply that the Vatican has no say on who runs: men seeking office as Christian Democrats usually require a favorable nod from the Vatican, but a candidate cannot even enter Sicily's political arena until the Mafia has given him firm approval. If the Mafia rejects someone who has received Vatican approval, he wisely withdraws. This rarely happens, however, because the Mafia and the Vatican collaborate in advance, discussing at secret conferences which men are 'qualified'. Once in office, such a parliamentarian will do the bidding of both his supporters with puppet-like obedience.

Postwar Italy has been rife with major problems, of which any number derive from Mafia activities; kidnappings and assassinations are among those to have made the newspaper headlines in recent years. Not all of the Vatican's dirty linen has been washed in printer's ink, and a notable omission is the Church's close connection with the Brotherhood in Sicily. It can only be said that because of the position and prestige of both the Vatican and the Mafia, newspapermen in Italy (foreign correspondents included) have treated the Roman Catholic hierarchy with a degree of awe and respect.

The complicity between the Vatican's political party, its Christian

Democratic leaders and its organizers in Sicily and the Mafia is demonstrated with well-documented examples, few of which ever make the headlines of the foreign press (especially in the United States and Canada). The monopolists, the owners of vast land-holdings, the North Italian holding companies (some of which are owned or partially owned by the Vatican), and the Banco di Sicilia are all partly responsible for the prevailing state of things in Sicily and for the preservation of conditions favorable to the Mafia. The Christian Democrats govern Sicily, and the Mafiosi are the ones who vote in their districts and intimidate the opposition, especially the Communist Party. Cabinet members in Sicily are not averse to being seen in public with Mafia leaders who seek to displace uncooperative public officials. The Sicilian Mafia keeps as its primary goal the infiltration of all important government bureaus, both in Sicily's regional government administration and in Rome itself within the federal government structure so that its power continues unabated with the benefit of inside information at all levels.

This applies to national politics of course, in which the Church has a major stake, since it had been the power behind the Italian government for at least 35 years when the Christian Democratic Party was formed and took office. In local matters relating to Sicily, there is another group of Mafiosi — mostly families with power — some of which concern themselves with the sale of agricultural and horticultural products, while others deal with the slaughtering of animals, the letting of arable or pasture land, or the kidnapping of well-to-do people for huge ransoms. These families avoid clashing with each other, and so there is a dichotomy of power and interest in the wholesale fruit and vegetable markets, meat markets, flower markets, flour and bread markets in which — through threats, random gun shots, kidnapping and even murder — enforcement is maintained.

Sicily's Mafiosi, through support from the Church — but not any direct help, it should be acknowledged — having infiltrated regional governments, have a hold on public contracts and can extract a percentage from the activities of Sicily's new industrialization. At election time their collaboration is considered indispensable, and candidates will do anything to secure it. While the old, peasant-type Mafiosi have all but moved out of the picture, today's Sicilian Mafiosi are well-dressed, well-educated, slick, middle-class men (no women permitted in the hierarchy, either) who are well-versed in muscling in on business deals, organizing protection rackets and raking in millions in kickbacks.

It is no secret to anyone in Italy that the Mafia control the Sicilian vote. In the four Mafia-infested provinces of western Sicily where the Mafia is at its strongest (there is no Mafia in Sicily's East or in the cities of Catania and Siracusa), hardly a town exists where a candidate could win an election without the endorsement of the local capo-Mafia even after he has won approval from his local priest or bishop. These candidates, incidentally, could win an election without even making a single campaign speech — and in a number of cases that is exactly what has happened. One Christian Democrat member of Italy's Chamber of Deputies has not made a single campaign speech to his constituents in Sicily and yet he is re-elected every time. His only campaign is to be seen in Sicily with one of the top Mafiosi at a public function. Everybody gets the message. . . .

The one factor that ensures the corruption in Sicily is poverty. Keeping the majority of the Sicilians poor is part of the Church's overall strategy, which is supported by the Mafiosi who stand to profit from such conditions. Being poor in Sicily, having to make a living where not enough jobs exist, is to live a nightmare that many foreigners know practically nothing about. My friend Danilo Dolci (about whom more later) has explained in great detail some of the ways poor Sicilians earn enough to buy bread for their kids: there are men who are known as *panerare* who wait outside large villas hoping to carry a baron's parcels for a tip; there are people who are called *munnezzare* who collect horse manure from Palermo's streets and peddle it as fertilizer; there are street magicians who do tricks for people who will toss them a coin; there are women who walk the streets renting leeches for bloodletting; there are one-man lottery sales people who for a small coin sell you a chance on a basket of groceries; there are fire-eaters and story-tellers who entertain street gatherings for coins; there are people who specialize in queuing at government offices to pick up legal documents for other people; there are people who pick up cigarette butts, dumping the tobacco into a paper bag to be sold by weight later on; there are men and women who are paid by a doctor or lawyer to lure clients away from another; there are hawkers of perfumes, good-luck charms, fountain pens, postcards and so on; there are even teachers who run private schools for pickpockets.

Since Danilo Dolci described these poor souls in one of his books on Sicily in the early 1960s, nothing has changed. Nor can any change be expected so long as Sicily's and Italy's political leaders continue to show tolerance bordering on connivance with the Mafia, together with the Vatican. It is in Sicily that Danilo Dolci, a poet and architect from the hated North, has emerged as the Vatican's most pestilential enemy. Known by the noble sobriquet of the Sicilian Gandhi, the Trieste-born Dolci is a hero, a legend and an extraordinary person who may also be, indeed, a great one.

All this has not barred him from becoming a most hated man. Yet his worst enemies — the Mafia and the Vatican — have not been able to extinguish him. Although Dolci is hated in powerful Italian circles, he has won unbounded admiration outside Italy for his dramatic work among Sicily's wretched poor: hundreds of volunteer pilgrims have come from Switzerland, Sweden and England — people who pay their own expenses to be able to work for the gentle, round-faced rebel.

In the early 1950s Danilo Dolci was a successful architect, the author of several professional books in his field and well respected in Italy. It was while making a tour of Sicily that he abandoned classical ruins to work with human ruins. The appalling ignorance of the people, their degraded and poverty-stricken lives in filth-littered streets, plus their superstition, apathy and misery all preyed on his mind. Believing that Sicily could never benefit by the tiny trickle of American foreign aid, Dolci settled himself in the starving fishing village of Trapetto. He did not have a cent in his pocket when he married a semi-literate widow with five children, at which time he adopted five more. Then, possessed of the guts of a bull-elephant, Dolci began his campaign for social reforms, using Mahatma Gandhi's methods of non-violence.

The first battle he staged was a hunger strike. Widely publicized, it brought some help to Trapetto. The next battle, however, brought the police. Dolci had rounded up 20 unemployed men to work without pay on a road which needed fixing, but for which no Christian Democratic government ever seemed to allot any funds. It was a strike in reverse, for when the law ordered him to go away, Dolci and his helpers calmly kept working. Dolci had forewarned his men that any show of violence on their part would destroy the effect of their action. Infuriated, the police arrested him for 'trespassing on public property'. In Palermo he was tried on five counts and sentenced to seven weeks in prison. The nature of the unprecedented crime and the ludicrous aspects of the trial brought publicity from all over the Continent. Before long, spontaneous Danilo Dolci committees sprouted up in Europe and began sending money. Embarrassed Italian politicians of the party in power, the Christian Democrats, tried to palm him off as a Communist agent, after his acceptance of the Lenin Prize for a volume of poetry.

Thanks to the financial aid resulting from press attention and also to the volunteer foreign social workers who came and stayed as long as their money held out, Dolci created some minor miracles. He built a shelter, known as the Village of God, for destitute families and orphans. He also built a dam on a small river for irrigation, two modest-sized hospitals, a pharmacy and many sewers and roads. After he moved his headquarters to the larger town of Partinico, which he considered a bigger challenge, he tackled the problem of agriculture. With 40 foreign volunteers he undertook to teach the peasants new methods and aid the cultivation of new crops, how best to employ fertilizer and water, how to carry out intensive cultivation, and so on.

In recent years Dolci has been using week-long 'sit-downs' in various small hill towns of western Sicily to draw attention to the need for water. One of these attracted international publicity and a measure of success. In flyblown Roccamena, Dolci staged in the fall of 1963 a nine-day fast and a mass sit-down in front of the only church. Joining the peaceful protest were movie star Vittorio Gassman, author Carlo Levi, other cultural figures from Europe, and 600 townspeople: they spent entire nights outdoors on straw mats, and Gassman, during dull moments at night, would entertain by reciting passages from Dante's *Divine Comedy* while standing in the glare of auto headlights as makeshift footlights.

The Bruca Dam project over the Belice River near Roccamena had been delayed for 30 years by Italian politicians, and especially by Christian Democrats in the postwar period. Although Rome had earmarked $12.8 million for the Bruca Dam in 1952, the money disappeared, and the project never began. Similarly, the $1.6 million that the government put up for preliminary work vanished. Roccamena (which had lost 170 families, a total of 700 people out of a population of only 3000, through emigration to the North) remained without water to eke out a living from the arid but potentially fertile soil that lay waste in the parched countryside. Most of it was owned by the Church and a few large wealthy landowners who had the backing of the Vatican and the Mafia. What little water there was, for too long had been used for the advantage of the few while millions of gallons from the unharnessed Belice River were wasted. As Dolci's publicity mounted, so did the pressure on Rome. The Ministry of Public Works finally bent and issued a communiqué stating the Bruca Dam would be built.

Roccamena's situation came about as a result of Vatican strategy: where poverty, misery and ignorance fester, the Vatican gains and holds strength. Italy's southern regions provide excellent hosts for this centuries-old practise. The situation, ironically, is aggravated by the *Cassa per il Mezzogiorno* (Southland Development Fund) which, instead of bringing economic relief to an insular backwater such as Sicily, has become a gigantic patronage organization, often awarding development contracts on strictly political considerations.

Several knowledgeable economic observers, admitting that this sort of thing goes on in any country, feel that in Italy the Christian Democrats, the Catholic hierarchy and the Mafia have promoted it. One Italian economist, a scholar with a thorough understanding of Italy's South, maintains that loans are made, credit is secured, fertilizer is distributed and contracts are awarded on a fairly strict basis of loyalty to the Christian Democratic Party. Because this practice is no secret, the bishops and local politicians do not have to advertise the fact, but they do impress upon stubborn individuals the hard time ahead for anyone who persists in supporting activities not approved by the Vatican. So entrenched is this system of economics and politics that it is no surprise to meet many people who take the position that, despite the formal government machinery that suggests democracy, Sicily is nothing more than a 'holding' in the hands of the Vatican.

Adding to the complexity and the poverty is the paradox that Sicily is a land of large estates; feudal barons in medieval times staked their claims to large holdings, laying the foundations for today's society. Much of Sicily's land is owned by some 60 princes, 200 marquises, 80 counts and 200 barons who, as the old nobility, are tied to the Vatican, and in nearly all cases, have amicable relations with the Mafia. Influential in regional politics, this upper crust rules the roost by pushing Christian Democratic candidates (sometimes they run for office themselves), all of whom, as explained earlier, must be approved by the Mafia. In protecting its land interests, the Sicilian nobility also protects the Vatican's land interests and its financial interests in some of the new industrial plants. People have long been critical of this state of affairs, but not until Danilo Dolci came upon the scene with his innovatory social reforms, causing more trouble than even the Sorcerer's Apprentice, has any opposition been aimed at the twins of old nobility, the Mafia and the Church. While Dolci puts into practice the Catholic Church's humanitarian and charitable ideas, the Vatican opposes him not on philosophical or theological grounds but on commercial principles. Because of Dolci there is the danger, among other things, that the Vatican's most valuable resource — its church-going believers and the funds they bring — could be diminished.

Paradoxically, Dolci is well-liked by the local priests who know him personally and is regarded with some admiration for his spunk by Mafia chiefs who have wisely hesitated to bump him off from fear of creating a martyr and a movement. It is said in Sicily that if Danilo Dolci has not been assassinated by now, he never will be. The man, however, is viewed as no friend of the Vatican in Rome's papal circles and is considered a Number One pest by the Christian Democratic Party.

Often accused of flirting with Communism and opening the way to a Red-backed renaissance in Sicily, Dolci asks no quarter in his struggles against the Catholic hierarchy and the Mafia. For the record, Dolci's collisions with the mainland Chistian Democrats are mostly ignored by the Pope and his inner circle, who consider him smallfry and who would not want to elevate him by a confrontation.

Although the Vatican has preferred not to quieten Dolci, the Bank of Sicily has seen fit to do otherwise. This bank, known among the natives as the Mafia's bank, is a financial arm of the Pope, and an overseer of the Vatican's holdings in the western end of Sicily. As such, it has tried to make short shrift of the Gandhi of Sicily without much obvious success. The Bank of Sicily scandal has kept things relatively peaceful for the time being, fortunately for Dolci. Carlo Bazan, the president of the Bank of Sicily, was arrested in 1967 on charges of alleged irregularities. Bazan, a Christian Democrat and a member of a noble Vatican family, for one thing had hired over an eight-year period nearly a hundred members of his family for various key posts inside the bank. While nepotism is not unknown in Palermo and does not necessarily constitute a legal offense, Bazan was accused of having doctored records and overlooked payments due on loans to members of his family or his in-laws. Bazan's trial, at the time of writing, has been held up all these years as a result of a squabble as to where the proceedings should take place — in Palermo or in Rome.

In spite of the friendly working relationship between the Vatican and the Mafia, a wing of the latter organization was not above trying to pull a fast one on the Vatican — it almost got away with palming off $14.5 million worth of fake securities on the Vatican bank. This was attempted through an Austrian underworld character with good Mafia connections in the United States and a good connection with the Vatican. The plot was foiled at the last minute. Although several FBI men visited the Vatican and talked with Bishop Paul Marcinkus and Monsignor Giovanni Benelli, then Pope Paul's closest adviser, in the end the FBI decided not to take the case any further since the fake securities ring had been broken anyway. The only missing link in the gang was a Vatican personage who would have been arrested the moment he set foot on American soil.

A central figure in the scheme was a priest by the name of Don Alberto Barbieri, a member of the Pauline Fathers Order of Rome (who often called himself Monsignor Pretta). From one Leopold Ledl of Vienna, he received a number of counterfeit securities (stocks from Pan American, Chrysler and the First National City Bank), and they were sold to his Order (the Pauline Fathers), apparently without the knowledge of the Vatican. The face value of these fake stocks came to nearly a billion US dollars, but they were purchased by the Pauline Fathers through Father Barbieri for the sum of $14.5 million. A bundle of these stocks was taken to the Vatican bank and an arrangement was made for them to be sold on the open market, using the Vatican's good name to help the sale. In all good faith, Bishop Paul Marcinkus, head of the Vatican bank, took on the handling of the transactions, as part of the normal routine of his office.

Because the transactions had to go through the Bank of Rome, an alert bank clerk detected them as counterfeit, and they were confiscated. The whole mess was hushed up, but Father Barbieri was given a secret trial, found guilty, defrocked and given a prison term. The file on his case, which ordinarily would be available, was not available to me because, I was told, it could only be extracted on Barbieri's signature. Having served his prison term, the ex-priest — who took up residence in Ostia, not far from Rome — found work in a bookstore. He refused to put his signature to the release of the file.

Meanwhile, in the United States, the man who delivered the fake securities to Leopold Ledl in a Munich hotel, Vincent Rizzo, received a 25-year prison sentence. Ledl, arrested by the Vienna police, earned a prison sentence for possession of fake securities. When the FBI went to the Vatican to question officials of the Vatican bank, they talked to Bishop Marcinkus who, giving his full cooperation, answered as many questions as he could. But when eventually the two American agents wanted to talk to Monsignor Benelli (who is now the Archbishop of Florence, a cardinal and a man tipped as the next pope), he did not invite them into his office. He spoke to them in the corridor outside his door. The Pope's closest advisor told them, smilingly, to forget the whole thing as quickly as possible. As to whether the Pope knew anything about the fake securities, Benelli replied to the FBI men that even if he knew the answer to that question, 'Why should I tell you?'

CHAPTER XXXVI

'And Lead Us Not Into Temptation . . .'

SCANDALS ARE nothing new to the Vatican, over the centuries the Vatican has become adept at dealing with them. These are some Vatican scandals that never quite made the headlines.

The unreported scandal of Italy's Leonardo da Vinci Airport is an example of a shady Vatican business deal. In 1952 the City of Rome decided that its airport at Ciampino, which was ideally situated, would soon be inadequate, despite the fact that its three runways could have been extended to accommodate jet planes. But instead of allocating funds for Ciampino's expansion, the Italian government (under Vatican prodding) bought up large areas of land in the coastal town of Fiumicino. As an airport site, Fiumicino had nothing to recommend it. A marshland near the mouth of the Tiber, it had in 1944 been rejected by the US Air Force because of shifting sands, frequent fogs and occasional flooding. After the site had been recommended to the government by the Vatican-owned Società Generale Immobiliare, the Italian government bought it for $21 million from Prince Torlonia, who was prominent in many Catholic organizations and whose family had played a large role in Vatican history.

This land was purchased even though nearby Casal Palocco, which was threatened by neither fog nor flood, was available for purchase at a much lower price. Had the existing airport at Ciampino been expanded or the Casal Palocco land been purchased, the government would not have had to appropriate $7.2 million to shore up the shifting sands of Fiumicino before concrete for the runways could be laid. It took workmen at Fiumicino five years to control the sand, their labors often having to be interrupted by heavy fogs that descended over the site.

In 1955 Italy allocated $22.4 million to complete the new airport. Several years later, in 1959, the Italian Ministry of Public Works received an additional $6.64 million to make the airport operative. Another $8 million was given over to make the connecting roadways to the city limits. All this was done in clear violation of Italian law which states that all financial allocations for public works of an extraordinary nature must be discussed by Parliament and that a bill must be passed for any withdrawals from the treasury. The contract to put in the runways was awarded to the Manfredi Construction Company; it is no small coincidence that Manfredi belonged to the Vatican. The contract to build the main terminal was put up for public bidding in which eight construction companies participated. Provera & Carrassi, a Vatican-owned company, won the bid at $5.12 million. It proceeded to build the terminal building, but on the 376th day of work discovered it had 'underestimated' the total cost. Without any publicity, the sum paid to Provera & Carrassi was raised by $4.38 million. Not until the final accounting had been made was it learned that Provera & Carrassi had received 80 per cent over its original 'low' bid.

A contract was given to the Castelli Construction Company (also Vatican-owned) to put up the hangars. The sum to build this was listed on the budget as $4.54 million, but on the government's final expense accounting, the Castelli company had received several other large payments in addition. The same happened with the amount paid to the Vaselli Company, another Vatican-owned firm, which got the contract for building the connecting roadways.

Several shady Vatican business deals took place in 1958 as a result of the building projects which were undertaken in connection with the 1960 Rome Olympics. The Vatican owned more than 102 million square feet (9.68 million square meters) of property within Rome's city limits, which were acquired through quiet purchase, inheritances, donations and foreclosures over a long period of time. Without any kind of public announcement, the National Italian Olympic Committee purchased large areas of this land from the Holy See for an unspecified sum and erected some 15 stadiums at a cost of almost $29 million. To connect the sport structures located in the northern part of the city with those in the southern sector, Rome built the Olympic Highway. Not making any kind of logical sense, this highway followed a contorted route, because it was placed on land that the city of Rome had purchased from front companies owned by the Vatican. In all cases involving the building of the Olympic structures, every Vatican-owned company filed a petition for bankrupty as soon as the installations had been finished — so that when some of them began to sprout major cracks and crevices, including the Olympic Highway, the Vatican companies could not be sued because they were 'no longer in business'. Nor could the Vatican be sued because the Rome City government had not dealt with the Vatican directly but with the front companies.

Not all of the Vatican's scandals involve business deals, however.

There is, for instance, the time in 1972 when the Vatican, for reasons of its own, threw cold water on a major international initiative that was attempting to cope with the problem of world poverty, world economic problems and world monetary problems. Ironically, the Vatican had supplied its own team of experts and had cooperated for four years to coordinate a strategy for Catholic and Protestant churches, ignoring denominational boundaries. It then suddenly torpedoed the joint effort to narrow the gap between the world's rich and poor countries.

With no publicity, early in 1968, the Geneva-based World Council of Churches and the Vatican's Pontifical Commission on Justice and Peace agreed to work out ways and means together to fight world poverty. Several exploratory meetings were held with excellent results, and from these a new organization was formed called the Joint Commission for Society, Development and Peace — Sodepax. Sodepax's assignment was to put into action a machinery that would deal directly with poverty, both in the rich countries and the poor. Its first head was a Jesuit, Rev George Dunne, who put his full energies into the project.

Through Father Dunne, Sodepax minced no words with the richer countries or with some of the totalitarian regimes among the poorer nations. For instance, in a 1970 conference in Austria — at Baden, just outside Vienna — Sodepax delegates passed tough resolutions against the racial policies and practices in the Republic of South Africa, Australia and the United States and against the systematic use of torture in Haiti, Vietnam, Brazil, Greece and Zanzibar.

Back in Rome, Vatican diplomats became uptight about these resolutions, for Father Dunne had pushed for them with no instructions from the home office, besides which the energetic priest was considered impetuous and was personally disliked by some members of the Curia. Even Pope Paul VI had his doubts about both Dunne and Sodepax, despite the fact that the new organization had already begun to tackle some of the sticky problems facing the world's poverty. When Father Dunne — again without prior instruction from Rome — urged Sodepax to set a good example by moving its headquarters from the marble palace in Geneva to one of the poor African or Asian countries, the Vatican decided to wield the ax. It felt that Sodepax had become a rival of the Pontifical Commission on Justice and Peace and that Father Dunne needed some wind taken from his sails. When Sodepax's charter was up for a three-year renewal, the Vatican hedged and insisted that not only should its responsibilities be redefined along more limited lines, but that it also should be disciplined by appointing a new general secretary (because Father Dunne was being assigned to another Vatican job in a different part of the world). Moreover, the Vatican made it known that its financial contribution to Sodepax was being substantially reduced; the Vatican suggested that the annual $300,000 be reduced to $60,000 and that Sodepax be forbidden to raise funds or accept gifts of money. Shortly after, Sodepax went the way of all flash! And Father Dunne gave up the priesthood.

Another international Vatican scandal that should have been reported involves the traffic of nuns between India and Europe. It is no startling news that there is a shortage of nuns today, a fact that the Vatican is having to face. When a confidential report was made to the Vatican that many of Germany's 7000 convents and holy orders had been buying poverty-stricken girls from Kerala, a southern state in India, Curia officials preferred to ignore it. That was in 1966; yet the practice is still quietly going on, with Vatican officers turning a blind eye — despite the disapproval of a number of priests.

When the report, which carried a reference number of Jr-Nr G 24 505/64 and signature by Cardinal Julius Doepfner of Munich, was sent to the Pope in 1966, the nun-running traffic had already been going on for six years. Most of the girls going to Germany to work at menial jobs, mostly as domestics in convents, were taking their religious vows in India or after they arrived in Germany. The cost per woman came to about $700, including air fare to Frankfurt, and the money was paid to an Indian priest, Father Cyriac Puthenpura, who sent the girls to his counterpart in Germany, Father Hubert Debatin.

With its large Roman Catholic population, the State of Kerala is one of India's poorest with very low employment, and young girls there can expect a bleak future. Father Puthenpura had little difficulty, therefore, in recruiting young girls for nunneries abroad. Most of them have come from two Kerala dioceses, Tiruvalla and Trivandrum. Many of the girls who were received by Father Debatin were then sent to such areas as the industrial Ruhr, the Black Forest and Cologne. A goodly number of the recruits were put to work in Catholic hospitals as domestics or as trainee nurses.

Two German Jesuit priests got wind of what was going on — Father Ludwig Wiedenmann and Father Joseph Otto — and they undertook an investigation for Cardinal Doepfner. Father Wiedenmann made a trip to India and learned from a government official there, a passport officer, that hundreds of passports had been issued to young Keralese girls going to Germany under religious patronage. When the passport official communicated his concern to Delhi over the inordinately large number of passports being issued, nothing came of it. And when Father Wiedenmann brought the matter to the attention of the

German Embassy in India, he was told to mind his own business. A report was then made to Bonn, in February 1965, on the flow of nuns from India to West Germany recommending that support be given to 'a carefully thought-out and executed action'.

The Vatican's rationalization for the traffic of Indian nuns is, basically, that sending young girls away from their homes to do menial work in a foreign country is the duty of underdeveloped countries to repay Western aid. It is also claimed that the Church provides pastoral help for the girls who are confused or have uncertain religious leanings. In addition, the Vatican holds to the view, not yet made public, that the idea of sending Keralese recruits to Germany and also to Italy (where more than a thousand are now working in nunneries) is not bad in itself — particularly since the girls do 8 to 12 months of preparatory training in Father Puthenpura's Secular Institute in Ettumanoor before going to Europe. At the end of 1981 the Vatican still showed no inclination to stem the flow of womanpower, no doubt because it needs to keep outdated monastic structures functioning and these women provide a good source of cheap labor.

CHAPTER XXXVII

The Vatican as a Tax Evader

BACK IN 1975 newspapers had a field day when a California law student, William Sheffield, sued Pope Paul VI for the sum of $428.50 because a Swiss monastery did not deliver the new-born Saint Bernard dog he had purchased. Headlines at the time read:

- POPE LOSES PIP OF A SUIT OVER A PUP
- VATICAN IS DOGMATIC IN COURT
- PUP 1, POPE 0

Mr Sheffield, who is today an attorney in Santa Ana, goes down in Vatican history as the only person ever to have sued a pope. He also goes down in history as the only man who ever sued the Pope successfully, for an Alameda County superior court judge awarded him a $428.50 default judgment against Paul VI on the grounds he never received delivery of the puppy for which he had paid a $60 deposit to a Roman Catholic monk in Switzerland. In his suit, which took some six years' litigation, Sheffield named the Roman Catholic Church doing business as the Bishop of Rome, the Holy See, and Pope Paul VI — contending that the Pope was ultimately responsible for the Church's business obligations.

The incident started when Sheffied ordered the puppy from the Hospice of the Great Saint Bernard in 1968. Soon after, he was informed by Father Bernard Cretton of the eleventh-century monastery on the Swiss–Italian border that the litter of pups had died and that his deposit was not returned because it had been used in servicing his account and in feeding the mother dog. Throughout the court proceedings Pope Paul ignored the suit, and after the superior court awarded the plaintiff his loss and expenses, the Pope ordered that the money not be paid. Sheffield still has to collect. This incident alone, demonstrates the Vatican's attitude to unpaid bills; its stand on tax, however, is revealed by its behavior towards the Italian government's petition for unpaid taxes.

During the mid-1960s when the business barometer was showing its low opinion of Italy's economy, the then prime minister — Aldo Moro — was caught in a crossfire between politicians who wanted to tax the Vatican on its stock market holdings and Vatican lobbyists who sought a preferential arrangement whereby the Vatican would be provided with an exemption. A law had been passed in 1962, when Amintore Fanfani was the prime minister, establishing a dividend tax (*cedolare*) on shares quoted at the stock exchange. To avoid rocking the boat, Aldo Moro resorted to an old fighter's trick: he stopped trying to be a good referee and, instead of pushing the Vatican back to its corner, he stalled.

The Moro strategy was simply this: he asked the Vatican to submit a statement of its holdings as a prelude to obtaining an exemption. This worked up to a point, and the tug-of-war over the Vatican tax matter subsided. The matter lay dormant for several years, while the red-herring campaign to get Italy to pass a divorce law — vigorously opposed by the Vatican — took priority. Since Italy was one of the few civilized countries without a divorce law, the campaign reached an unprecedented intensity. Eventually, this matter, too, lost much of its heat and petered out.

In 1967 the leftist Rome weekly, *L'Espresso*, suggesting that some kind of secret deal had been made between the Italian government and the State of Vatican City, wanted to know why 'the biggest tax evader in postwar Italy' was not coughing up like other law-abiding companies and citizens. *L'Espresso* calculated that the Vatican had saved up to $36 million in unpaid taxes. Italy's Socialist finance minister, Luigi Preti, refuted this figure, and in an unprecedented public accusation said from the floor of the Senate that the Vatican had earned $5.2 million in Italian stock dividends in 1965 and that if it had paid the 30 per cent *cedolare* tax, the sum would come to $1.6 million.

Denying Preti's figures as being 'absurd' and 'clearly baseless', an unofficial Vatican spokesman admitted to some reporters that the actual amount involved was a sum approaching $160,000. The same source cited the Lateran Treaty of 1929 between the Holy See and Italy in which there is provision for the recognition of the Vatican as a sovereign independent state and as a state exempt from Italian taxation. Even *L'Osservatore Romano* put in its two lire worth when, eschewing its usual ecclesiastic verbiage, stated in more earthly and immediate terms that the amount of money, in any case, was 'holy money, entirely earmarked for charity'.

When Giovanni Leone took over the premiership in 1968, he made it known in a state-of-the-union message that the Vatican would have to pay its tax arrears. Monsignor Fausto Vallainc, then the Vatican's press officer, countermandered that the Vatican contributed heavily to Italy's income with its investments and tourist attractions, that several other countries (including the United States) gave the Roman Catholic Church tax exemptions, that taxing Holy See income violated treaties regulating church-state relations in Italy and that the tax would reduce the fund available for religious and social projects carried out by priests in Italy and in other parts of the world. Minister Preti publicly rejected these claims:

'It is true,' he declared, 'that Holy See activities are advantageous for the tourism influx to Italy and that this increases state incomes, but I cannot see why these should serve as reasons for the Vatican to be exempted from taxes. Also I think the Vatican has no grounds in pointing to the treatment it enjoys in other countries where the Holy See is exempt from taxes. The Italian law clearly indicates there are no exemptions for any foreigners having Italian stock holdings. The noble aims that the Holy See pursues here and elsewhere in the world are highly respected in Italy, and by all political parties, but this is no reason for tax-free treatment.'

From the time of the Lateran agreements of 1929, the Vatican has a history of 'tax evasion' that has often smacked of comic opera. Although the third document of the Lateran Pacts, known as the Concordat, provided tax exemptions for 'ecclesiastical corporations', it became necessary during the 1930s and the early 1940s to give the Vatican treasury added protection. Mussolini's Fascist regime bent over backwards to give special dispensations to the Holy See on matters of taxes.

In October 1936 Mussolini imposed a 5 per cent tax on all Italy's corporations to help underwrite a large loan needed to pay for the war in Abyssinia. Moreover, the regime levied a 3.5 per cent tax on every thousand lire worth of real estate holdings to run for a 25-year period; this latter tax was created to absorb the interest costs on the war loan. Decree 1743 of October 5, 1936, set up this tax schedule, but Article 3 of the decree exempted the Vatican from paying either of the two levies. None of this was mentioned in the controlled Fascist press, nor did the Vatican's semi-official daily mention it. Foreign correspondents stationed in Rome at the time had no knowledge of it, either.

Vatican-owned companies also benefited from tax exemption: they were freed of a special duty ordered in October 1937, Decree 1729, which required a graduated tax payment on the capital stock of every corporation. Early in 1938 when the tax program got under way, a special order exempted the Vatican's corporations from paying this levy. Again, in 1940, after Italy had instituted a sales tax (IGE, which is still in existence today), Mussolini's minister of finance, in a circular dated June 30, freed the Vatican and all churches from paying the new tax. Exemption from the IGE sales tax remains to this day. Lastly, in 1942, a law was passed, 'in the spirit of our Concordat', which did not require the Vatican to pay existing assessments on dividends.

In a devious move to keep such special privilege from public knowledge, the finance minister published an official roster of organizations that were not eligible for taxation on dividends (all of which were Vatican-affiliated companies) during the year-end holiday season when the public would not notice it, and then had it published, not in the government's official bulletin, but in an obscure state bulletin called *Rivista di Legislazione Fiscale*. The decree, Number 4800, was dated December 31, 1942, but was not published until 1943. It appeared in 1943 on page 1963 of volume 2, and it escaped the attention (as was to be expected) of every foreign correspondent stationed in Rome.

The preferential treatment the Vatican received from Mussolini's Fascist regime was what Church officers wanted the newly formed postwar republic to honor. By and large, fiscal truths about the Vatican — such as preferential tax treatments — are invariably kept out of print by a sympathetic Italian press and by the corps of foreign reporters in Rome. Deferring to the notoriously thin skin of the Vatican on money matters, most of the correspondents I knew at Rome's *Stampa Estera* (Foreign Press Club) avoided the subject in their dispatches — a subject which when broached tends to touch the spring that could open Pandora's box and sacrifice the Vatican's feelings on the altar of subterfuge *ad absurdam*. I myself was cabled at least twice by my Stateside editors to lay off on the subject of the Vatican's finances. The editors 'justified' the censorship by explaining that the local archdiocese which would use its considerable clout and good standing with the publication's owner, who would then very likely carpet the offending editor.

At the end of 1981, the Vatican still had not paid a single lire of the *cedolare* taxes it has owed the Italian government from the 1960s. This is not to mention those it owes for the 1970s and the 1980s. The Vatican did, however, say late in 1968 that it would pay taxes on its Italian stock earnings but requested a statement from the Italian government as to how much would have to be paid. Moreover, it asked permission to pay the tax in installments because it did not have the necessary funds to meet a large bill. Mysteriously, the Italian government has never submitted such a statement to the Vatican. Not so mysteriously, the Vatican has yet to make a single payment.

CHAPTER XXXVIII

Is The Vatican Going Broke?

BY THE time Pope Benedict XV died in 1922, the Vatican, which had had its share of financial troubles during and after World War I, was sailing in choppy waters, for Benedict XV had given far more money to charity than he should have. From the day he had assumed the pontifical chair in 1914, he never once looked into the apostolic honey bowl, giving out the Church's money faster than it was coming in. So free and easy was Benedict with money that in his desk drawer he used to keep large sums which he would hand out to any priest who hit him with a sob story. Without once giving any thought to where the Vatican's income came from, the over-generous Pontiff made handsome grants to convents, schools and missionary settlements.

There is an authenticated story about the time Pope Benedict had given a private audience to a visiting bishop, then engaged in building a convent in Palestine. As the bishop was about to leave, the Pope asked him why the building of the new convent was moving so slowly, and the answer was that, alas, more money was needed. The Pope nodded, opened the center drawer, foraged around but found nothing, smiled sheepishly, pulled open the bottom drawer on the side of the desk and spilled out the contents. 'Here,' he said, 'take this!' and pushed $6250 in loose bills and coins towards the flabbergasted clergyman.

If Pope Benedict was sloppy with money, his successor, Pius XI, was more so. On the first day he took office, Pope Pius handed out $26,000 to some German cardinals for a needy cause. Within months, still having made no accounting of the Vatican coffers, Pius handed out $62,500 to a sanatorium in France, $156,000 in aid to Russia, nearly $10,000 to the poor of Rome, more than $50,000 to the victims of a conflagration in Smyrna, $12,500 to a Catholic institute in Cologne, $81,000 to Germany, $22,000 to Vienna for hungry children, and $20,000 for Japanese earthquake victims.

Such largesse had to herald a day of reckoning, and it came when Monsignor Dominique Mariani, an aide on the committee for the management of the Holy See's property, made a complete inventory and found that the Vatican was broke. Swift action had to be taken. Under Monsignor Mariani's careful guidance, with the Pope's blessing and cooperation, the Holy See began to take control of its financial affairs, and gradually proper bookkeeping put the Vatican on the road to balancing its books.

Given that money may be the root of all evil, Vatican policies since the 1930s have kept the wolf from the door . . . until the fall of 1979 when it made a historic disclosure. For the first time ever, the Vatican revealed the state of its finances, divulging that it had lost $20.2 million that year. In July 1981, while Pope John Paul II was in hospital recovering from gun wounds in an unsuccessful assassination attempt, 15 cardinals met to investigate the Vatican's finances. The commission found that there would be a $25 million deficit at the end of 1981. It is not known whether the 1979 $20.2 million deficit or the 1981 figure are accurate figures.

Both in 1981 and 1979, after the cardinals completed their meetings, the Vatican issued a statement suggesting that there should be a more intimate 'collaboration on the part of local churches'. This message was primarily for the United States and intimated that Catholic Americans should increase their contributions to the Vatican. In effect, this meant that the annual Peter's Pence collection, which is taken up at the end of June each year in every diocese in America, would have to come up with a much more substantial sum than in past years.

The origin of Peter's Pence has been traced as far back as AD 787 when it was first collected in England. The levy remained in force until the time of King Henry VIII, in the early part of the sixteenth century. It then spread to other northern lands. Still other countries adopted the Peter's Pence levy and for centuries it persisted in many places. Existing records in Portugal, Poland and certain of the Italian states do not make clear which revenues derived from Peter's Pence and which from the feudal tribute, the price of papal protection. The Reformation brought an end to Peter's Pence, but in the middle of the nineteenth century, during the reign of Pope Pius IX, it reappeared — first in France, then in Austria and Germany, and later in Ireland. In the United States Peter's Pence was revived in 1868 in Baltimore when the second Plenary Council decided to have a collection in all American churches for the Pope once a year. At the turn of the century, France was the principal contributor to Peter's Pence, but now first place has been taken by the American Catholic Church. As for the money received each year, the Pope is not accountable to anyone as to how it is administered.

During the reign of Paul VI (now considered by Vatican officers as having been an 'unpopular' Pope), the Peter's Pence payments dipped to $6 million. Since John Paul II came to the throne, however, contributions have risen, to $12 million at the end of his first year. The Vatican brass has not been able to explain, however, why the payments then started to go down again. The cardinals several years ago were asked by the Vatican to give the Pope suggestions as to how to deal with the uncertainty of the flow of the Peter's Pence payments and other voluntary, variable sources of payment.

The knotty finances of the Holy See, coupled with the fact that it has never published a balance sheet, present a dilemma, born of the irony that Christianity originated with a poor Man who preached poverty and practiced it for 33 years that the Church shows considerable material wealth.

Trying to glimpse the Vatican's business operation is like looking through a kaleidoscope. With each shake, the entire picture changes, while the shapes and colors of the individual pieces stay the same. Since the Vatican's complex business operations have been cloaked in obscurity, the public image of the Roman Catholic Church has remained by and large that of a charity. As one of the greatest fiscal powers in the world, however, the Vatican, like Rome, was not built in a day, and its wealth was not accumulated overnight.

The Vatican's financial empire got a heady start in 1929 when Mussolini and Pope Pius XI signed the Lateran Pact, which, in exchange for surrendering 16,000 square miles (41,440 square kilometers) of Italy, gave the Vatican compensation of about $90 million. Pius called in banker Bernardino Nogara, an Italian Jew who had converted to Catholicism, to advise him on what to do with it. Nogara, an architect by profession, suggested that one-third of it should be put into gold (which is kept at Fort Knox today) and the rest invested. He formulated a policy that the Vatican's investment program should not be restricted by theological considerations, and, when he died in 1958, Nogara left a network of prospering holdings, an established investment policy and the belief, expressed by one of his successors, that he was 'the best thing to have happened to the Church since Our Lord Jesus Christ'.

As the world's largest religious business concern today, the Vatican is firmly entrenched in numerous companies engaged in real estate, plastics, electronics, steel manufacturing, cement, textiles, chemicals, food products and construction. It is one of Italy's largest bankers, owns several large Italian insurance companies and is a heavy investor on the New York Stock Market — to the tune of over $2 billion. Indeed, it is a formidable international financial power with a corporate wealth that is in excess of $20 billion.

Generally speaking, it is not Vatican strategy to own companies directly but to control holding companies. For instance, the SNIA–Viscosa Company of Milan, which produces more than 70 per cent of Italy's artificial and synthetic fibres, is not directly owned by the Vatican, but it is linked to two Vatican-owned companies — the CISA–Viscosa Company, which produces viscose fibres and rayon, and the Saici Company, which manufactures cellulose and holds considerable stock in a cotton plant.

The Vatican-owned Italgas controls subsidiary gas companies in 36 Italian cities (including Rome, Venice, Florence and Turin) and others that deal in tar, iron ore, coke for steel mills, distillates, drinking water, gas stoves and appliances and industrial ovens. Italcementi, a distantly controlled Vatican interest, is the world's sixth largest producer of cement and owns a financial institution, Italmobiliare, which bought eight banks over five years in what is considered to be one of the most brilliant financial maneuvers in Italy's recent economic history. Of the some 180 medium and long-term credit institutes in Italy, at least a third receive pontifical funds and put Vatican money into industry, public works, utilities, property, hotels, tourism and agriculture.

In the light of these facts the question of whether the Vatican is going broke or not needs a microscope examination. True, things started to go downhill for the Vatican after the Franklin National Bank (New York) failure; this was the twentieth largest bank in America, in which the Vatican had a substantial financial stake through its main representative, Michele Sindona (see Chapter XL), who had acquired the bank with the purchase of a million shares at $40 apiece. To offset its losses in the Franklin National collapse and because the Peter's Pence income did not cover the operating expenses of the State of Vatican City), the Vatican opted to increase its visible income by conning affluent Catholics — pleading poverty and appealing for much more money. American Catholics in the United States and Canada were the special targets of this drive for the simple reason that the Vatican power structure, mostly Italians, is firm in its belief that when it comes to politics and international affairs, the American people as a whole are *bambini* (infants). They are regarded as unsophisticated, politically, and somewhat gullible. By a simple manipulation of its income figures (which were never specified), the Vatican sought to con North Americans to increase its coffers.

This is how the scheme worked: the deficit figure of $25 million, as announced by the Pontifical Commission of Cardinals, is not exactly accurate, for it is based on the Peter's Pence income and the income derived from the sale of postage stamps and coins and tickets to the Vatican Museum. It is a deficit for the State of Vatican City, but it is not a deficit for the Vatican itself, since Vatican city is just a part and a separate operation of the Vatican. A church-going Catholic is easily confused if he does not make the distinction that Vatican City is not the Vatican and that the Vatican is not Vatican City. The distinction is fully clear to every Italian I have ever met, but it is not made clear to people in North America.

The so-called $25-million deficit would disappear if placed against all of the Vatican's earnings from all sources — which we know to be around $2 billion annually. The next question is if the American Catholic Church can afford to come to the Vatican's rescue, even if that $25-million deficit were an honest figure. Catholic figures for the United States show 30 archdioceses, 123 dioceses and 22,394 parishes and missions, whereas the latest available official statistics for Canada show that there are 17 archdioceses, 46 dioceses and 6063 parishes and missions. Canada's total Catholic population, out of a population of 23.8 million, comes to over 8.7 million; in the United States there are more than 65 million Catholics. (The population figures could be disputed since figures for practicing Catholics and born Catholics vary considerably, even if the Vatican prefers not to make such a distinction.)

Given that the Catholic Church in the USA and Canada does indeed possess substantial material riches — such as church buildings, elementary schools, high schools, universities, rectories, convents, orphanages, homes for the aged, hospitals and cemeteries, not to mention uncounted and untaxed real estate — the fact remains that North American dioceses do not have cash. There is no money for spending or for 'foreign aid to Rome'. Although the Church in North America is rich in property, it is poor in cash. The bulk of its wealth is tied up in schools and hospitals that use most of the cash taken in the Sunday collections. Nearly every parish and diocese has deepening financial troubles.

Unnoticed by many people, the Vatican has practiced a rigid policy of not sending any money to the US for charitable purposes, whether the need is pressing or not. This is because the hierarchy in Rome, including such recent beloved Popes as Paul VI, John XXIII and Pius XII and the present incumbent, believe that the United States is the richest country in the world and can therefore take care of poorer countries. This attitude extends to Canada as well.

In addition to Peter's Pence, the Vatican requires of US churches what are called *supplimenti* (additional contributions). These are usually percentages of other collections that are taken throughout the year, and they are all managed by the American Board of Catholic Missions. One of these annual mission collections is for the Society for the Propagation of the Faith, and the contributions from all sources around the world come to a total of about $30 million each year, nearly $7 million of which comes from the United States and all of which goes to Rome. Other collections are those for the Catholic Relief and Bishop Relief and the Catholic Near East Society.

Over and above the funds and percentages that are forwarded to Rome are the so-called *Ad Limina* visitations by the various bishops and the offerings to Rome for quinquennial faculties. Various 'taxes' are levied on American bishops, who must pay at least one visit to the Pope every five years, at which time they are expected to present a donation to the Pope. The average gift ranges between $2000 and $3000, but archbishops from a few of the richer American jurisdictions will go as high as $5000. Taking into account the *Ad Limina* visitations, the annual Peter's Pence contribution and the *supplimenti*, it is estimated that the 123 dioceses in the United States and the 46 dioceses in Canada give a total of about $20 million a year to Rome. With the Vatican now pleading poverty and actively seeking an increase in the *Ad Limina* contributions, the aforementioned sums were expected by the Vatican to be greatly increased during the 1980s.

However, the North American Catholic Church is in a bad way, financially. Many of the dioceses are on the brink of bankruptcy, and many of the education systems have had to be cut or curtailed. But the Vatican prefers to ignore these hard facts.

CHAPTER XXXIX

The Gorilla in the Vatican

AFFECTIONATELY KNOWN by the Vatican brass as Gorilla, the most important American inside the State of Vatican City is generally conceded the following attribute: he has the fastest pair of fists this side of the Atlantic Ocean and wields the most lethal set of elbows which got their basic training on dozens of rugby fields. Bald, in his early sixties, six feet two inches (1.8 meters) in height, 220 pounds plus (15¾ stone), with shoulders like those of a water buffalo, Bishop Paul Marcinkus is a sure bet to become a cardinal before the decade is out. He is also the one cleric who stands a good chance of being elected the first American pope ever, if and when another Conclave is held while he is still in robust good health.

For many years Bishop Marcinkus was Pope Paul VI's personal bodyguard whenever he went abroad. Marcinkus got the job quite by chance: it was while on a trip to one of Rome's basilicas downtown when a massive crowd came towards the helpless Pope Paul and the then-Monsignor Marcinkus took charge in 1964 of the potentially dangerous situation. Using his powerful shoulders and operating his elbows like two pistons, the cleric cleaved a path for the Pontiff and saved him from being badly trampled. He impressed everyone with his Herculean might — but particularly Paul VI, who appointed him his bodyguard. And that was how he got the nickname The Gorilla; in Italian, it does not always refer to the animal and can mean, in slang, bodyguard. Nobody calls Paul Marcinkus 'Gorilla' to his face, though he has admitted to me he rather likes it, since it is really a term of affection used by his colleagues and superiors.

Built on the lines of a Notre Dame fullback, the ordinarily gentle prelate is an athlete who excelled in such sports as basketball, boxing, rugby and baseball. In fact, it was he who started the first-ever baseball team behind the Vatican walls — he was the catcher, manager and clean-up man. Before its first game, the Vatican nine received a special papal blessing, but apparently that was more of a jinx because it did not help score many runs in games against the US military teams stationed in Italy. Manager Marcinkus's only alibi was that the squad needed pitchers, which may explain why his team lost by such scores as 23–0 and 42–1. The only run the Vatican ever scored in a baseball game was a ninth-inning homer hit by Marcinkus himself. But as far as his career with the Vatican is concerned, Bishop Marcinkus is batting a cool 1.000.

The son of a Lithuanian immigrant who became a skyscraper window-cleaner, Father Marcinkus went to Rome in 1950 after getting his law degree in Chicago. In Rome, he studied canon law at the Gregorian University run by the Jesuits, and after winning a doctor of divinity degree in 1953, he entered the Vatican's diplomatic school. Assigned to the Vatican's Secretariat of State as an interpreter (a role he still fills from time to time whenever a VIP American, like the President of the United States, has an audience with the Pope), Marcinkus was supposed to have remained in Rome long enough to complete a specialized graduate course in law. Today, although he no longer serves as a papal bodyguard, he does carry out several important jobs: one of his responsibilities is to plan all the details of a trip whenever the Pope takes off — either in Italy or abroad; another of his responsibilities is overseeing the management of the Vatican City State. The title he carries for this latter is pro-president of the Pontifical Commission for Vatican City State (the job is essentially that of 'mayor' of Vatican City), which makes him responsible for relations with Vatican personnel and any staff problems. Though these two jobs are lesser in the Vatican scheme of things, it is Marcinkus's most important job that makes him one of the big powers inside the Vatican: he is in executive control of the Vatican's Institute for Religious Works (which is the official name of the Vatican bank and which is probably the classiest euphemism for any financial organization anywhere), a post that makes him responsible for handling the investment of hundreds of millions of dollars belonging to Roman Catholic orders and charities in all parts of the world. The Institute also manages the foreign portion of the Holy See's substantial securities portfolio. Most of the investments the Vatican has outside Italy are American.

Founded in 1942 by Pope Pius XII in order to transfer money from Fascist Italy to religious orders and charitable institutions all over the globe, the Vatican bank is one of the world's most mysterious financial entities. Housed within the walls of a seventeenth-century fortress within spitting distance of Vatican City's supermarket and pharmacy, the Vatican bank functions as a normal bank in that it has lay cashiers and tellers, accepts deposits, opens new accounts, cashes checks and transfers money. One of the big differences between the Vatican bank and other banks is that its clientele is select.

Accounts may be opened only by people who live or work in Vatican City, by diplomatic persons accredited to the Holy See, by members of the Curia, by heads of religious orders and by Italian citizens who are members of the royal Vatican families (ordinary priests and nuns from outside the Vatican are now also able to open accounts in the Vatican bank). Pope John Paul II, although he arrived with only $10 in his pocket when he left Poland to go to the Conclave after the sudden death of John Paul I, has a personal account; his account number is 16–16, and because he earns not a penny in salary as Pope, his total deposit is tiny.

Such is not the case with the other 10,500 accounts, however, of which 1047 are in the names of religious institutions. The Vatican's financier in America, Michele Sindona (see Chapter XL), had an account in the Vatican bank, but after the Franklin National Bank collapse and Sindona's imprisonment, his account was closed by papal order and Sindona's Italian lire were transferred to the Banca Cattolica del Veneto (owned by the Vatican) and his foreign account was transferred to a bank in Switzerland. Clients who hold an account in the Vatican bank, which gives 14 per cent interest in lire accounts and nearly 8 per cent on foreign money accounts, are not taxed on their interest, as is the case with accounts in Italian banks at the rate of 15 per cent.

Unlike Swiss banks with their famous numbered accounts, the Vatican bank does not engage in this practice — which might come as a surprise considering that the Vatican makes a fetish of secrecy about almost everything. Because the Vatican bank is owned by a foreign country (the State of Vatican City), it is not subject to Italy's banking laws, and therefore several types of legal and illegal fiscal operations (illegal in the eyes of the Italian law) are possible, such as the transfer of Italian lire in large quantities outside Italy.

This therefore means that some clients can use the Vatican bank as a place to launder what the Italian people refer to as 'dark money'. Dark money is not necessarily dirty money, but it is money that Italian citizens do not want the Italian authorities to know about for one reason or another, and this is when the Vatican bank is a handy tool. The way it usually works is that a banking officer in one of Rome's banks is entrusted with a large cash sum of lire, which he deposits in the name of someone who has an account in the Vatican bank, which then transfers the money by check to a Swiss bank in the name of the original holder of the lire. Such transactions are common in Italy today, and the shady characters who serve as the middlemen are paid a substantial bribe (known as *bustarella* in Italian slang).

While all this is against Italian law, it is certainly not against any laws of the Vatican City State. Vatican banking officials are not unaware of the network, but it sympathizes with the fear that well-to-do Italian Catholics have about Communism, the Red Brigades and the weak lira. The Vatican bank, however, did clamp down on a recent mini-racket involving the change of foreign currency for lire. Quite often when the official Italian rate was as much as 8 per cent lower than what dollars, for example, were fetching in exchange at the Vatican bank, some people discovered that by changing dollars at the Vatican, they made a nice profit for themselves. The Vatican got wise and issued a new rule saying that anyone who wanted to change money had to have an account there.

There is a documented case of a Vatican cleric who used the Vatican bank to swindle money for himself. Monsignor E P Cippico, a young prelate employed by the Vatican archives, got entangled in a series of financial deals that eventually brought him to ruin. When World War II ended, Italy was subject to currency restrictions; many Italian businessmen discovered that in order to purchase goods for import, they could transfer funds through the Vatican, since the Vatican was exempt from Italy's currency regulations. Cippico, who enjoyed moving in high-society circles and who had good personal contacts in the Vatican, served as a go-between for people who wanted to get their money out of the country. All went well until Cippico agreed one day to underwrite the production costs of a movie on the life of Saint Francis of Assisi. To conceal the outflow of money, Cippico merely enlarged his operation, and while the film never got past the first reel, more and more people who had entrusted him with large sums of money saw no return. The roof caved in on Cippico. He was arrested by the Pope's Gendarmerie, made to stand a Vatican inquiry, found guilty, defrocked and put into detention. Later, he stood trial in an Italian court and was convicted of fraud. Still later, he was set free by a court of appeal.

Bishop Marcinkus has what the Vatican considers an impressive track record in a high-risk-job — one for which he admitted he was quite unqualified because he had had no formal training, knew very little about economics and was not much good at arithmetic to boot. Bishop Marcinkus got into some hot water, however, when the Vatican took a bath in the collapse of Michele Sindona's complex financial empire. Marcinkus had had dealings with Sindona, agreeing to invest in Sindona's banking interests, but when the empire, which included the Franklin National Bank, went down the drain, so did an estimated $160 million in Vatican funds.

Curia officers raised a cry for Marcinkus's head to be put on the chopping block, but Pope Paul came to his rescue and took the blame by admitting he gave the final approval on the misguided deals with Sindona. The Gorilla bounced back.

When John Paul II came to power, the big American prelate emerged as one of the new Pope's favorite people in the Vatican. Part of this may have come about because Marcinkus had done some heavy speculating with Vatican funds in gold, and because that had worked well, the Vatican had managed to offset a goodly portion of its Sindona/Franklin Bank losses. Marcinkus also ran into some good luck when he made a quick sale in one day earning the Vatican bank the sum of $14 million on paper in the New York Stock Market. Ironically, had he made the same transaction just one day later, Marcinkus would have earned more than $100 million for the Vatican, but the Pope was nevertheless pleased with the $14 million.

Notwithstanding Marcinkus's business acumen, Pope John Paul appointed a commission of cardinals to oversee his work. Since few of these cardinals had any relevant background or experience, and since Marcinkus had become adept in international financial matters, the princes of the Church do not interfere in his work or even make suggestions as to what he should be doing. Their function, up to now, has been to look at the semi-annual balance sheet submitted to the Pope by Marcinkus and to nod appreciatively at the plus sign they see on the bottom line. The Vatican balance sheets, which are among its most carefully guarded secrets, do not contain any indication of where the money actually goes or where it comes from. This document is considered so sensitive that the cardinals themselves can only look at it right there in a Vatican office with Marcinkus in attendance; they cannot take a copy away with them.

For his work as head of the Vatican bank, Bishop Marcinkus earns a salary of only $6000 a year. To unwind, he takes every Wednesday afternoon off to play golf (and sometimes tennis). A few years back when Rome was the scene of a two-man-team world golf championship match, Marcinkus got permission from his superiors to compete, but he had to cancel when he could not find a sufficiently good golfing partner on the Vatican staff.

Extremely popular with the some 3000 people of all ranks who work in the State of Vatican City, the cigar-smoking Illinois giant is not the kind to make waves inside the Vatican. He is a good team man. He is adept at handling the nuts and bolts of the Vatican world, and he does it all with an admirable sense of humor. It was Marcinkus's quick wit that came up with a quip about the Vatican concern for money that summarizes him and his job: 'You can't run the Church on Hail Marys!'

CHAPTER XL

The Vatican Howard Hughes

WHEN THE Vatican asked a successful Milan lawyer and businessman to be its special business representative in the United States (but strictly on the q.t.), he accepted the job, even though he could not speak one work of English. He would attend to that pronto. Just as he had amassed a megafortune of $450 million by applying himself diligently from the day he first started out selling lemons from the back of a cart in Sicily, so too did he tackle the learning of the Queen's English with the same intensity and dedication. Aware that he had no aptitude for languages, he nevertheless booked a flight to London, established himself in a Bayswater hotel, watched BBC television all afternoon and all evening, read every word in the *Financial Times* and the *International Herald Tribune* with the aid of a dictionary each morning and chatted as much as he could with the hotel's chambermaids, waiters, desk clerks and assorted personnel using basic English. At the end of three weeks, during which he concentrated 18 hours a day on English, he went back to Milan and ordered his polyglot secretary to speak to him at all times only in English. By the time he was ready to go to America for the Vatican, Michele Sindona's English was fairly good.

In 1969 the Vatican needed a man like Sindona. Having already carved for itself a firm niche in the world of big business and having become the financial power behind many of Italy's companies in the postwar period, The Vatican had enough foresight to see that it could not allow itself to be placed in the embarrassing position of sitting at the bargaining table with Italian union leaders — especially the Communist unions — demanding not only more pay but 'more economic and social justice'. Moreover, the Vatican could not in good conscience ever face the likelihood in a shaky Italian economy of firing workers or closing down plants that were not making money. Small wonder then that the image of Vatican capitalism hung like an albatross around the neck of Pope Paul VI. The Vatican decided to initiate a plan where it would, discreetly, bit by bit, shed its business, industrial and financial holdings on the peninsula, while it escalated its investments beyond Italy's shores. Enter Michele Sindona. . . .

Judging Signor Sindona to be a financial fox, Pope Paul believed with incredible naïveté that the Sindona magic would work miracles for the Vatican. It was a task Hercules might have baulked at. But Sindona knew that he had muscle — the kind of muscle that could lead the Vatican through some dense business jungles. What apparently loomed large in Pope Paul's eye was the way Sindona had once come through with Sicilian chutzpah back in 1962 when the Archbishop of Milan — then Cardinal Giovanni Montini (and later Pope Paul VI) — sought to build an old folks' home, *Casa della Madonnina*, and Sindona offered his banking connections to raise some $2.5 million. Which he did. After that the two men became friends, and Cardinal Montini often relied on Sindona's financial acumen.

Hardly anybody outside Italy's banking circles at the time knew of Sindona, much less anything about him, thanks to a passion for anonymity which kept his associations and operations perpetually hazy. Yet, in a few decades, Sindona had, from nothing, formed 22 international companies, all of them interlocking and overlapping, and had become perhaps Italy's richest man. In August 1973 the *Fortune* magazine caught up with the Sindona story, he was worth in the vicinity of $450 million — all accomplished through buying and selling companies. The Sicilian-born Milan financier had stealthily amassed a megafortune and had become 'The Vatican's Howard Hughes'.

Unlike the reclusive American tycoon, Michele Sindona came from a very humble stock; his grandfather was a chicory seller, and his father an employee of the local farmers' association. Young Sindona, born in the tiny town of Patti near Messina, Sicily, in 1920, attended Jesuit schools where he demonstrated no proclivity for either mathematics or economics. When of age, he found a way to avoid conscription into Mussolini's army through the brother-in-law of a cousin who had considerable pull inside the Vatican. (This same man, Monsignor Amleto Tondini, who worked in the office of the Vatican Secretary of State, was later instrumental in introducing Sindona to powerful lay figures involved in the Vatican's financial operations — such as Massimo Spada, a Roman nobleman, then head of the Vatican bank, who upon retirement in 1962, took an executive post with one of Sindona's companies and who provided the social opportunities that enabled Sindona to meet key Vatican business bureaucrats.)

While studying law at the University of Messina, Sindona took an active part in the local Catholic students' federation, during which time he curried the friendship of one of Sicily's most powerful archbishops, noted for the record number of new churches he built in his archdiocese. After Sindona started his own legal practice, he had no lack of clients, many of whom included important Catholic laymen with interests in America.

In 1947, when he was 27 years old, Sindona left Sicily for Milan where he started a firm specializing in international taxation. American capital was beginning to flow into an Italy recovering from the ravages of war, and Sindona built a reputation as a legal expert able to unravel the mysteries of Italian balance sheets and Italian taxes to Italian–American investors. Meanwhile, he had met a banker who owned a small private bank, the Banca Privata Finanziaria, and a steel foundry. the man, getting on in years, was seeking to get out of the steel company: he found Sindona. Sindona's career switched: Sindona rapidly revamped the foundry and sold it for a fat profit to the American Crucible Company — whose vice-president, Daniel Porco, later resigned to become Sindona's chief sidekick in the United States.

The bank, in the meantime, fell into Sindona's hands shortly after he acquired the foundry, and it became the base for Sindona's game — the takeover of international financial operations. One of these included getting hold of a block of 10 per cent of the shares of the Libby food company in Italy, which he then sold to Nestlé's at a profit of several million dollars. Sindona then set up a holding company called Fasco in the new tax haven of Liechtenstein under the direction of Daniel Porco. In 1956 Sindona linked up his Banca Privata Finanziaria with two foreign private banks, Hambros of London and Continental Illinois National Bank & Trust Company of Chicago. The latter bank had connections with the Vatican's so-called finance ministry, the Institute for Religious Works (of which Bishop Paul Marcinkus is in executive control today).

What undoubtedly gained for Sindona the favor of both Cardinal Egidio Vagnozzi, head of the Prefecture for the Holy See's Economic Affairs, and Bishop Marcinkus was the way he freed the Vatican from the association of uncomfortable bedfellows on the Vatican-controlled Banca Unione board (which included a pro-Communist family, the Feltrinelli publishing clan). Sindona purchased the Banca Unione from the Vatican, taking the Vatican off the hook. Under his management, Unione, an old Milan institution with only two branches, aimed its sights at a market that was until then unexplored — the workers with savings of less than $500. To do this, Unione offered them interest rates in excess of what other banks were offering. Unione's deposits rose from $70 million to $165 million, while the number of accounts went from 5210 to 8562 practically overnight.

Apparently wowed by this mastermind maneuver, and equally

impressed with the personal recommendation given by David Kennedy, who had been president of the Continental Illinois National Bank & Trust Company of Chicago, and who then was, in 1969, Treasury Secretary in President Richard M Nixon's first cabinet, the Vatican brass commissioned Sindona to unload Italy's largest real estate and construction company, the $175-million Società Generale Immobiliare — the same company that had built the huge Watergate apartment and office complex in Washington for $70 million of Vatican money, SGI was also responsible for dozens of other construction projects, including the posh Cavalieri Hilton Hotel in Rome for which the Vatican, through a front company, put up three-quarters of the capital.

Sindona bought out the Vatican's controlling interest in SGI, sold 16 per cent to Gulf & Western Industries, kept a 40 per cent controlling interest for himself and held on to 5 per cent for the Vatican. Although Sindona was later to lose his holding in SGI in the 1974 Franklin Bank disaster, the Vatican managed through two front companies to hold on to Watergate which it administered through Giuseppe Cecchi, vice-president of Watergate Improvements, He stayed on the scene to keep an eye on things until the Vatican finally sold Watergate. (During the heat of the Watergate scandal — with which the Vatican had nothing to do, of course — I asked an office tenant what it was like having the Pope as his landlord, and he quipped: 'Well, he's like any other landlord, I guess, but I will say he never bugs us!') That the Vatican could continue to own and run Watergate came as a result of a complicated Sindona maneuver that was carried out through the 5 per cent of SGI that the papacy held on to at his behest.

It was from such operations, with typically clandestine tactics, that Sindona became a most favored man inside the Vatican where all his friends and admirers were in the top ranks. It was never altogether clear, whenever Sindona completed one of his spectacular business deals in Italy, whether the deal was Vatican business or Sindona business or both. When Sindona bought something from the Vatican, however, he was in effect not buying it for himself but for the Vatican, thereby enabling the Vatican to hide behind the Sicilian superman. Whenever the Pope wanted to get rid of inconvenient holdings, therefore, Sindona was called into consultation by the Vatican's top brass. Since the buyer often turned out to be Sindona himself, Italy's business fraternity was justifiably suspicious: Sindona was acting as a front for papal interests. Whenever Sindona made any kind of move that involved large amounts of capital, even Vatican insiders were never sure whether he was using his own money or Vatican money because in true Sicilian style he kept tight lipped about everything he did, especially where it concerned his clients, who — particularly the Vatican — preferred to remain phantom backers.

Just as it was difficult to pin down exactly when Sindona was acting on the Vatican's behalf and when he was acting on his own behalf, his purchase of the *Rome Daily American* in September 1971 (when it was in its 27th year of publication) was equally rife with uncertainty. Had the Vatican bought up an American newspaper, or had Sindona decided to add publishing to his multiple list of varied activities?

After his name appeared several times on the *Daily American's* masthead as president, Sindona replaced it with the name of one of his in-laws, Giuliano Magnoni. Soon after the takeover, the *Daily American* started to carry late US stock market listings and tried to widen its readership from the Americans residing in Italy to those all over the Mediterranean basin. For a while it seemed that the *Daily American* was planning to invade the advertising and circulation markets of the well-established Paris-based *International Herald Tribune* in which both the *Washington Post* and *The New York Times* have heavy financial stakes, but by this time, during the spring of 1975, Sindona sold the daily to a syndicate of Italian businessmen. During the some four years that the paper was owned by Sindona, no one was able to determine — least of all its editors and reporters, who indeed were the most curious of all — whether the *Daily American* had been acquired with Vatican money or with Sindona money.

With or without Vatican backing, nevertheless, the Sindona empire flourished during the late 1960s, helped considerably by his Vatican connections about which he kept a low profile. By shunting money from one company to another, as required, he managed to expand his holdings. In 1971, however, Sindona made a bad decision. He attempted to take over Bastogi, a large Milan-based holding company, with a tender offer for its shares, but powerful business interests in Milan and government officials in Rome ganged up on him and blocked the takeover. This was done not only because Sindona was looked down upon as 'that onion-munching maverick from Sicily' but also out of *cattiveria* (a wicked or hostile action based usually on plain ornery meanness). Ethnic prejudice was a factor too: in Italy's North, Sicilians are not generally held in high esteem.

Apparently Guido Carli, then governor of the Bank of Italy, shared some of this racism, for it was known that he disliked Sindona. Once when the two men were seated side by side in first class on an Alitalia flight from New York to Rome, Sindona made an attempt to strike up a conversation with Carli. The latter snubbed him, covered his eyes with a black sleeping mask and simulated sleep for seven hours, thereby snuffing any attempt on Sindona's part to get on the good side of him.

When the Bank of Italy displayed its displeasure at the Sicilian's attempt to gobble up Bastogi, amounting to a kiss of death for Sindona, the Hambros Bank, which had bought nearly 25 per cent of Sindona's Banca Privata Finanziaria, severed its relations with him. Convinced he was the target of northern discrimination and also *persona non grata* in his own country, the deflated merchant banker decided to give up Italy. He agreed to test the waters in the United States for the Vatican as the Pope's Number One business agent — but no one was to know of his papal affiliation for as long as it could be kept a secret. In America Sindona already owned three companies — Oxford Electric, Interphoto and Angus Inc. They provided him with a good front for the job he had to do.

After his affair in London with the English language, Sindona transferred himself to New York City, and, in July 1972, using his freshly acquired English, he plunged into the business of business: he purchased 52 per cent interest (1.6 million shares) in Talcott National, a 115-year-old finance firm, for $27.3 million, and a 21.6 per cent interest in the Franklin New York Corporation, the holding company for the Franklin National Bank — a million shares at $40 apiece when it was selling at $32 over the counter.

As a result of the diversification of investments outside Italy through Sindona, the Vatican portfolio today includes stocks in Chase Manhattan, Celanese, Colgate, General Foods, Procter & Gamble, Standard Oil, Unilever and Westinghouse. A substantial part of the development of lower Manhattan by the Uris Building Corporation and Tisham Realty & Construction was provided by Vatican money. Some Sindona money — or perhaps Vatican money — also went into the building of the New York World Trade Center.

Ever energetic, Sindona also tried to make 'new friends' in the United States when he offered to donate $1 million to President Nixon's 1792 campaign fund on the proviso he remain anonymous (a goodly portion of this money was the Vatican's). He was turned down because secret campaign contributions had become illegal.

The financial fortunes of Franklin, which was the twentieth largest US bank, began to decline when it was learned that the bank had lost some $39 million because of unauthorized trading in foreign currencies. After the Franklin bank collapsed late in 1974, thereby earning the distinction of being the biggest American bank failure of all time, Sindona got his fingers burned. The Banca Privata Italiana of Milan had previously gone into liquidation as some $300 million could not be accounted for. The Italian authorities, seeking the

Sicilian's extradition, issued an arrest warrant charging that he had illegally taken money out of his Milan bank and faked a balance sheet to cover up the deficit. Meanwhile, the Securities & Exchange Commission filed a civil suit in Federal Court which charged Sindona with several violations of rules.

In the wreckage of Sindona's fizzled banking empire, there were rumors in Rome that the Vatican had reportedly lost some $60 million through the Sindona-controlled Banca Unione and Banca Privata Italiana. Swiss banking experts, however, computed the Vatican's losses as exceeding $250 million, and some Italian newspapers set the figure at $750 million, a considerable sum if it were true. Such estimates prompted a Vatican press officer to admit there had been 'limited losses' but, alas, no specific figure was given. The Vatican was later to change tactics and issue a statement stating it had only lost about $144,000. This was patent nonsense: in point of fact the Vatican's real losses on the collapse of the Franklin came to about $56 million.

Embarrassed Catholic magnates now began maneuvering to separate the Sindona shadow from theirs. Bishop Marcinkus insisted he had indeed only met Sindona once (not true). The Vatican's 'finance minister' at the time, Cardinal Vagnozzi, even went so far as to claim he had personally never met Michele Sindona at any time (not true). Neither of the two Church officers bothered to recall the many times they and Sindona had gone together to Assisi to 'meditate' during retreats.

As head of the Prefecture for the Holy See's Economic Affairs, the bespectacled Cardinal Vagnozzi used the occasion to make the first public declaration ever of the Vatican's assets throughout the world, which he put at less than $125 million. He backed up this statement by adding that the Vatican's productive assets consisted of 'mixed property, real estate and moveables — stocks and bonds'. Under further questioning Cardinal Vagnozzi admitted that some but not all of the Vatican investments had recently been transferred out of Italy to the United States and other countries. The Vatican was trying, he said, 'like any other prudent administration,' to invest in areas where 'there are likely to be better returns and where the burden of taxation is less'. The cardinal also insisted that Sindona's only business affiliation with the Vatican was the sale of Società Generale Immobiliare.

Some facts to the contrary, however, put this assertion in doubt. For instance, in February 1973 when the American Stock Exchange stopped the trading in Vetco Industries because a Los Angeles investment adviser had gathered together nearly 27 per cent of Vetco's outstanding share and options (in violation of SEC regulations), it was learned that 20 per cent of the 27 per cent (454,000 shares worth about $16.8 million) had been acquired by the Vatican through a Liechtenstein investment company in which Sindona had a substantial interest. In settling with the SEC by paying a fine of $307,720, the Vatican sold all its Vetco shares at a profit — but refused to make any public comment at this embarrassing time.

The Vatican also had a 22 per cent equity participation (worth approximately $19.2 million) in Geneva's Finabank (the Banque de Financement), another Sindona banking operation, and remained completely mum when the Swiss government early in 1975 closed the bank temporarily after heavy foreign exchange losses had been noted. The Finabank also controlled Hamburg's Bankhaus Wolff which closed its doors shortly before Franklin National died. No one actually knows whether Sindona ever used any Church money in his attempt to rescue Franklin National.

Indicted on 66 counts of fraud stemming from his operation of Franklin National, Sindona, free on bail, disappeared from his plush condominium flat in New York City's exclusive Hotel Pierre on August 2, 1979, and did not reappear until October 16. He explained to the authorities that he had been abducted and displayed a bullet wound in his left leg, which he said he had suffered in an attempt to escape from his kidnappers. Sindona went on trial early in 1980, during which evidence was presented by the prosecution showing that he had used the name of Joseph Bonamico (which means good friend in Italian) on airline tickets which flew him from New York to Vienna, from Munich to Frankfurt and from Frankfurt to New York during the period he claimed to be in the hands of his abductors. Found guilty of 65 charges, which covered perjury and the misappropriation of $45 million from Franklin National, Sindona was given a 25-year prison term and fined $207,000 — in addition to receiving a 30-month prison term and a $25,000 fine for having faked his kidnapping.

During the two and a half months of his disappearance, Sindona had gone to Europe to settle some matters of a personal and financial nature and to get the support of the Vatican for his scheduled trial in Manhattan's Federal District Court. Because Sindona had never mixed with the Mafia in Sicily, he did not venture into Italy to solicit help from a 'Godfather' who could influence Vatican personages to come to his defense. Instead he went to Frankfurt where he had a secret meeting with a good Vatican connection of his, the papal nuncio, Monsignor Guido del Mestri, who traveled from Bonn in an ordinary suit to meet him in a downtown hotel. Monsignor del Mestri agreed to intercede and get two cardinals and a bishop who knew Sindona well to attest to the character of the defendant, Michele

Sindona, in court. Later when Sindona's chief defense counsel, former federal judge Marvin E Frankel, flew to Rome to get the videotapes that the three prelates had made, he was prevented from doing so by Vatican Secretary of State Cardinal Agostino Casaroli.

Cardinal Giuseppe Caprio, Cardinal Sergio Guerri and Bishop Paul Marcinkus had made the videotape depositions, but Frankel was told by Cardinal Casaroli that they could not be used because they would subject the three prelates to a secular court's jurisdiction, thereby creating a precedent that would be detrimental to the Vatican's general interest. It is not known whether Pope John Paul II also had a hand in the matter, but, in any case, Sindona's defense attorney could not introduce any of the videotape depositions at the trial. Several clerics inside the Vatican, who firmly believed that Sindona had not stolen any money from Franklin National and had instead used millions of his own dollars to save the bank, felt that what the Vatican had done to its former business representative was a 'cowardly act that smacked of a double-cross'.

CHAPTER XLI

Afterword

IN GENERAL, I have not cited my sources for statements of facts. All of these are people whose names were listed at the outset, but especially the trio of clerics who are involved with the Vatican system on a day-to-day basis. I have not felt it necessary to name sources, as I am thoroughly convinced as to their reliability, and, additionally, recognize that attribution would harm those close to the Pope and those integrated in daily Vatican operations. I would like to state, moreover, that my sources are mostly primary and only occasionally secondary.

It was not my purpose in this book to bemean the Roman Catholic religion in the eyes either of Catholics or non-Catholics. I make no judgment on the validity of the faith, for I accept the fact that the Catholic religion gives many people solace and joy. Furthermore, I have not sought to rebut any of the Catholic tenets. I have concerned myself with certain imperfections and failings among the men who run the Church and its administrative body, the Vatican. My experience of writing about the Catholic Church in previous books tells me that this book will bring me the disfavor of some readers who will find it convenient to classify me as an anti-Catholic. As a journalist, however, I seek always to be as professionally objective as humanly possible and let the facts speak for themselves.

Whoever takes it upon himself to write about the Vatican could easily give the impression that he is an expert. There are, in my opinion, no experts on the Vatican. There are, indeed, Vatican-watchers, Vaticanists, Vatican observers and Vaticanologists, but there are no Vatican experts. As witness this story:

During an audience one day when a dozen cardinals, bishops and assorted clerics were present and Pope Pius XII was in one of his rare good moods, he asked two young priests the same question: 'How long have you been in the Vatican?' The first man replied: 'Three weeks.' 'Then,' said the Pope, 'you are an expert on the Vatican!' The second man gave as his reply: 'Three years.' 'Then,' said the Pope, 'you know nothing about the Vatican!'

APPENDIX

The Popes

The name of each Pope is given with his family name in parenthesis and the dates of his pontificate in square brackets.

John Paul II (Karol Wojtyla) [1978-]
John Paul I (Albino Luciani) [1978-34 days]
Paul VI (Giovanni Montini) [1963-1978]
John XXIII (Angelo Roncalli) [1958-1963]
Pius XII (Eugenio Pacelli) [1939-1958]
Pius XI (Achille Ratti) [1922-1939]
Benedict XV (Giacomo Della Chiesa) [1914-1922]
Pius X (Giuseppe Melchiorre Sarto) [1903-1914]
Leo XIII (Gioacchino Pecci) [1878-1903]
Pius IX (Giovanni Mastai Ferretti) [1846-1878]
Gregory XVI (Bartolomeo Alberto-Mauro-Cappellari) [1831-1846]
Pius VIII (Francesco Saverio Castiglioni) [1829-1830]
Leo XII (Annibale Della Genga) [1823-1829]
Pius VII (Barnaba Chiaramonti) [1800-1823]
Pius VI (Giovanni Angelo Braschi) [1775-1799]
Clement XIV (Giovanni Ganganelli) [1769-1774]
Clement XIII (Carlo Rezzonico) [1758-1769]
Benedict XIV (Prospero Lambertini) [1740-1758]
Clement XII (Lorenzo Corsini) [1730-1740]
Benedict XIII (Pietro Orsini) [1724-1730]
Innocent XIII (Michelangelo dei Conti) [1721-1724]
Clement XI (Giovanni Albani) [1700-1721]
Innocent XII (Antonio Pignatelli) [1691-1700]
Alexander VIII (Pietro Ottoboni) [1689-1691]
Innocent XI (Benedetto Odescalchi) [1676-1689]
Clement X (Emilio Altieri) [1670-1676]
Clement IX (Giulio Rospigliosi) [1667-1669]
Alexander VII (Fabio Chigi) [1655-1667]
Innocent X (Giovanni Pamphili) [1644-1655]
Urban VIII (Maffeo Barberini) [1623-1644]
Gregory XV (Alessandro Ludovisi) [1621-1623]

Paul V (Camilio Borghese) [1605–1621]
Leo XI (Alessandro de' Medici) [1605–one month]
Clement VIII (Ippolito Aldobrandini) [1592–1605]
Innocent IX (Giovanni Facchinetti) [1591–two months]
Gregory XIV (Niccolo Sfondrati) [1590–1591]
Urban VII (Giovanni Castagna) [1590–one month]
Sixtus V (Felice Peretti) [1585–1590]
Gregory XIII (Ugo Boncompagni) [1572–1585]
Pius V (Antonio Ghislieri) [1556–1572]
Pius IV (Giovanni de' Medici) [1559–1565]
Paul IV (Gian Pietro Carafa) [1555–1559]
Marcellus II (Marcello Cervini) [1555–two months]
Julius III (Giovanni Ciocchi del Monte) [1550–1555]
Paul III (Alessandro Farnese) [1535–1549]
Clement VII (Giulio de' Medici) [1523–1534]
Adrian VI (Adrian Florensz Dedal) [1522–1523]
Leo X (Giovanni de' Medici) [1513–1521]
Julius II (Giuliano Della Rovere) [1503–1513]
Pius III (Francesco Todeschini Piccolomini) [1503–two months]
Alexander VI (Rodrigo Borgia) [1492–1503]
Innocent VIII (Giovanni Cibo) [1484–1492]
Sixtus IV (Francesco Della Rovere) [1471–1484]
Paul II (Pietro Barbo) [1464–1471]
Pius II (Enea Piccolomini) [1458–1464]
Calixtus III (Alfonso Borgia) [1455–1458]
Nicholas V (Tommaso Parentucelli) [1447–1455]
Eugene IV (Gabriel Condulmaro) [1431–1447]
Martin V (Oddo Colonna) [1417–1431]
Gregory XII (Angelo Correr) [1406–1415]
Innocent VII (Cosimo de' Migliorati) [1404–1406]
Boniface IX (Pietro Tomacelli) [1389–1404]
Urban VI (Bartolomeo Prignano) [1378–1389]
Gregory XI (Pierre Roger de Beaufort) [1370–1378]
Urban V (Guillaume de Grimoard) [1362–1370]
Innocent VI (Étienne Aubert) [1352–1362]
Clement VI (Pierre Roger) [1342–1352]
Benedict XII (Jacques Fournier) [1334–1342]
John XXII (Jacques Duèse) [1316–1334]
Clement V (Bertrand de Got) [1305–1314]
Benedict XI (Niccolo Boccasini) [1303–1304]
Boniface VIII (Benedetto Gaetani) [1294–1303]
Celestine V (Peter of Morrone) [1294–five months]
Nicholas IV (Girolamo Masci) [1288–1292]
Honorius IV (Jacobus Savelli) [1285–1287]
Martin IV (Simon de Brie) [1281–1285]

Nicholas III (Giovanni Orsini) [1277–1280]
John XXI (Petrus Juliani) [1276–1277]
Adrian V (Ottobono Fieschi) [1276–two months]
Innocent V (Peter of Tarentaise) [1276–five months]
Gregory X (Tedaldo Visconti) [1271–1276]
Clement IV (Guy Fulcodi) [1265–1268]
Urban IV (Jacques Pantaléon) [1261–1264]
Alexander IV (Rainaldo, Count of Segni) [1254–1261]
Innocent IV (Sinibaldo Fieschi) [1243–1254]
Celestine IV (Goffredo Castiglioni) [1241–two months]
Gregory IX (Hugo, Count of Segni) [1227–1241]
Honorius III (Cencio Savelli) [1216–1227]
Innocent III (Lothar of Segni) [1198–1216]
Celestine III (Giacinto Bobo) [1191–1198]
Clement III (Paolo Scolari) [1187–1191]
Gregory VIII (Alberto de Morra) [1187–two months]
Urban III (Uberto Crivelli) [1185–1187]
Lucius III (Ubaldus Allucingolus) [1181–1185]
Alexander III (Roland Bandinelli) [1159–1181]
Adrian IV (Nicholas Breakspear) [1154–1159]
Anastasius IV (Conrad de Suburra) [1153–1154]
Eugene III (Bernard) [1145–1153]
Lucius II (Gerardo Caccianemici) [1144–1145]
Celestine II (Guido of Castellis) [1143–1144]
Innocent II (Gregory Papareschi) [1130–1143]
Honorius II (Lambert Scannabecchi) [1124–1130]
Calixtus II (Guido of Burgundy) [1119–1124]
Gelasius II (John of Gaeta) [1118–1119]
Pascal II (Rainerius) [1099–1118]
Urban II (Odo of Châtillon-sur-Marne) [1088–1099]
Victor III (Dauferius; Desiderius) [1086–1087]
Gregory VII (Hildebrand) [1073–1085]

BIBLIOGRAPHY

[This is a minimal listing of references that were consulted by the author. For readers who want to familiarize themselves with the Catholic Church and the Vatican, several of the listed sources have useful bibliographies which cover most of the areas dealt with in this book.]

ABBOTT, WALTER M., S.J. (editor), *The Documents of Vatican II*, Association Press, New York, 1966.

Annuario Pontificio 1981, Libreria Editrice Vaticana, Rome, 1981.

ARADI, ZSOLT/TUCEK, JAMES I./O'NEILL, JAMES C., *Pope John XXIII*, Dell, New York, 1961.

ARMSTRONG, APRIL OURSLER, *What's Happening to the Catholic Church?*, Echo Books, Garden City, New York, 1967.

BALK, ALFRED, *The Religion Business*, John Knox, Richmond, Virginia, 1968.

BARZINI, LUIGI, *From Caesar to the Mafia*, Hamish Hamilton, London, 1971.

BERNSTEIN, MARCELLE, *The Nuns*, Bantam, New York, 1979.

BLANSHARD, PAUL, *American Freedom and Catholic Power*, Beacon, Boston, 1949.

BLANSHARD, PAUL, *Communism, Democracy and Catholic Power*, Beacon, Boston, 1951.

BLANSHARD, PAUL, *God and Man in Washington*, Beacon, Boston, 1960.

BLANSHARD, PAUL, *Paul Blanshard on Vatican II*, Beacon, Boston, 1966. 1966.

BLAZYNSKI, GEORGE, *Pope John Paul II*, Sphere, London, 1979.

BOKUN, BRANKO, *Spy in the Vatican 1941–45*, Praeger, New York, 1973.

BOLTON, GLORNEY, *Roman Century*, Viking, New York, 1970.

BROER, WOLFGANG, *Mein Job Ist Papst*, Amalthea Verlag, Vienna, 1980.

CARROLL-ABBING, J. PATRICK, *But For the Grace of God*, Dell, New York, 1965.

CAVALLARI, ALBERTO, *Il Vaticano Che Cambia*, Mondadori, Milan, 1966.

CHAMBERLAIN, E. R., *The Bad Popes*, New American Library, New York, 1971.
CIANFARRA, CAMILLE, *The Vatican and the War*, Dutton, New York, 1944.
CLEARY, JON, *Peter's Pence*, Fontana, London, 1974.
CORDERO, FRANCO, *Against the Catholic System*, Calder & Boyars, London, 1972.
CRAIG, MARY, *Man From A Far Country*, Hodder & Stoughton, London, 1979.
CUNNINGHAM, JAMES F., *American Pastor in Rome*, Doubleday, New York, 1966.
DALLA TORRE, GIUSEPPE, *Memorie*, Mondadori, Milan, 1965.
DE BROUCKER, JOSE, *The Suenens Dossier*, Fides, Notre Dame, Indiana, 1970.
DE LA BEDOYERE, MICHAEL (Editor), *Objections to Roman Catholicism*, Lippincott, Philadelphia, 1965.
DUPONT, YVES, *Catholic Prophecy*, Tan, Rockford, Illinois, 1970.
DURRELL, LAWRENCE (Translator), *Pope Joan by Emmanuel Royidis*, World, London, 1954.
ELFENBEIN, HIRAM, *Organization Religion*, Philosophical Library, New York, 1968.
ELLIS, JOHN TRACY, *American Catholicism*, Doubleday, Garden City, New York, 1965.
ERSKINE, JOHN, *The Human Life of Jesus*, Morrow, New York, 1945.
FALCONI, CARLO, *L'assistenza Italiana Sotto Bandiera Pontificia* Feltrinelli, Milan, 1957.
FALCONI, CARLO, *The Popes in the 20th Century*, Little Brown, Boston, 1967.
FITZSIMONS, M. A. (Editor), *The Catholic Church Today: Western Europe*, Notre Dame, Indiana, 1969.
GAER, JOSEPH, *How The Great Religions Began*, New American Library, New York, 1954.
GALLAGHER, J. P. *Scarlet Pimpernel of the Vatican*, Collins, London, 1967.
GANNON, ROBERT I., *The Cardinal Spellman Story*, Doubelday, Garden City, New York, 1962.
GHEERBRANT, ALAIN, *The Rebel Church in Latin America*, Penguin, Harmondsworth, 1974.
GOLLIN, JAMES, *Worldly Goods*, Random House, New York, 1971.
GORRESIO, VITTORIO, *Il Papa e il Diavolo*, Rizzoli, Milan, 1973.
GRAHAM, ROBERT A., *Vatican Diplomacy,* Princeton University Press, New Jersey, 1965.
GREELEY, ANDREW M., *The Making of the Popes*, Futura, London, 1979.
GUITTON, JEAN, *The Pope Speaks*, Meredith, New York, 1968.
HALES, E. E. Y., *The Catholic Church in the Modern World*, Doubleday, New York, 1960.

HARDON, JOHN A., *Religions of the World*, Doubleday, New York, 1968.
HEBBLETHWAITE, PETER, *The Runaway Church*, Collins, London, 1975.
HEBBLETHWAITE, PETER, *The Year of Three Popes*, Collins, London, 1978.
HOLLIS, CHRISTOPHER, *The Church and Economics*, Burns & Oates, London, 1961.
HOOK, SIDNEY, *Religion in a Free Society*, University of Nebraska Press, Lincoln, 1967.
HUEGLI, ALBERT G. (Editor), *Church and State Under God*, Concordia, St. Louis, 1964.
HUGHES, PHILIP, *A Short History of the Catholic Church*, Burns & Oates, London, 1967.
HUTCHINSON, RAY, *The Gospel According to Madison Avenue,* Bruce, New York, 1969.
JOHNSON, PAUL, *Pope John XXIII,* Hutchinson, London, 1974.
KAISER, ROBERT BLAIR, *Pope, Council and World*, Macmillan, New York, 1963.
KAVANAUGH, JAMES, *A Modern Priest Looks at His Church*, Simon & Schuster, 1967.
KERWIN, JEROME G. *Catholic Viewpoint on Church and State*, Hanover House, Garden City, New York, 1960.
KITTLER, GLENN D., *The Papal Princes*, Funk & Wagnalls, New York, 1960.
KÜNG, HANS, *Structures of the Church*, Notre Dame University, Indiana, 1968.
KÜNG, HANS, *Truthfulness*, Sheed & Ward, New York, 1968.
LA PALOMBARA, JOSEPH, *Interest Groups in Italian Politics*, Princeton University Press, New Jersey, 1964.
LARSON, MARTIN A., *Church Wealth and Business Income*, Philosophical Library, New York, 1965.
LARSON, MARTIN A. and LOWELL, C. STANLEY, *The Religious Empire*, Luce, Washington, 1976.
LECKIE, ROBERT, *American and Catholic*, Doubleday, Garden City, New York, 1970.
LEWY, GUENTER, *The Catholic Church and Nazi Germany*, McGraw-Hill, New York, 1964.
LO BELLO, NINO, *The Vatican Empire*, Simon & Schuster, New York, 1968.
LO BELLO, NINO, *Vatican, USA*, Simon & Schuster, New York, 1972.
LOMBARD (pseudonym), *Soldi Truccati*, Fetlrinelli, Milan, 1980.
LUCIANI, ALBINO, *Illustrissimi*, Little Brown, New York, 1978.
MANHATTAN, AVRO, *The Vatican Billions*, Paravision, London, 1972.
MANHATTAN, AVRO, *Catholic Power Today*, Lyle Stuart, New York, 1967.

MANHATTAN, AVRO, *Vatican Imperialism in the 20th Century*, Zondervan, Grand Rapids, Michigan, 1965.
MARTIN, MALACHI, *The Final Conclave*, Stein & Day, New York, 1978.
MARTIN, MALACHI, *The Popes and The Cardinal*, Popular Library, New York, 1972.
MAYNARD, THEODORE, *The Story of American Catholicism*, Doubleday, New York, 1960.
McGURN, BARRETT, *A Reporter Looks at American Catholicism*, Hawthorn, New York, 1967.
McGURN, BARRETT, *A Reporter Looks at The Vatican*, Coward-McCann, New York, 1962.
McKNIGHT, JOHN P., *The Papacy*, McGraw-Hill, London, 1953.
MEADOWS, DENIS, *A Popular History of the Jesuits*, Macmillan, New York, 1958.
MORGAN, RICHARD E., *The Politics of Religious Conflict*, Pegasus, New York, 1968.
MORLEY, HUGH, *The Pope and The Press*, Notre Dame Press, Indiana, 1968.
MURPHY, FRANCIS X., *John XXIII: The Story of the Pope*, Avon, New York, 1959.
MURPHY, WALTER F., *The Vicar of Christ*, Cassell, London, 1979.
MUTCHLER, DAVID E., *The Church As A Political Factor in Latin America*, Praeger, New York, 1971.
NEVILLE, ROBERT, *The World of the Vatican*, Harper & Row, New York, 1962.
NICHOLS, Peter, *The Pope's Divisions*, Faber, London, 1981.
NICHOLS, PETER, *Italia, Italia*, London, 1973.
NICHOLS, PETER, *The Politics of the Vatican*, Praeger, New York, 1968.
O'CONNOR, JOHN (Editor), *American Catholic Exodus*, Chapman, London, 1968.
O'CONNOR, JOHN, *The People Versus Rome*, Random House, New York, 1969.
O'HAIR, MADALYN MURRAY, *What On Earth Is An Atheist?*, American Atheist Press, Austin, Texas, 1969.
OREFICE, PIERO, *Il Saio e La Tiara*, Rizzoli, Milan, 1979.
OSTLING, RICHARD N., *Secrecy in the Church*, Harper & Row, New York, 1974.
PACKARD, REYNOLDS and ELEANOR, *Balcony Empire*, Oxford University Press, New York, 1942.
PALLENBERG, CORRADO, *Vatican Finances*, Owen, London, 1971.
PALLENBERG, CORRADO, *The Vatican From Within*, Harrap, London, 1961.
PANERAI, PAOLO and DE LUCA, MAURIZIO, *Il Crack*, Mondadori, Milan, 1975.

PELLICANI, ANTONIO, *Il Papa di Tutti*, Sugar Editore, Milan, 1964.
PEPPER, CURTIS BILL, *An Artist and the Pope*, Davies, London, 1968.
PEYREFITTE, ROGER, *Knights of Malta*, Panther, London, 1971.
PEYREFITTE, ROGER, *Les Cles de Saint Pierre*, Flammarion, Paris, 1955.
PFEFFER, LEO, *Church, State and Freedom* (revised edition), Beacon Press, Boston, 1966.
PHIPPS, WILLIAM E., *Was Jesus Married?*, Harper & Row, New York, 1970.
PICHON, CHARLES, *The Vatican and Its Role in World Affairs*, Dutton, New York, 1950.
PUCCI, ENRICO, *La Pace del Laterano*, Editrice Fiorentina, Florence, 1958.
PUTZ, LOUIS J., *the Catholic Church, U.S.A.*, Fields, Chicago, 1956.
RANKE, L. VON, *Die Römischen Päpste in den Letzten Vie Jahrhunderten*, Munich, 1923.
RHODES, ANTHONY, *The Vatican in the Age of the Dictators [1922–1945]*, Holt, Rinehart & Winston, New York, 1973.
RIEMER, GEORGE, *The Jesuits*, Little Brown, Boston, 1971.
ROBERTSON, ALEXANDER, *The Roman Catholic Church in Italy*, Morgan & Scott, London, 1903.
ROBINSON, HENRY MORTON, *The Cardinal*, Simon & Schuster, New York, 1950.
ROSA, ENRICO, *I Gesuiti*, Civiltà Cattolica, Rome, 1957.
ROSSI, ERNESTO, *Pagine Anticlericali*, Samona e Savelli, Rome, 1966.
RYNNE, XAVIER, *Letters From Vatican City*, Farrer, Strauss & Giroux, New York, 1963.
RYNNE, XAVIER, *The Fourth Session*, Farrer, Strauss & Giroux, New York, 1965.
SCHILLEBEECKX, EDWARD, *Jesus, An Experiment in Christology,* Seabury Press, New York, 1979.
SCHMITT, KARL M., *The Roman Catholic Church in Modern Latin America*, Knopf, New York, 1972.
SCHONFIELD, HUGH J., *Those Incredible Christians*, Geis, New York, 1968.
SCHONFIELD, HUGH J., *After the Cross*, A. S. Barnes, New York, 1981.
SELDES, GEORGE, *The Vatican: Yesterday, Today, Tomorrow*, Harper, New York, 1934.
SHARKEY, DON, *White Smoke Over the Vatican*, Fallon, Dublin, 1960.
SMIT, JAN OLAV, *Angelic Shepherd: The Life Of Pope Pius XII*, Dodd Mead, New York, 1950.
STEWART, OLIVER, *Divorce, Vatican Style*, Dimension Books, New Jersey, 1971.
SWEENEY, FRANCIS (Editor), *The Vatican and World Peace*, Colin Smythe, London, 1970.
SWIDLER, LEONARD and ARLENE (Editors), *Bishops and People*, Westminster, Philadelphia, 1970.

TARDINI, DOMENICO, *Pio XII*, Tipografia Poliglotta Vaticana, Rome, 1960.
TEDESCHI, MARIO, *La Guerra dei Cent'Anni*, Edizioni del Borghese, Rome, 1970.
TEMPLETON, CHARLES, *Act of God*, Little Brown, Boston, 1977.
VAN LIERDE, PETER CANISIUS, *The Holy See at Work*, Hawthorn, New York, 1962.
VON ARETIN, KARL OTMAR, *The Papacy and the Modern World*, Weidenfeld & Nicolson, London, 1970.
WAAGENAAR, SAM, *The Pope's Jews*, Library Press, La Salle, Illinois, 1974.
WAKIN, EDWARD, *The De-Romanization of the American Catholic Church*, Macmillan, New York, 1966.
WALL, BERNARD, *The Vatican Story*, Harper, New York, 1956.
WECHSBERG, JOSEPH, *The Merchant Bankers*, Little Brown, New York, 1966.
WEBB, LEICESTER C., *Church and State in Italy [1947–1957]*, Melbourne University Press, Australia, 1958.
WELLS, DAVID F., *Revolution in Rome*, InterVarsity Press, Illinois, 1972.
WELLS, JOEL, *A Funny Thing Happened to the Church*, Macmillan, London, 1967.
WHALE, JOHN (Editor), *The Pope From Poland: An Assessment*, Collins, London, 1980.
WILLIAMS, MICHAEL, *The Catholic Church in Action*, Kenedy & Sons, New York, 1958.
WILSON, IAN, *The Turin Shroud*, Penguin, Harmondsworth, England, 1978.
WLASCHIN, KEN, *To Kill The Pope*, New English Library, London, 1971.
YOURCENAR, MARGUERITE, *Memoirs of Hadrian*, Secker & Warburg, London, 1949.
ZOLLI, ISRAELE, *Il Nazareno*, Istituto Delle Edizione Academiche, Udine, 1938.

INDEX